The July Revolution
Barcelona 1909

T0154545

The July Revolution
Barcelona 1909

Leopoldo Bonafulla

Translated by Slava Faybysh
Introduction by James Michael Yeoman

The July Revolution: Barcelona 1909
by Leopoldo Bonufulla

Translation and citations, as noted © 2021 Slava Faybysh
Introduction and citations, as noted © 2021 James Michael Yeoman

ISBN 978-1-84935-410-3
E-ISBN 978-1-84935-411-0
Library of Congress Control Number: 2020946133

AK Press   AK Press
370 Ryan Avenue #100   33 Tower Street
Chico, CA 95973   Edinburgh, EH6, 7BN
USA   Scotland
www.akpress.org   www.akuk.com
akpress@akpress.org   akuk@akpress.org

The addresses above would be delighted to provide you with the latest
AK Press catalog, featuring several thousand books, pamphlets, audio and
video products, and stylish apparel published and distributed by AK Press.
Alternatively, visit our websites for the complete catalog, latest news and
updates, events and secure ordering.

Cover design by John Yates, www.stealworks.com
Printed in the United States of America on acid-free paper

Contents

Introduction
by James Michael Yeoman

It would be useful to reconstruct the historical truth of the events of July, distorted as it has been by the insolent assertions that traditionalists of all stripe have dared to proffer in statements and protests, even more useful if we consider the fact that history has never recorded such a powerful revolutionary movement in which the revolutionaries had put such sentiments of human decency into practice. Maybe such decency was its own punishment.

So begins *The July Revolution*, an analysis of the Tragic Week of Barcelona in 1909 by the anarchist publisher Leopoldo Bonafulla. While the Tragic Week has attracted brief flashes of historical interest—most recently around its centenary in 2009[1]—the number of sustained studies of this event and the broader Restoration

---

1. My thanks to Mary Vincent, Matthew Kerry and the Red Deer's Writing Collective for their thoughts on this piece.
This is particularly true in Spanish and Catalan scholarship. See for example Juan Avilés Farré, *Francisco Ferrer y Guardia: Pedagogo, anarquista y mártir* (Madrid: Marcial Pons, 2006); Francisco Bergasa, *¿Quién mató a Ferrer i Guardia?* (Madrid: Aguilar, 2009); Ramon Corts i Blay, *La Setmana Tràgica de 1909: L'Arxiu Secret Vaticà* (Barcelona: Publicacions de l'Abadia de Montserrat, 2009); Antoni Dalmau, *Set dies de fúria: Barcelona i la Setmana Tràgica (juliol de 1909)* (Barcelona: Columna, 2009); Pere Gabriel Sirvent, 'La Setmana Tràgica: Una revolta política?' *L'Avenç* 348 (2009): 32–41; Dolors Marín, *La Semana Trágica. Barcelona en llamas, la revuelta popular y la Escuela Moderna* (Madrid: La Esfera de los Libros, 2009); Antoni Moliner Prada, ed., *La Semana Trágica de Cataluña* (Alella: Nabla, 2009); Josep Pich Mitjana, ed., *La Setmana Tràgica (1909): Sagnant, roja, negra o gloriosa* (Barcelona: Universitat Pompeu Fabra, 2009); Josep Termes et al., *Els fets de la Setmana Tràgica (1909): Actes de les jornades organitzades pel CHCC* (Barcelona: CHCC and Generalitat de Catalunya 2010). See also the literature review and anthology edited by Eloy Martín Corrales, *Semana Trágica: Entre las barricadas de Barcelona y el Barranco del Lobo* (Barcelona: Bellaterra 2011).

period (1874–1931) pale in comparison to those of the Spanish Second Republic (1931–1936/9) and Civil War (1936–1939), particularly in Anglophone literature.[2] Added to this, there is a notable lack of English translations of primary sources on modern Spain, and almost none for any period outside the 1930s, making this translation of Bonafulla's study a welcome and important new resource for anyone interested in popular protest, anarchism, anti-clericalism, anti-colonialism, and the tumultuous history of one of Europe's most vibrant and radical cities.[3]

At its most basic, the Tragic Week was a popular insurrection which erupted across Catalonia in from 26 July to 2 August 1909. What began as demonstrations against the conscription of working class men to fight in a deeply unpopular colonial project in Morocco developed into a general strike across the region. Barcelona was the epicenter of conflict, as protesters clashed with security forces on the streets and began destroying the property of the Catholic Church. By the end of the week between a third and a half of Barcelona's religious buildings were burned by protestors in the most spectacular eruption of anticlericalism in Spain in almost a century. The repression that followed was brutal, as hundreds of anarchists, socialists, republicans, unionists, and freethinkers were arrested, imprisoned, and exiled. Most infamously, blame was shouldered by the radical anarchist pedagogue Francisco Ferrer i Guardia, who was executed by firing squad on 13 October, following a trial widely regarded as a sham both in Spain and internationally.

Like any major historical event, the Tragic Week and its significance has been the subject of a range of interpretations. In her influential 1968 work *The Tragic Week*, Joan Connelly Ullman

---

2. Notable exceptions include Joan Connelly Ullman, *The Tragic Week: A Study of Anticlericalism in Spain* (Cambridge: Harvard University Press, 1968); Temma Kaplan, *Red City, Blue Period: Social Movements in Picasso's Barcelona* (Berkeley: University of California Press, 1992); and Angel Smith, *Anarchism, Revolution and Reaction: Catalan Labour and the Crisis of the Spanish State, 1898–1923* (New York: Berghahn, 2007), 175.

3. One of the best English-language studies of Barcelona through this era is Chris Ealham, *Anarchism and the City: Revolution and Counter-Revolution in Barcelona, 1898–1937* (Oakland: AK Press, 2010). Earlier version available at: https://libcom.org/files/Class,%20Culture%20and%20Confict%20in%20Barcelona_0.pdf.

saw the events as primarily the result of radical republicans, who sought to direct the anger and energy of Barcelona's popular classes towards the Church and away from genuine social revolution.[4] A decade later, Joaquín Romero Maura portrayed the events as a decisive turning point in the history of Spain's huge anarchist movement: a moment when the nineteenth-century tactics of spontaneous uprising were finally revealed as the "ghosts of past errors" and were soon replaced by the "modern" strategies of revolutionary syndicalism.[5] Like Ullman, Romero Maura highlights how capitalists and factories were spared from the violence while the city's religious institutions burned, seeing this as evidence of the lack of class consciousness amongst the protesters, who saw the removal of the Church from public life as panacea for all of Spain's problems.[6] In both readings, the Tragic Week was portrayed as more akin to a pre-modern revolt than a true revolution.[7]

In following decades, works by Joan Culla and José Álvarez Junco have questioned both Ullman and Romero Maura, stressing that while the Tragic Week had no clear leadership—either anarchist or republican—the popular unrest can still be regarded as rational (Culla) and reflective of the distinctly modern mobilizing political cultures in the city (Álvarez Junco).[8] More recently both Angel Smith and Maria Thomas have emphasized the political nature of anti-clericalism during the Tragic Week, inverting Ullman's position to argue that the protesters regarded attacking the Church as essential to the revolution: as constitutive of social change rather than a distraction from it.[9] For all of these scholars,

---

4. Ullman, *The Tragic Week*, 322–332.

5. Joaquin Romero Maura, *La rosa de fuego: Republicanos y anarquistas: La política de los obreros barceloneses entre el desastre colonial y la semana trágica, 1899–1909* (Barcelona: Ediciones Grijalbo 1975), 472.

6. Romero Maura, *La rosa de fuego*, 521 and 536–37.

7. On this distinction see Samuel Cohn, "The 'modernity' of medieval popular revolt," *History Compass* 10:10 (2012): 731–741.

8. Joan B. Culla i Clara, *El Republicanisme lerrouxista a Catalunya: 1901–1923* (Barcelona: Curial 1986), 212; José Álvarez Junco, *The Emergence of Mass Politics in Spain: Populist Demagoguery and Republican Culture, 1890–1910* (Brighton: Sussex Academic Press, 2002), 148–151. See also the more extensive Spanish-language version of Álvarez Junco's above work, *El emperador del paralelo: Lerroux y la demagogia populista* (Madrid: Alianza 1990), in which 371–418 covers the Tragic Week.

9. Smith, *Anarchism, Revolution and Reaction,* 179–80; Maria Thomas, "The

the anticlerical violence witnessed during the Tragic Week was less a symptom of the "primitive" or "undeveloped" political strategies of the Spanish working class and more the product of a deep-felt antipathy to the Church, which was regarded as a concrete and powerful enemy on the path to progress. These views were whipped up in Barcelona from the turn of the century onwards, by both the anarchist movement—which had maintained an intense anti-clerical position since its inception in the 1860s—and in the popular demagoguery of the radical republican Alejandro Lerroux following his arrival in the city's politics in 1901. In one of the more interesting studies of the last few years, Josep Pons-Altés and Miguel López-Morell have attempted to shift the focus of the Tragic Week away from the anticlerical violence, which dominates almost every other study. By bringing in analysis of the many other areas in Catalonia where unrest broke out in 1909, they show how outside Barcelona attacks on the Church were rare and instead the Tragic Week took a clearly revolutionary, republican form.[10]

It is not the intention of this introduction to settle these ongoing historiographical debates, but rather to situate the following piece within them, returning to the words and observations of a participant in the events and their aftermath. The historical value of Bonafulla's work resides not in its historical "accuracy": as noted by the translator of this work, the original edition published in January 1910 was rushed, full of errors of fact and slippages in spelling and typography. Bonafulla also assumes a great deal of knowledge on behalf of the reader, throwing in individuals, events and themes with little introduction, to the extent that approaching this work cold may leave the reader slightly bewildered. Nevertheless, this work provides something unique to anyone interested in the experience of popular unrest, revolutionary possibilities and state repression. Part eyewitness account, part reconstruction from press and legal sources, *The July Revolution* stands as the only extended

faith and the fury: The construction of anticlerical collective identities in Spain, 1874–1931," *European History Quarterly* 43:1, (2013): 73–95.

10. Josep M. Pons-Altés and Miguel A. López-Morell, "Barcelona and the Tragic Week of 1909: A crazed mob or citizens in revolt?," *International Journal of Iberian Studies* 29:1 (2016): 3–19.

contemporary anarchist piece of writing on the Tragic Week. As such, we see how a prominent radical publisher made sense of this event and the repression that followed: how the eruption of violence was seen as an inevitable response to the machinations of capitalism, the state and its colonial ambitions, and religion; how the Tragic Week "did not have a leader" but was rather the spontaneous impulse of "unknown heroes" amongst the Barcelona working class; and, crucially, how the Spanish state used the events of 25 July–2 August to justify a ruthless repression against the anarchist movement, culminating in the execution of Ferrer. While Bonafulla may not be able to provide us with a wholly reliable account of *what happened* over these days, weeks, and months, few other sources can tell us *how it felt* to be a part of them and *what they meant* to an anarchist at the time.

I

The short-term origins of the Tragic Week lay in the "grossly insensitive" decision of the Spanish government to call up conscript reservists in early June 1909 following an escalation of conflict in Spanish-controlled Morocco.[11] In the minds of many of Spain's conservative and liberal reformers, expansion into Moroccan territory and markets would off-set the damaging loss of Cuba in 1898 and limit French interests in the area, which had been formalized alongside the Spanish claims in 1904. Business interests, Catholic expansionists, and the military all began to push for action in Morocco, culminating in the 1908 expedition from the Spanish outpost of Melilla into the surrounding Rif Mountains, on the premise of protecting Spanish mining interests from Berber tribes. Guerrilla fighting escalated through 1909, culminating in an attack on a Moroccan railway line in early June. It was this intensification of fighting that prompted the conservative government of Antonio Maura to call up the reservists.[12] Both the colonial maneuvers of

---

11. Smith, *Anarchism, Revolution and Reaction*, 175.
12. On the growing Spanish presence in Morocco and the escalation of conflict in 1909, see Sebastian Balfour, *Deadly Embrace: Morocco and the road to the Span-*

the government and the conscription system—which allowed rich young men to buy their way to exemption from service, while the poor were forced to leave their homes and families—were loathed by the Spanish working class, while antimilitarism and anticolonialism were shared across the Spanish left, especially within the anarchist movement, which had generally been supportive of Cuban independence in the previous decade and was ideologically hostile to the Army.[13]

The July Revolution begins with a discussion of this situation in Morocco, viewing the escalating conflict as the result of entangling business and imperial interests. It was, to Bonafulla, to the anarchist movement, and to a wide sector of Spanish society, "a bourgeois war... the result of a ruinous association of professional politicians and the banking elite" (p. 46). The reader is introduced to a range of companies and figures in these opening passages, such as *Compañia Norte Africana* and the Count of Romanones, a wealthy Liberal businessman and newspaper proprietor, whose "scheming" with both French and German interests had resulted in the grotesque exploitation of Morocco. We are left in no doubt as to Bonafulla's view on why the conflict arose in Morocco: beyond all the details, the political intrigue and international treaties, it was the "transparent greed and egoism" (p. 53) of the capitalist class that lay at the root of the call-up and the protest which followed.

With the Spanish parliament in recess, the only arena where popular anger at the call-up could be expressed was the streets.[14] A series of public anti-war protests erupted across the country, most notably in Barcelona, where predominantly female crowds conducted mass demonstrations as troops embarked at the city's port. News of heavy Spanish casualties on Monday 19 July radicalized these protests further, prompting huge anti-war demonstrations across Catalonia. Cries of "Death to the police!" "We're fighting for

---

ish Civil War (Oxford: Oxford University Press, 2002), 3–30.

13. Álvarez Junco, *La ideología política del anarquismo español (1868–1910)* (Madrid: Siglo XXI, 1991) 272–277 and Rafael Núñez Florencio, *"Patria y ejercito desde la ideología anarquista,"* Hispania: Revista Española de Historia, 178 (1991): 589–643.

14. Álvarez Junco, *The Emergence of Mass Politics*, 144.

the mines, not our country!" "Down with Maura!" "Send the friars!" and "Long live freedom!" were raised as soldiers made their way to the ships, while the national anthem was whistled and jeered by angry crowds.[15] Bonafulla gives a vivid picture of these protests, stressing that they were both spontaneous and an "absolutely just" response to reservists being called "to die in Africa" (p. 55). This was no planned insubordination, nor an attempt by militants to provoke unrest, but rather the product of the despair of "tearful, desperate people" (p. 56).

Several groups now began to make plans to transform these demonstrations into a more concerted protest movement, and on Thursday 22 July a committee formed of anarchists, syndicalists, socialists, and republicans called a general strike, to begin on Monday 26. The strike was supported by the majority of Barcelona's working class, and soon spread to other towns in Catalonia. This politicized industrial action rapidly developed into popular unrest in Barcelona, as barricades were erected in working-class *barrios* (districts), dividing the city between a popular insurgency of the left, freethinkers, and progressive educators on one side, and the army and quasi-military Civil Guard on the other. Clashes between these two blocs became increasingly violent, while the middle classes and ruling elites of the city closed their businesses and withdrew to their homes.[16]

After paralyzing the city's economy and clashing with the forces of order, protesters turned against the Catholic Church. These attacks began on the first night of the Tragic Week, as men and women gathered by a Catholic School in the industrial district of Pueblo Nuevo, before destroying the nearby streetlights and torching the building.[17] Over the following week dozens more burnings would follow across the city, often with little or no resistance from

15. Cited in Pons-Altés and López-Morell, "Barcelona and the Tragic Week," 6.
16. Ullman, *The Tragic Week*, 167–282, provides perhaps the most comprehensive account of the day-by-day developments; see also Maura, *La rosa de fuego*, 509–42; Xavier Cuadrat, *Socialismo y anarquismo en Cataluña (1899–1911): Los orígenes de la CNT* (Madrid: Ediciones de la Revista de Trabajo, 1976), 382–92; Dalmau, *Siete días de furia*, 97–105.
17. Ullman, *The Tragic Week*, 192–93.

local residents.[18] Bonafulla's account of the church burnings in Chapter 2 of *The July Revolution* is relatively brief, though it does give a sense of their scale and spread, listing off dozens of institutions that were targeted across Barcelona's districts. Religious artefacts and the material wealth of the Church were also targeted: rather than looting, protestors destroyed what they found in the churches and convents, seemingly motivated by "a consuming passion to destroy everything in sight."[19] Crowds "in search of the dark secrets behind cloistered walls" ransacked religious cemeteries and disinterred the bodies they found there, seeking to prove rumors of the sexual perversions of priests by exposing of the abused bodies of nuns.[20] A desire to expose and purify runs through all of these acts: when morning arrived the sun would now shine onto the exposed, roofless stone shells of Church property, gutted of its objects and no longer able to shelter the secrets of its dead.[21] For Romero Maura, this curiosity and distrust at what occurred behind church walls, and the desire to expose it, is central to understanding the Tragic Week, reflective of a complete disconnect between the Catholic Church and the working class in Barcelona.[22] As Bonafulla notes, similar comments were made from the federalist leader Francisco Pi y Arsuaga, who warned in his analysis of the Tragic Week that the Church had become "a friend to the meek in appearance only" (p. 111) and that "the secrecy of monastic life has favored evil thinking" (p. 109). Bonafulla would appear to concur, stating in his own analysis of the burnings that the people were "venting their

---

18. The exact number of church properties burned varies in different accounts: Ullman, *The Tragic Week*, 286, cites the official report of the Bishop of Barcelona, who stated that twelve churches and thirty to forty convents were destroyed; Romero Maura, *La rosa de fuego*, 516–17 states that twenty one churches and thirty convents were burned, and five others rescued by Carlists and local residents. Álvarez Junco, *The Emergence of Mass Politics* claims that "some fifty churches, monasteries and church schools" were burned, while Pons-Altés and López-Morell, "Barcelona and the Tragic Week," 3–4 states that "almost 100 religious buildings were attacked." Whatever the exact figure, it is clear that a large proportion (just under 50%) of Barcelona's religious institutions were attacked in some way.

19. Smith, *Anarchism, Revolution and Reaction*, 180.

20. Álvarez Junco, *The Emergence of Mass Politics*, 146.

21. This point is drawn from a talk given by Mary Vincent at the University of Sheffield on 8 May 2018.

22. Romero Maura, *La rosa de fuego*, 524–33.

collective hatred" and exposing "the crimes of a murderous regime" (p. 70).[23]

Similar forms of anticlerical violence marked the first months of the Spanish Civil War in 1936, when once again hundreds of religious buildings were burned, artifacts destroyed, and the bodies of nuns dug up and paraded in streets across Republican Spain. Yet, unlike the violence at the start of the Civil War, the Tragic Week saw relatively few attacks on members of the clergy. By the end of the week one Marist Brother, one Franciscan Monk and one priest had been killed, alongside 104 civilians (both protesters and onlookers), two civil guards, five members of the military, one municipal policeman and one security guard.[24] This was in stark contrast to the wave of violence in 1936, in which over 4,000 priests and 2,300 monks were killed in what is regarded as "the greatest anticlerical bloodletting Europe has ever seen."[25] While clearly distressing for those that valued the Church's architecture and material possessions, it is perhaps the focus of violence against property as opposed to people that led an anarchist like Bonafulla to depict the Tragic Week as a moment of revolutionary "decency," conducted by "brave" crowds (p. 67-68), acting in a "correct, measured—all too measured" manner (p. 114), while those few who engaged in murder or looting were merely "isolated cases committed by the vile scum spawned by a perverse society" (p. 67).

At midnight on Friday 30 July the Church of San Juan in the district of Horta was burned and a nearby convent school was ransacked, becoming the last religious buildings to be attacked during the Tragic Week. Military and Civil Guard reinforcements had been arriving over the previous day and began to disperse protesters and ensure a return to "order" in the city. Public transport resumed over

---

23. Natalie Zemon Davies's work on early modern anticlerical violence make for interesting comparisons with the Tragic Week, see "The rites of violence: Religious riot in sixteenth-century France," *Past and Present* 59 (1973): 51–91 and "Writing 'The rites of violence' and afterward," *Past and Present* 214, Supplement 7 (2012): 8–29.

24. Ullman, *The Tragic Week*, 285–56; Romero Maura, *La rosa de fuego*, 515.

25. Mary Vincent, "'The keys of the kingdom': Religious violence in the Spanish Civil War" in *The Splintering of Spain: Cultural History and the Spanish Civil War, 1936–1939*, ed. Chris Ealham and Michael Richards (Cambridge: Cambridge University Press, 2005), 68.

the weekend and on Monday 2 August workers returned to the factories.[26] As the rebellion was quelled and repression began it was clear that blame would be shouldered by the radical left. The syndicalist federation Solidaridad Obrera and its paper were closed under martial law and high-profile anarchists and labor leaders fled the city. A number of those who stayed were accused of directing the rebellion, alongside senior figures in the radical republican party. In total over 2,000 people were arrested in Barcelona, of whom five were executed, including Ramón Clemente García, a young coalman with (unspecified) mental disabilities who was accused of dancing in the streets with the disinterred corpse of a nun.[27] Clemente García's case occupies the whole of Chapter 5 of *The July Revolution*, which makes clear the anger and indignation felt by Bonafulla towards this sentence. The reader gets a snapshot here of the swift, uncompromising, and exemplary "justice" that was handed out in the aftermath of the Tragic Week. While it is impossible to know the truth of the incident in question—his defense attorney claimed Clemente García was simply moving the body he had discovered in the street (p. 126)—all those called to testify in this case were clear that he had not taken up arms (which made him innocent of the major crime of rebellion) and was not mentally capable of answering for his actions in court. In Bonafulla's words, Clemente García was "a good example of illiteracy and the failure of the Church as educator of the people" (p. 138). The same Church that had failed "the boy" was, for Bonafulla, responsible for his death, with the "higher and lower clergy" demanding a "show of force" following the attack on its property and prestige (p. 138).

In the trials that followed fifty-nine further protesters were given life sentences in prison and 178 were exiled from the city, including Bonafulla, who began writing *The July Revolution* account during his internal exile in Siétamo (Aragon). Bonafulla reproduces a number of accounts from the exile groups, giving a valuable insight into this punishment that was used repeatedly over the turn of the century, often against known anarchists against whom little concrete evidence of crimes could be brought. For Bonafulla the

---

26.   Ullman, *The Tragic Week*, 261–82.
27.   Ullman, *The Tragic Week*, 291.

"humiliating" experience of being paraded through rural villages and kept in "filthy jail cells, wretched hospitals, or in the barracks of the Civil Guards," unable to work and without support from the authorities, was enough to cause "one's fists to clench" (p. 140). The only positive aspect of this experience was the general kindness, hospitality, and solidarity shown to them by the local populations, rather patronizingly described in a letter co-signed by Bonafulla as "simple folk" (p. 144). The most intense stage of repression was only just beginning to ease as Bonafulla finished his work. International protests across the European and American left had flared up strongly against Maura's government in the months from August to October, almost entirely focused on the decision to blame the Tragic Week on the radical educator Francisco Ferrer. At first these protests called for Ferrer's release, and then exploded in furious response to his execution on 13 October. While the response in Spain was initially muted in comparison, the Liberal party, supported by the parliamentary socialists and republicans, used this moment to force Maura out of office just over a week after Ferrer's death, a process depicted in Chapters 12 and 13 of *The July Revolution*.[28]

II

In the following section I will discuss the major groups involved in the Tragic Week, giving a sense of the background and outlook of the three main mobilizing forces of the Barcelona working class: the anarchist and syndicalist movements, the radical republicans and, to a lesser extent, the socialists.

Anarchism had strong roots in Spain. The Spanish branch of the First International (FRE), founded in 1870, generally favored the ideas and strategies of Mikhail Bakunin to those of Karl Marx. Politicized labor organization in Spain thus tended towards decentralized organization and radical, confrontational tactics, particularly in southwest Andalusia and Barcelona, where the anarchist

---

28. See Ullman, *The Tragic Week*, 307–321.

movement became hegemonic amongst the working class.[29] In contrast, the Spanish socialist movement, founded after a split from the FRE in the early 1870s, favored a more "orthodox" strategy based on legalist unionism and centralized control—reflected in their national union (UGT)—and sought power through government in their parliamentary party (PSOE). Despite their strength in Madrid and northern industrial areas such as Asturias and Vizcaya, the PSOE-UGT failed to make any significant gains in national politics until after the First World War and was always a minority presence in Barcelona.[30]

The anarchist movement was repressed soon after it emerged. Following the brief First Spanish Republic (1873–1874), the Bourbon monarchy returned to power following the *pronuncamiento* (military coup) of General Manuel Pavía, and the FRE was declared illegal. The anarchist movement returned to legality only in the 1880s, re-establishing their national federation (now known as the FTRE), which soon claimed around 50,000 adherents. This flourishing was, however, soon undermined by schisms between anarcho-collectivists who favored a union-orientated strategy, and anarcho-communists, who regarded small-group direct action as the only legitimate revolutionary tactic. As the FTRE unraveled in the late 1880s, the movement was cut adrift from the majority of the Spanish working class.[31] Even more damaging was the upsurge in anarchist violence in the 1890s, as a tiny minority in the movement took up the strategy of "propaganda by the deed" (terrorism) in an effort to shock the working class into revolution. This decade was marked by anarchist outrages across Europe and the Americas, both in the form of targeted assassinations of state officials and indiscriminate public bombings, cementing the image

---

29. The best study in English of the origins of the anarchist movement in Spain remains George Esenwein, *Anarchist Ideology and the Working Class Movement in Spain, 1868–1898* (Berkeley: University of California Press, 1989), 11–38. In Spanish, see Josep Termes, *Anarquismo y sindicalismo en España: La Primera Internacional (1864–1881)* (Barcelona: Crítica, 1977).

30. On the early socialist movement see Paul Heywood, *Marxism and the Failure of Organised Socialism in Spain, 1879–1936* (Cambridge: Cambridge University Press, 1990), 1–28.

31. Esenwein, *Anarchist Ideology*, 78–133.

of the anarchist as the "mad bomber" in the public imaginary.[32] Three major anarchist attacks took place in Barcelona: an attack on General Martínez Campos on 24 September 1893 by the printer Paulino Pallás; the bombing of the Líceo opera house by Santiago Salvador on 7 November 1893; and the bombing of the Corpus Cristi Procession on 7 June 1896 by an unknown assailant. In response the Spanish state enacted a brutal and indiscriminate repression, arresting hundreds of known anarchists and radical activists and holding them in Montjuich castle, where they were deprived of food, drink and sleep, beaten, gagged, manacled, forced to sit on hot irons, and subject to sexual abuse. A wave of protest erupted around Europe at the excesses of "Black Spain," cast as a backwards land where the Inquisition had returned, with Prime Minister Antonio Cánovas del Castillo at its head as a reincarnation of the infamous Grand Inquisitor Tomás de Torquemada. Some revenge was secured in August 1897, when the Italian anarchist Michele Angiollio shot Cánovas dead at a Basque spa town, yet this did nothing to repair the enormous damage that had been inflicted upon the movement following the turn to terrorism.[33]

We can see the legacy of the anarchist experience of the 1890s in Bonafulla's discussion of the repression that followed the Tragic Week, which returns to the themes of Inquisitorial Spain—now with Prime Minister Antonio Maura cast as the Inquisitor-General—beholden to a corrupt Church and the malicious interests of capital. Bonafulla frames this repression as "cruel brutality... more inquisitorial, if that is possible, than during the times when the agony of barbaric passions touched even the children of the children of the torture victims" (p. 81). More concretely, we can see direct parallels in the response of the Spanish state to popular acts of violence, with the mass arrests, torture, sham trials, and

---

32. Richard Bach Jensen, "Daggers, rifles and dynamite: Anarchist terrorism in the nineteenth century," *Terrorism and Political Violence*, 16:1 (2004): 116–153; Constance Bantman, "The era of propaganda by the deed," in *The Palgrave Handbook of Anarchism*, ed. Carl Levy and Matthew Adams (London: Palgrave Macmillan, 2018), 371–87.

33. See James Michael Yeoman, *Print Culture and the Formation of the Anarchist Movement in Spain* (London and New York: Routledge, 2020), 62–119.

exemplary punishment that followed the Tragic Week, as well as a similar international outcry that followed. A year after the death of Cánovas the Spanish state faced an existential crisis. By the late nineteenth century Cuba was Spain's last significant imperial possession, and a major factor in the Spanish economy. A grueling war for independence had begun in Cuba in 1895, which eventually prompted US intervention in April 1898. Three months later the Spanish had been defeated, and Cuba, the Philippines, and Puerto Rico were lost. This "Disaster" was a massive blow to the Spanish national psyche: at a time when other European powers were consolidating huge global empires, Spain was now a second-tier nation, humiliated and ignored on the international stage. The effects of this moment were profound, setting in motion many of the fractures that would result in the Civil War of 1936–39. A clamor for "regeneration" went up from all sides of society, from republicans and socialists to reformist conservatives such as Maura.[34] As discussed earlier, one potential source of "regeneration" for imperialists and business interests was sought in Morocco, where Spain had held protectorates since the 1880s. Amongst liberals, education reform was viewed as a source of national salvation, while regionalism was the route taken by a growing section of the Catalan bourgeoisie. While they shared a desire to change the existing order, these tendencies were often as hostile to one another—and to the socialist and anarchist movements—as they were to the established elite.[35]

Amongst the most dynamic new political actors at this moment were the radical republicans, who saw an overthrow of the Bourbon Restoration as the only viable solution to Spain's perceived malaise. This group formed in the first years of the twentieth century under the leadership of Alejandro Lerroux, a journalist and populist demagogue who had broken the liberal parties' duopoly in Barcelona in 1901 by winning a seat in the *Cortes* (parliament).

---

34. An excellent study of the war and its impact in Spain is given in Sebastian Balfour, *The End of the Spanish Empire, 1898-1923* (Oxford: Clarendon Press, 1997).

35. Pol Dalmau, *Press, Politics and National Identities in Catalonia: The Transformation of La Vanguardia, 1881-1931* (Brighton: Sussex Academic Press, 2017) does a good job of charting these tendencies through the lens of one of Catalonia's most important families, see esp. 93-160.

Lerroux had previously been close to the anarchist movement, styling himself as a revolutionary and holding dramatic mass meetings in which he violently denounced the Catholic Church and the growing strength of bourgeois Catalan regionalism. Bonafulla himself praised Lerroux's "noble aims" in 1900, echoing the sentiment of much of the anarchist movement.[36] While his decision to stand for parliament provoked anger from his former anarchist colleagues, he nevertheless remained close to several figures in the movement, in particular its minority of middle-class activists such as Francisco Ferrer.[37] Both Ferrer and Lerroux were implicated in the attempted assassination of King Alfonso XIII in 1906, in which Mateo Morral—a worker at Ferrer's school—had thrown a bomb at the King's wedding procession, leaving his target unharmed but killing twenty-four soldiers and civilians. Ferrer was arrested and accused of funding and inspiring the attack, and while he was eventually acquitted in 1907—following a strong international campaign for his release—the Spanish authorities remained convinced of his guilt and his school was permanently closed. Lerroux, meanwhile, spent much of the following years in prison and in exile.[38]

When agitation began in 1909 Lerroux was in Argentina, though his party retained considerable support in Barcelona through its network of *ateneos* (social spaces) and the youth movement, which attracted support from some well-known anarchists and was popular amongst the city's lower-middle-class.[39] The *lerrouxistas* responded to the anti-war protests with rhetorical enthusiasm, yet refused to give political direction to the growing movement. As discussed above, Ullman makes a strong claim that it was this group that encouraged the outburst of church burnings that defined the Tragic Week, as its leaders in the city sought to dissipate genuine revolutionary activity through anticlericalism. This analysis is alluring. For all their talk of overthrowing the Restoration monarchy, in practice the radicals had largely remained

36. Smith, *Anarchism, Revolution and Reaction*, 163.
37. Romero Maura, *La rosa de fuego*, 491–92.
38. The best study of Lerroux is Álvarez Junco, *El Emperador* and its abridged English translation, *The Emergence of Mass Politics*.
39. Smith, *Anarchism, Revolution and Reaction*, 170.

committed to working within the existing political settlement. However, more recent scholarship has generally downplayed the likelihood of any group directing the Tragic Week in such a coherent manner, even if the events could broadly be seen as a "republican" rebellion.[40] Nevertheless, while Lerroux and his followers did not "lead" the Tragic Week in a direct sense, since 1901 they had helped to create a broad, anti-clerical, anti-bourgeois atmosphere amongst Barcelona's popular classes, in which he and his party overlapped considerably with the city's other major mobilizing force: the anarchist movement.[41]

Repression against anarchism relaxed following the "Disaster" of 1898, prompting an unparalleled expansion of the movement. Over the turn of the century, anarchist groups recovered their strength in their traditional heartlands of Andalusia and Catalonia, and reached out into new areas of support, from Gijón on the northern coast to Tenerife in the Canary Islands; from Vigo on the Atlantic to Valencia on the Mediterranean. The movement was quick to re-establish its national federation, now named the FSORE, which surpassed the size of the socialist UGT within a year of its founding. New ideas and initiatives blossomed, including an upsurge in anarchist-feminism, spearheaded by the pioneering activists Soledad Gustavo and Teresa Claramunt. While much of the movement remained highly patriarchal in both theory and practice, it was at this point that a sustained attention to the dynamics of gender oppression was ingrained into anarchist ideology and culture in Spain, most notably in its demands for co-education of boys and girls and equal rights in the workplace.

The re-emergence of anarchism in Spain went hand-in-hand with a shift in focus of revolutionary strategy. Rather than immediate, violent action, the movement turned towards education, or a "raising of culture," as key components of building an enlightened revolutionary working class. A huge range of intellectual fields were brought into anarchist thinking and discussion, from the revolutionary potential of synthetic food to the sociological necessity for

---

40. Pons-Altés and López-Morell, "Barcelona and the Tragic Week," 3–19.
41. Álvarez Junco, *The Emergence of Mass Politics*, 148–149.

birth control and public hygiene.[42] In order to harness the power of their faith in "progress," the anarchist movement targeted schooling as a key site of struggle, especially as Spain had one of the worst illiteracy rates in Europe, with around sixty-five percent unable to read or write to a measurable standard, a figure which was far worse in working-class and rural areas and amongst women. Anarchists sought to emancipate the Spanish masses from this "ignorance," setting up improvised schools and night classes in social centers and union premises which could impart education free from the influence of the Catholic Church and bourgeois reformers.[43]

The pinnacle of this drive towards education was the Modern School established by Francisco Ferrer in Barcelona in 1901, which soon became a symbol across Europe and the Americas for advanced, radical pedagogy.[44] Ferrer was from a middle-class background in Barcelona, and in the late nineteenth century had been a supporter of the revolutionary republicanism of Manuel Ruiz Zorrilla. After joining Zorrilla's failed attempt to overthrow the monarchy in 1885, Ferrer and his family moved to Paris, where he was drawn into the French anarchist milieu and befriended key activists such as Louise Michel, Eliseé Reclus, and Jean Grave. He also became deeply interested in the radical, "integral" schooling pioneered by Paul Robin, which called for an educational environment attuned to the individual wants and needs of every student. Following Robin, Ferrer began to form ideas for a school promoting radical education, which would be experiential, non-religious, and gender-free; an education of both body and mind that broke down spurious, bourgeois boundaries between intellectual and physical work. In 1901 Ferrer received a huge inheritance (around a million francs) from a wealthy widow he had been tutoring and returned to Spain to put his ideas for libertarian schooling in practice.[45]

---

42. See Richard Cleminson, *Anarchism, Science and Sex: Eugenics in Eastern Spain, 1900–1937* (Oxford: Peter Lang, 2000).
43. On both of these paragraphs see Yeoman, *Print Culture*, 120–197.
44. On the impact of Ferrer in the US see Paul Avrich, *The Modern School Movement: Anarchism and Education in the United States* (Princeton: Princeton University Press, 1980).
45. Juan Avilés Farré, *Francisco Ferrer y Guardia: Pedagogo, anarquista y mártir* (Madrid: Marcial Pons 2006), 17–99. For Ferrer's account of his school's opening

Libertad) provided the movement with a combination of high culture and organizational information, with its editors Soledad Gustavo and her husband Federico Urales becoming the de facto elite of anarchist culture.[50]

The repression of the 1890s lingered longer in Barcelona than elsewhere in Spain, but the city soon began to reassert its position as the most important site of anarchism and anarchist publishing in Spain. The first major periodical to appear in this period was *El Productor*, the creation of thirteen anarchist groups who met in Gràcia early 1901 to reorganize the anarchist presence in the city. The editors of this paper were two anarchist activists who had recently returned from exile: the textile worker and pioneering anarchist-feminist Teresa Claramunt and the shoemaker and labor activist, Joan Baptista Esteve, better known by his pseudonym Leopoldo Bonafulla.[51] Reports vary on the nature of Claramunt and Bonafulla's relationship: in some accounts the two were simply close colleagues, though others claim they were a couple. Either way, the two formed a dynamic pairing, and soon made *El Productor* one of the most important publications of the movement. A year later Claramunt and Bonafulla undertook a propaganda tour through Andalusia, passing through numerous towns in the provinces of Cádiz, Seville, Huelva, Málaga, and Granada, where they were joined by local activists in meetings of thousands of people.[52]

Claramunt and Bonafulla led the way in the resurgence of anarchist publishing in Barcelona. It was soon joined by Ferrer's *La Huelga General*, which generally contained more theoretical pieces than the worker orientated *El Productor*. Many others followed, including José Prat's influential journal *Natura*, Luis Bulffi's neo-Malthusian *Salud y Fuerza*, and *La Tramontana*, one of the very few anarchist publications to be published in the Catalan language. *El Productor* was frequently forced to suspend its publication following repression, and in 1906 the paper closed for good. However, Bonafulla continued to contribute to every major

---

50. Yeoman, *Print Culture*, 40–61 gives an overview of anarchist print culture in this period.
51. Smith, *Anarchism, Revolution and Reaction*, 117.
52. Yeoman, *Print Culture*, 147–48.

periodical of the movement and published a string of pamphlets in the following years, including *Generación libre* (1905), a critique of neo-Malthusianism, and in 1908 launched a new weekly named *El Rebelde*. Bonafulla's interpretation of anarchism was deliberately broad. Having experienced the fractures between anarcho-collectivists and communists in the 1880s and 1890s, he saw firsthand how hardline positions could damage the unity of the movement. *El Productor* was open to differing positions on contentious issues such as the role of anarchists in labor organizations, and Bonafulla himself was flexible in his attitude to other political groups, encouraging collaboration with socialists and republicans during labor unrest. During a citywide general strike in support of the Metalworkers Federation in 1902, which paralyzed Barcelona for over a week, Bonafulla had called for broad working class solidarity, although his insistence on more combative stance towards the employers was a tacit critique of the socialists' calls for conciliation. His role in this strike resulted in a spell in prison, during which time he received financial support from the Liberal politician José Canalejas. When news of this assistance broke anarchist opinion was scathing, and Bonafulla began to lose his high standing within the movement. While he continued to contribute to the cultural sphere of the movement, he was left somewhat outside of the developments within anarchist organization in the following years, the most important of which was the incorporation of syndicalism into anarchist thought and practice.[53]

Syndicalism signified revolutionary trade unionism, combined with a commitment to collective, direct action that made workers the instrument of change. As such, it was broadly compatible with anarchist ideology, indeed in many respects it could be seen as a development from nineteenth-century anarchist-collectivism, albeit with greater emphasis on tactics such as the general strike, boycotts, and sabotage.[54] While syndicalism owed a great deal

---

53. Smith, *Anarchism, Revolution and Reaction*, 118, 120, 123–4, 128.
54. For a broad overview see Marcel van der Linden and Wayne Thorpe, "The rise and fall of revolutionary syndicalism," in *Revolutionary Syndicalism: An International Perspective*, ed. Marcel van der Linden and Wayne Thorpe (Aldershot: Scolar

to ideas and practices from countries such as Britain, Ireland, the USA, Australia, Argentina, Brazil, and South Africa, it was in France that it found its most prominent supporters and thinkers. Sections of the international anarchist movement were inspired by the growing success of the French Confédération Générale du Travail (CGT), which adopted revolutionary syndicalism at its IX Congress in 1906.[55] Syndicalist ideas had been gradually filtering into Spain from France since the turn of the century, gaining strong support in Catalonia, where syndicalism was seen as a means to bypass the long-standing problems within anarchist organizing, providing a means of mass mobilization for the revolution that was both coherent and coordinated, yet also autonomous and worker-led.[56]

In 1907, fifty-seven workers' societies in Barcelona came together to constitute the Federación Local Solidaridad Obrera de Barcelona (known as Solidaridad Obrera, hereafter SO), which sought to coordinate socialist, radical republican, and anarchist groups in the city, providing a united organization that represented the entire workers' movement. SO portrayed itself as independent of all political positions—including anarchism—defining itself as a "purely syndicalist" organisation which would fight solely for the economic interests of its affiliates. In 1908 it expanded into a regional federation, encompassing all of Catalonia and claiming the support of 20-25,000 workers. This expansion was aided by its periodical, *Solidaridad Obrera*, launched in October 1907 (reportedly with financial backing from Ferrer), and an almost entirely anarchist staff. SO's commitment to nonpartisan syndicalism was challenged from the outset. Both socialists and radical republicans in Barcelona tried to use SO to forward their own electoral objectives and opposed the organization when they failed to control it.

Press 1990), 1–24 and Marcel van der Linden, "Second thoughts on revolutionary syndicalism," *Labour History Review* 63:2 (1998), 182–196.

55. An excellent collection of case studies of the development of syndicalism outside Europe and the Americas is Steven Hirsch and Lucien van der Walt, eds., *Anarchism and Syndicalism in the Postcolonial World, 1870–1940: The Praxis of National Liberation, Internationalism and Social Revolution* (Leiden and Boston: Brill, 2010). Available at: https://libcom.org/files/Anarchism1870_1940.pdf. See also Ilham Khuri-Makdisi, *The Eastern Mediterranean and the Making of Global Radicalism* (Berkeley: University of California Press, 2010).

56. Yeoman, *Print Culture*, 198–202.

In contrast, the anarchist majority in SO wanted to ensure that the organization fulfilled its stated revolutionary goals, steering it away from parliamentary politics and towards confrontational industrial action. They portrayed SO as both the inheritor of the anarchist organizational tradition and a "modern" organization, suitable for the realities of the twentieth century. Syndicalist ideas soon began to spread across the rest of Spain, most notably in Gijón on the northern coast, where a local syndicalist federation (also named Solidaridad Obrera) formed in early 1909. SO's leadership was spurred on by the growing number of requests to join the federation from outside Catalonia, and soon put plans in place to hold a congress to confirm its expansion into a national body.[57]

While it gained strength across Spain through early 1909, in Catalonia SO was faltering. Conflict was growing within the organization, with its socialist faction critiquing the anarchists for attempting to dominate the supposedly apolitical federation, and regarding the plans for SO's national expansion as a direct challenge to the UGT (which it was). SO was also under attack from the *lerrouxistas*, who had broken from both SO and the wider republican coalition in 1908 and were now openly critiquing their former colleagues. In response, SO called for a boycott of Lerroux's paper *Progreso*.[58] Perhaps most damaging was the growing critique of SO by anarchists, including Bonafulla and Claramunt through their new publication *El Rebelde*. In a reversal of his earlier position, Bonafulla now maintained that the tendencies within SO should operate separately, and claimed that the federation's leadership was operating in an overly centralized and reformist manner.[59] As

57. On SO see Xavier Cuadrat, *Socialismo y anarquismo en Cataluña (1899-1911): Los orígenes de la CNT* (Ediciones de la Revista de Trabajo, 1976), 187–285, available at: http://www.cedall.org/Documentacio/e-books/Origenes%20de%20la%20 CNT/Socialismo%20y%20Anarquismo%20en%20Catalu%C3%B1a%20(1899- 1911)%20Los%20origenes%20de%20la%20CNT%20-%20X.%20Cuadrat.pdf; Antonio Bar, *La CNT en los años rojos: Del sindicalismo revolucionario al anarcosindicalismo (1910-1926)* (Madrid: Akal, 1981), 23–36, available at: https://anarkobiblioteka2.files.wordpress.com/2016/08/la_cnt_en_los_ac3b1os_rojos_-_antonio_bar.pdf; Smith, *Anarchism, Revolution and Reaction*, 128–139 and 166–184; Jason Garner, *Goals and Means: Anarchism, Syndicalism, and Internationalism in the Origins of the Federación Anarquista Ibérica* (Oakland, Edinburgh and Baltimore: AK Press, 2016), 59–65.

58. Smith, *Anarchism, Revolution and Reaction*, 164–8.

59. Romero Maura, *La rosa de fuego*, 473–4.

the SO coalition fractured, its strategy for industrial action was failing to achieve gains for its members, particularly in the textile industry around Ter valley where employers were slashing wages and threatening massive job losses.[60]

As the anti-war protests erupted in July 1909 SO was therefore in a delicate position. The federation's response was to call a general strike as early as possible, ahead of the socialists' own calls for a national general strike on August 2. SO's leadership met on Thursday 22 July and put plans in place for the strike to begin on Monday 26. Over the weekend, the city's socialists and republicans came on board with the plan. While this may suggest that the Tragic Week was orchestrated by SO, examination of the events suggest that their role was only part of a broader expression of popular anger. As was often the case in modern Spain, anarchists and radical unionists were certainly a major part in the popular mobilization and violence of July–August 1909, but neither movement instigated nor directed this popular rebellion, a fact acknowledged by both movements.[61]

What then was the Tragic Week? Was it, as was claimed by Bonafulla in the title of this work, a "revolution"? We have already seen that what occurred in Barcelona in 1909 was not directed, or planned in great detail, as we may expect from a model of revolutions based on the French or Russian examples. For Bonafulla, however, the revolutionary nature of the Tragic Week was not undermined by the fact that it was not directed by anarchists; indeed, to Bonafulla and many other anarchists a revolution could *only* take place if it was "spontaneous, a generalized expression of outrage" (p. 153). "Direction" of the revolution—as was advocated by Spain's socialists—was anathema to anarchists, as it violated their interpretation of the sacrosanct principle of the First International: "the emancipation of the working class must be conquered by the working class themselves." Many other anarchist commentators would agree with Bonafulla's analysis. Anselmo Lorezno, the most senior figure in the movement and veteran of the First International in Spain, was inspired by what had occurred in Barcelona

60. Smith, *Anarchism, Revolution and Reaction*, 139.
61. Romero Maura, *La rosa de fuego*, 512–3.

precisely because it had not been directed by his comrades: "this is amazing!"—he is reported to have exclaimed—"A social revolution has broken out in Barcelona, initiated by an entity so ill-defined, [ill-] understood, or [ill-] recognized that it is sometimes vilified as a mob and other times hailed as The People. No-one has instigated this revolution! And no one directs it!"[62] This interpretation of the development of uprising was fairly astute. In the aftermath of the Tragic Week denial that there was a "leader" of the protests, strike, and church-burnings became a central part of the movement's defense against claims by the Spanish authorities that anarchists—in particular Ferrer—were to blame for all that had occurred. To Bonafulla such claims were "a conspiracy" in themselves, a "sinister plan" to deny the true spontaneity of the events "at the behest of a fierce hatred" (p. 153).

Nevertheless, to frame the Tragic Week as a revolution is questionable, even if those involved felt that they were involved in one.[63] Without wanting to excessively debate terminology, "revolution" by most understandings would suggest some sense of—or potential for—tangible political and social change. Even failed revolutions, such as across Europe in 1848 (a failure to radicals, at least), the Paris Commune, or the 1905 Russian Revolution, had substantial effects on national and international society. This was not the case for the Tragic Week, which was instead closer to a violent mass protest.[64] We can see hints of this view throughout Bonafulla's account, which is frequently pessimistic about the prospects for the "revolution." Bonafulla states that the crowds were "sunk" and "without any hope of victory" (p. 74) by Wednesday 27 July, and two days later the protesters had apparently "lost any hope" of political support to further their cause, presumably a remark upon the inactivity of republican leaders (p. 77). While this tone was perhaps unsurprising, given that it was written in the aftermath of defeat and repression, it does slightly temper the enthusiasm Bonafulla displays at other points. His remarks that "it would have been crazy to expect

---

62. Cited in James A. Baer, *Anarchist Immigrants in Spain and Argentina* (Urbana and Springfield: University of Illinois Press, 2015), 72.
63. Álvarez Junco, *The Emergence of Mass Politics*, 149.
64. Álvarez Junco, *The Emergence of Mass Politics*, 161.

complete triumph of the revolution" (p. 77) question not only the consistency of his analysis, but also his very conception of revolution. If, as Bonafulla seems to suggest, the Tragic Week was both a stunning example of revolutionary spirit and almost immediately doomed to failure, where does that leave his view—and that of most anarchist commentators at this time—that the only valid model of social and political change was spontaneous, popular rebellion?

It is also notable that anarchist commentators themselves did not use the term "revolution" for long after 1910, instead referring to it as "the protest" or "the events of Barcelona." Indeed, as will be discussed later, aside from Bonafulla's account, there was very little discussion of the Tragic Week itself in the movement's publications, which instead focused almost exclusively on the repression that followed. In contrast, the events were claimed by radical republicans, who referred to the week as "Glorious," in contrast to the term "Tragic" which was circulating in the mainstream press within weeks, in reference to the disastrous loss of a huge amount ecclesiastical heritage. Perhaps most influential in this regard was Augusto Riera's *La Semana Trágica* (*The Tragic Week*)—an anthology of reportage and eye-witness accounts complied by the Barcelona-based journalist—published in late 1909, which helped to cement the term in popular discussion.[65]

III

Alongside labor militancy, radical education and educators were deemed the key factor in the disturbances. Over 100 progressive schools and educational centers were closed in Catalonia, as were many similar establishments outside the province. Bonafulla claims the total number of closures was "incalculable," with "the pettiest denunciation" enough to assure that any school that "operated without the proper certificate from the parish priest" would be targeted (p. 151). Key individuals in radical education were singled out for repression, most notably Ferrer, who was cast as the

65. Augusto Riera, *La Semana Trágica: Relato de la sedición é incendios en Barcelona y Cataluña* (Barcelona: Barcino, 1909).

figurehead of revolutionary ideas in Spain. He was arrested on 31 August and charged by military tribunal with being the decisive influence behind the insurrection. Few contemporaries genuinely believed these charges, and the prosecution barely attempted to prove them. Instead, Ferrer was attacked for being the source of seditious ideas, which the state regarded as equally dangerous to "social order" as outbursts of revolutionary activity. He was an obvious scapegoat for the rebellion: a recognizable figure to anarchists and the general public, whose punishment would demonstrate the state's commitment to crushing radical ideas. The educator was declared "the author and chief of the rebellion" and was shot by firing squad in Montjuich Castle on 13 October.[66]

Bonafulla's account of Ferrer's arrest and trial is designed to totally exonerate his comrade from any criminal activity during the Tragic Week. He details the "clumsy maneuvers" of the agents sent to arrest and implicate Ferrer in the events (p. 156), the "apocryphal" evidence used to condemn him (p. 164) and the farcical trial he was subjected to, which falsely claimed that Ferrer was "absolutely" the "leader" of the rebellion (p. 180) and "captain" of the churchburners (p. 175). Ferrer's defense was correct to state that he was targeted because of his educational work, which stemmed from a "hatred and the fear of educating the working class" (p. 200) common to Spanish authorities, and that the prosecutor's insistence that the Tragic Week must have had a leader and a "perfectly organized origin" (p. 202) misunderstood the nature of the events, and of social change in general. It was, clearly, not enough to prove that Ferrer was behind the events because they broadly correlated to his ideas, nor was it enough to base more concrete charges on hearsay (p. 206).

While all of these critiques are valid, the view that Ferrer had no involvement in the Tragic Week is unsustainable. Ferrer had supported the anticlerical violence of the Tragic Week, although probably did not directly take part in it; and while he could not have possibly orchestrated any of the developments alone he may have had a hand in some moves to escalate the events into a revolution. This is not to say that Ferrer was guilty of the crimes that

---

66. Ullman, *The Tragic Week*, 283–284; Avilés Farre, *Francisco Ferrer*, 232–242; Yeoman, *Print Culture*, 205.

he was charged and killed for, but rather that he *was* a committed revolutionary, and had seen the Tragic Week as a potential opportunity to realise the goals which had underscored his educational and publishing work in Spain since 1901.[67] Beyond the pretense of charging Ferrer with orchestrating the events of July 1909, the Spanish authorities were correct to identify him as a source of seditious, revolutionary ideas: he had "over the course of many years" been "distributing propaganda, recruiting people, and waiting for an opportune moment" (p. 194) to support a revolution, and he was proud of it. Ferrer's own declaration that he would be "happy to go before any tribunal that is charged with judging the Modern School's books" (p. 209) reflects this point, and gets to the heart of the real accusation being levelled at him.

The point of contention is thus not *whether* Ferrer's activities were a threat to the state—they were, and he wanted them to be— *but that the state saw this as deserving of death*, and carried out this decision through a sham trial, in order to preserve the thin veil of liberal rule of law that barely covered the authoritarian basis of the Restoration system. The broad, heavy-handed repression of the Tragic Week followed a pattern of instinctive, brutal state violence in response to episodes of popular unrest in Spain since the 1870s, often directed against high-profile members of the anarchist movement. This would be seen again in the following decade, and culminate in the coup of General Primo de Riviera in 1923 following years of employer and anarchist street violence in Barcelona, when Spain's liberal elites—including the bourgeoisie of Barcelona, where Primo's coup began—backed a quasi-fascist military dictatorship promising "order," rather than accept social reforms and a dilution of their power.[68]

Beyond Bonafulla's account, the anarchist reaction to the Tragic Week was both delayed and partial. All public communications to Barcelona were either severed or censored during the Tragic Week, and afterwards martial law was in place across the country until 27 September, curtailing all anarchist publishing in Spain. This made it

67.   Romero Maura, *La rosa de fuego*, 479–81.
68.   Smith, *Anarchism, Revolution and Reaction*, 345–354; Dalmau, *Press, Politics, and National Identities in Catalonia*, 183–189.

impossible for the movement to publish commentary on the events as they unfolded. This situation improved in November, marked by the arrival of a number of new anarchist periodicals, which between them established the Tragic Week and its repercussions as part of the collective memory of the movement. Unlike Bonafulla, few anarchist periodical papers examined the events of the Tragic Week in depth, and all refused to discuss anarchist participation in the events. Instead, they focused almost exclusively on the execution of Ferrer. Contributors saw Ferrer as part of a lineage of radical thinkers who had suffered at the hands of the Catholic Church, such as Jan Hus, Giordano Bruno, Galileo Galilei, and Michael Servetus. Ferrer's treatment was also explicitly linked to that of Christ, including in one postcard titled *Ecce Homo* ["behold the man": the words used by Pontius Pilate when he presented a scourged Jesus Christ to the Jerusalem crowd], which displayed Ferrer's bloodied head over a shroud, surrounded by a crown of thorns.[69] Another vivid evocation of Ferrer's death was a story published in the Seville paper *Al Paso*, in which the author-protagonist awoke to a downpour of blood, after which Ferrer's name was spelled out in the sky by a series of moons. As well as giving space for veneration and expressions of grief, this coverage of Ferrer's martyrdom was a boost to sales, as shown by the thousands of extra requests sent in for *Al Paso*'s proposed eight-page special issue on the "unforgettable" educator, which included his portrait and texts by Pyotr Kropotkin, Errico Malatesta, and Anselmo Lorenzo.

Ferrer became the most prominent martyr in Spanish anarchist culture to date, marked out by both his commitment to the anarchist cause and the baselessness of the charges which had condemned him. His works were regularly republished, and pamphlets and books on his martyrdom continued to be produced by the movement into the 1930s. Supporters of radical education, such as Samuel Toner, who had opened his own Modern School in Valencia in 1907, were keen to maintain the memory of Ferrer, and used their publications to commemorate the anniversary of his death. References to Ferrer also emerged in acts of naming.

69. This postcard can be viewed at: https://cartoliste.ficedl.info/article299.html?lang=fr.

Several anarchist groups adopted Ferrer's name directly—such as the "Ferrer" group of Estepona (Málaga) and Alcoy (Alicante)—or made reference to the date of his execution, as with the "13 October" groups in Málaga and El Ferrol. This latter group went on to publish *Cultura Libertaria* (El Ferrol, 1912–1913, 12 issues), a paper which declared the rational education promoted by Ferrer to be "the true religion."[70] Like the repression of the 1890s, Ferrer's trial and execution sparked a campaign of international protests against the Spanish state. Chapter 9 of *The July Revolution* gives a strong sense of the scale of this "towering, unanimous voice that announced the moment of solidarity with such apocalyptic ring" (p. 213). While Ferrer was still on trial, huge meetings were held across Europe and the Americas calling for his release, including in Liverpool, where Ferrer had visited and inspired an anarchist educational project in 1908.[71] These protests intensified after his execution, resulting in serious disturbances in cities such as Paris and Rome (outlined in Chapter 11). Ferrer's name and date of death were taken up by anarchist groups abroad, such as the "13 October" group of Havana and the "Ferrer" group of Las Cascadas (Panamá), who launched the periodical *El Único* in Cólon on the second anniversary of Ferrer's execution. Another "Ferrer" group was formed by Spanish migrants in South Wales. In the Netherlands, postcards of Ferrer's portrait and children's books about his life could be bought from anarchist publishers, and plays based on his life and execution became a popular feature of socialist clubs from Mexico to Beirut.[72] The strength of international condemnation of Ferrer's execution was comparable to that of the Dreyfuss affair in France earlier in the decade, a comparison made explicitly at the time by a number of commentators.[73] Beyond anarchist circles, Ferrer's status as the

---

70. On the construction of "Ferrer the martyr" see Yeoman, *Print Culture*, 205–208.

71. See http://www.solfed.org.uk/liverpool/working-class-history-anarcho-syndicalism-on-merseyside.

72. Khuri-Makdisi, *The Eastern Mediterranean* 21; Daniel Laqua, "Freethinkers, anarchists and Francisco Ferrer: The making of a transnational solidarity campaign," *European Review of History/Revue européenne d'histoire* 21:4 (2014): 467–484.

73. Álvarez Junco, *The Emergence of Mass Politics*, 147.

world's foremost radical educator was assured by his execution, as demonstrated by the Modern Schools that emerged in almost every continent from 1909 onwards. This was particularly pronounced in the USA, where a long-lasting Modern School movement emerged immediately after Ferrer's execution, supported by the "Francisco Ferrer Association," which included the novelists Jack London and Upton Sinclair amongst its members.[74]

However, the construction of "Ferrer the martyr" did not meet with uniform approval from Spanish anarchists, many of whom criticized this development as "idolatry." To Ricardo Mella, this was pure "fetishism," a "christianization" of Ferrer that was the work of "pseudo-revolutionaries" who "could not be anarchists." Anarchists also attacked parliamentary socialists and middle class educators who "mourned Ferrer as a freethinker and neglected his anarchism" and were critical of the international campaigns aroused by Ferrer's execution. When Belgian radicals began an international sub-scription to fund a statue to Ferrer—who had spent time in exile in Brussels following Mateo Morral's attack on Alfonso XIII in 1906—they were lambasted in the pages of *El Libertario* (Madrid), which suggested that the money would be better spent on rational schools.[75] There was a feeling that the ideas for which Ferrer lived and died were being overlooked in the construction of his mar-tyrdom, while his memory was appropriated for political gain. As Bonafulla relates, Ferrer warned against such "worrying about the dead" in his will, calling on those that had shared his ideas in life to dedicate themselves to "improving the conditions of the living" (p. 225) rather than creating idols.

The syndicalists of SO were also hesitant to invoke the mem-ory of the Tragic Week and decided that rather than "naming streets after [Ferrer]," the most fitting tribute would be to continue his work for revolutionary syndicalism, which was overlooked by non-anarchists and anarchists alike. If his death was to be remem-bered, it should not be in order to make Ferrer a saint—he was, after all, "no more than putrefied material"—but as a stimulus to

---

74. See Avrich, *The Modern School Movement*, 33.
75. The statue was erected in 1914, removed under German occupation in 1915, and returned in 1926. It can currently be visited on the Franklin Rooseveltlaan.

organization. This position is understandable, given that the Tragic Week was a disaster for SO, resulting in the closure of its paper and an end to the organizations' ambitions for national expansion. For many syndicalists, the best course of action was to move on from this event as quickly as possible.[76]

IV

Repression relaxed with the fall of Maura shortly after Ferrer's execution, allowing SO to resume its plans for national expansion. One year on from the Tragic Week the organization held a national congress, where representatives from across Spain agreed to form a single syndicalist federation, soon to be known as the Confederación Nacional del Trabajo (CNT). In its early years the CNT was dominated by its Barcelona sections, with almost all of its executive coming from the city. Nevertheless, both the organization and the strategy of syndicalism began to make inroads into anarchist constituencies, particularly in Gijón, Seville, and Valencia. At its first official congress in 1911 the CNT claimed the support of 30,000 members, around half of whom were based outside Catalonia.[77]

The CNT's 1911 Congress was held during a period of intense popular unrest in Spain, in some respects more widespread and potentially revolutionary than the Tragic Week. As in 1909, a call-up for troops to fight in Morocco provoked protest meetings through the summer of 1911, which were supported by syndicalists, socialists, and some republicans. At the same time, strikes began in Bilbao (24 August), Málaga (28 August), and the Asturian coalmining area of Mieres (5 September). When the CNT Congress began on 8 September, all of these strikes were escalating. Thousands joined anti-war protests in Madrid, while in Asturias around 20,000 miners came out on strike, completely halting work in the industry. In Vizcaya clashes took place between strikers and the Civil Guard, resulting in the closure of all workers' centers and the

---

76. Yeoman, *Print Culture*, 207–8.
77. See Smith, *Anarchism, Revolution and Reaction*, 189–206.

deployment of troops. As the Asturian and Málaga strikes ended, citywide strikes in solidarity with the Basque strikes took place in Zaragoza, La Coruña, El Ferrol, Vigo, Sevilla, Gijón, and Oviedo. In Valencia violence between workers and local authorities caused a number of deaths, which were followed by the burning of Church property. In a bid to regain control of the situation, Liberal Prime Minister José Canalejas suspended constitutional guarantees (19 September) and enacted press censorship (21 September). Within days the strike wave had petered out and the threat of a genuine, national general strike was averted.[78]

Like the Tragic Week, these strikes were not directed by any political group, and were subdued relatively quickly by repression. Once again, key figures in the republican and socialist movements were not prepared to declare themselves in favor of political revolution. The republicans were generally uninterested in such methods, while the socialists were paralyzed by their "sclerotic" leadership, which sought to moderate the strikes, despite the fact that a large section of UGT membership was keen for escalation. In contrast, the CNT clearly wanted to see revolutionary action, but lacked the means to fully instigate or direct it on a national scale. Official messages of support were sent to the workers of Bilbao and Málaga during the 1911 Congress, although there was no explicit discussion of using these incidents to provoke a national general strike. As with the Tragic Week, anarchists were certainly heavily involved in the strikes of 1911, and probably tried to use this moment for revolutionary ends, but they had not caused the strikes nor were they capable of directing them.[79]

Nevertheless, the movement was once again singled out for repression. The CNT was made illegal days after the 1911 Congress, its leading activists in Barcelona were imprisoned, and the confederation's periodical, *Solidaridad Obrera*, was suspended. In the following days hundreds more workers and activists were imprisoned across Spain, and by the end of September the situation looked bleak for the anarchist movement and the CNT. It

---

78. Cuadrat, *Socialismo y anarquismo*, 557–567, gives a blow-by-blow account of developments during the strike wave.

79. See Yeoman, *Print Culture*, 223–226.

would take the exceptional circumstances of the First World War, in which neutral Spain experienced unprecedented economic and social upheaval, for the CNT to resume its functioning. From 1914 onwards industries supplying both belligerent blocs boomed, sparking a huge shift towards urbanization and industrial employment. Many other areas experienced economic crisis, as international markets for Spanish exports collapsed and basic living standards were eroded following a dramatic spike in inflation. The CNT re-emerged in this context, gaining mass support from the working class for its anti-war stance.[80] Membership of the confederation rocketed from around 30,000 in 1915 to almost 800,000 in 1919. At the same time, anarchist ideas took a firmer hold of the organization, cementing its underlying principle as one of anarcho-syndicalism, advocating for anarchist revolution by syndicalist means.[81] This massive expansion made CNT the largest anarchist organization in world history, at the same time that anarchist and syndicalist movements elsewhere were surpassed by social democratic and communist counterparts. The organization only surpassed such numbers twenty years later at the outbreak of the Spanish Civil War, as it spearheaded the most profound—and perhaps only—anarchist revolution in history: the true "Revolution of July," which took place in 1936.[82]

One of the most striking aspects of the Spanish Revolution of 1936 was its attention to education. In the midst of Civil War, anarchists across Spain took it upon themselves to establish new centers, libraries, and schools for the working class, viewing cultural emancipation as integral to the victory of the anarchist cause. Women were crucial to this development, in particular the 20,000-strong anarchist-feminist "Mujeres Libres" group, who viewed radical education as the prime means to abolish hierarchies of gender.[83] In all of this activity we can see the legacy of the

80. Francisco J. Romero Salvadó, *Spain: 1914–1918: Between War and Revolution* (London: Routledge, 1999), 5–22, 31, and 44–5.

81. See Bar, *La CNT*, 338–39 and 490–92.

82. Amongst the best recent works on the anarchist movement during the Civil War is Danny Evans, *Revolution and the State: Anarchism in the Spanish Civil War, 1936–1939* (New York and London: Routledge, 2018).

83. On Mujeres Libres see Martha Ackelsberg, *Free Women of Spain: Anarchism*

anarchist educators of the early twentieth century, above all Ferrer, who had remained a key symbol of the movement's cultural strategy since his execution. Almost three decades after he was shot in Montjuich, as the success of libertarian communism seemed close, if not already in effect, educational groups and centers took up Ferrer's name and strove to emulate the ethos of the Modern School in the new revolutionary context.[84]

Unlike Ferrer, Bonafulla did not maintain his standing in the anarchist movement for long after the publication of *The July Revolution*. Although he took part in the inaugural congresses of the CNT, he was sidelined by a younger generation of activists over the following decade. Like his contemporary Ricardo Mella, Bonafulla had been instrumental in the reformation of anarchism in Spain over the turn of the twentieth century and had campaigned for the creation of a singular, worker-orientated organization to lead the anarchist revolution; yet was uncomfortable with this project as it became a reality. As the diffuse, decentralized movement of the 1890s and early 1900s became overwritten by the CNT, older militants like Bonafulla and Mella expressed their discomfort at a growing sense of "dogma" and "reformism" within the organization and withdrew from it. Bonafulla died in Barcelona in 1922, largely forgotten by the movement for which he had published, campaigned, and suffered for most of his adult life.

In the final paragraph of *The July Revolution* Bonafulla asks a poignant question, one which he could potentially ask himself in later years: "was this sacrifice productive?" His response is equally fitting, acknowledging that although "not as much as we would have hoped" had been achieved, the path to social change, to revolution, and a better world, to "the overwhelming flood of new ideas," had nevertheless been opened by the activists, educators, and ordinary people of Spain (p. 259), to whom he has written his account.

and the Struggle for the Emancipation of Women (Oakland: AK Press, 2005), available at: https://libcom.org/files/Ackelsberg%20-%20Free%20Women%20of%20Spain% 20-%20Anarchism%20and%20the%20Struggle%20for%20the%20Emancipation %20of%20Women.pdf.

84. Alejandro Tiana Ferrer, *Educación libertaria y revolución social (España, 1936–1939)* (Madrid: UNED, 1987).

Translator's Note

What would real social change feel like? Would it be exhilarating? Would it be about love or would it be about hate? Is it inevitable? Would it be logical? Or unhinged and crazy? In *The July Revolution*, Leopoldo Bonafulla shows us that it may be all these things—and also as painful as all births are.

The events of July 25–August 2, 1909 cannot exactly be called a revolution; when it was over, there was no fundamental change in government. Afterwards, there was massive repression—revolutionaries were killed, exiled, and imprisoned, and secular schools were shuttered. Nevertheless, this little-studied event (at least in the English-speaking world) can be seen as a prelude to the Spanish Civil War, which broke out twenty-seven years later, in 1936.

Bonafulla was there. He was an eyewitness, and he writes from that perspective. Of course, it's quite possible, maybe likely, that his account was biased. After all, he was personally involved, and many of his friends and associates were killed or exiled. Furthermore, the last events the book describes took place in November 1909, and the book was published in January 1910. It was rushed and replete with typographical errors. Of course, we should always think critically when reading historical accounts, no matter how polished or well-researched, but this amateur quality gives the book a certain force.

Yet for translators, there is a conundrum: should the typos be corrected? It's a double-edged sword. What is more important? To faithfully preserve the hasty, slapdash feel, or to create a translation that is comprehensible and readable to an English speaker?

I've chosen to correct the typos for a number of reasons. Firstly, these typos were mostly (but by no means entirely) corrected in later Spanish editions. Secondly, even if it was written for an average reader in early twentieth-century Spain (an average literate person, that is—illiteracy rates were extremely high), the text would be very difficult for an average English-speaking reader today. Even nowadays, long sentences are the norm in Spanish, but this was especially true over one hundred years ago. And although these sentences remain long in the translation, many of them are even longer in the Spanish, in some cases *significantly* longer, with sentences routinely spanning over a page.

But not only are the sentences long and convoluted, the concepts are difficult, too. Bonafulla casually throws around references to historical figures, politicians, and writers without explaining who they were—without *having to* explain. Back then people like Antonio Maura, don Jaime, Torquemada, King Alfonso XIII, Alfred Naquet, Rosas Samaniego, Azorín, etc., were well known individuals; today they have fallen into relative obscurity. So the combination of typos, extremely long sentences, and multitudes of obscure references would simply make this book unreadable to an English speaker. And as a translator, since I want people to read this, I have to make some compromises. That's why I corrected the typos and shortened sentences here and there. James Yeoman's in-depth introduction and footnotes will hopefully help readers understand the many references and concepts Bonafulla wrote about.

But notwithstanding these compromises that translators often have to make, one of the overall goals of translation is to try to put readers into the shoes of another person, in another time and in another place. That's difficult, in both small and large ways—words mean different things in different places, and they change meaning over time. Take the simple example of the word *convento* vs. convent. Merriam-Webster defines convent as "a local community or house of a religious order or congregation; especially: an establishment of nuns." In other words, monasteries and friaries are convents. But it seems to me the vast majority of modern English speakers don't see it that way. And this creates a problem because in Spanish, the word *convento* does include religious houses of both men and women. Clearly, the revolutionaries did not only burn down establishments of nuns. Therefore, I've generally translated *convento* as "convents and friaries." (I left monasteries out because I thought having to use all three words for the single word *convento* would have made it too unwieldy. Another small compromise, this time between readability and meaning.)

Some words look the same in two different languages and have the same root but mean different things. Any English speaker studying Spanish, or vice versa, will eventually have to deal with what is known as "the false friend." An example is the word "eventually" in the previous sentence. Here my assertion is that language learners will eventually—or *definitely*—come across this phenomenon at some point. However, if this were translated into Spanish using the word *"eventualmente,"* it would imply that language learners *may or may not* come across this, since *eventualmente* means "perhaps."

But an even bigger challenge is how to deal with words that have *overlapping* sets of meanings, words that mean the same thing in one context, but completely different things in another. For example, let's take a look at benign/malignant and *benigno/maligno*. In Chapter 3 of this book, Doctor don Ricardo Cortés, bishop of Eudoxia, writes:

> It would be endless and perhaps useless at this time to insist on the enormous effort to repudiate all the slander and fantasies circulated by the *malignidad revolucionaria* latching on to appearances interpreted in a twisted manner by the mob.

In the realm of medicine, both sets of words refer to diseases like cancer, and benign/*benigno* are both sometimes used to describe mild weather. Aside from this, though, their meanings diverge. Merriam-Webster defines malignant as "evil in nature, influence, or effect: injurious" and "passionately and relentlessly malevolent: aggressively malicious."

Meanwhile, the Royal Spanish Academy defines *maligno* as *"propenso a pensar u obrar mal"* and *"de* índole *perniciosa."* In English, roughly, "tending to think or act in a bad/evil way" and "of a pernicious nature" (pernicious/*pernicioso* both roughly mean "highly injurious or destructive").

In comparing these definitions, two things stand out. First, the English word malignant seems much more negative than *maligno*. Second, *maligno* has one connotation that doesn't exist in the English at all: tending to *think* in a bad/evil way.

In the context of the above quote, this is relevant. During Tragic Week, the revolutionaries set fire to many religious establishments, and this bishop is responding to those events after they are over. He is not merely insulting the revolutionaries; like several of the other religious representatives highlighted by Bonafulla in Chapter 3, he is also bewildered at why they decided that the Church was their enemy—look at all these good deeds we have done, how we help the poor, and yet *these revolutionaries always think the worst of us*. He seems exasperated. (We can only guess, but I believe Bonafulla would say this is a fake exasperation).

Now let's take a look at the opposite term benign/*benigno* (while the meanings of the words themselves may be different, in both languages, benign/malignant and *benigno/maligno* are opposites). Bonafulla used this word at the very beginning of his book, and again in the final chapter. In Chapter 1, fourth paragraph, he writes:

> . . . if we consider the fact that history has never recorded such a powerful revolutionary movement in which the revolutionaries had put such *benignidad* into practice. Maybe such *benignidad* was its own punishment. The truth is that they proceeded *benignamente*, and so that must be noted.

And in the last chapter, he writes, ". . .the recently-ousted government was universally declared to be the cause of the rebellion and the *benignidad* of the revolutionaries was praised."

Ignoring any definitions related to the weather or medicine, the Oxford English Dictionary defines benign as "gentle and kind." Meanwhile, the Royal Spanish Academy defines *benigno* as "*afable, benévolo, piadoso*," or "affable, benevolent, and (something like) pious." It would be a stretch to say that gentle and affable are the same thing, but they are somewhat close; kind and benevolent are synonyms; but what is interesting is that *benigno* means "*piadoso*" (something like pious) while benign does not.

Now let's look at *piadoso* versus pious. These two words also have overlapping meanings. According to the OED, pious means "devoutly religious" or "making or constituting a hypocritical display of virtue." And the Royal Spanish academy has three definitions for *piadoso*: "*Benigno, blando, misericordioso, que se inclina a la piedad y conmiseración; Que mueve a compasión; religioso, devoto*," roughly "*benigno,* soft, merciful, and tending towards *piedad* and commiseration/sympathy; inspiring compassion; religious, devout." To sum it up, these two words both mean something like "devoutly religious," but *piadoso* also means "merciful and compassionate," while pious can have negative connotations.

Consider the following sentence: "She may be an atheist, but she is more Christian than most Christians." (I'm not making value judgments about the word Christian or atheist here, only discussing their definitions.) If we substitute the word pious for the underlined word Christian, it changes the meaning entirely, but *piadosa* would work well there.

I thought about using Christian/unchristian for *benigno/maligno* but decided against it because I felt that the definition of the word Christian as underlined above cannot be separated from its main definition. While I think unchristian would work well in the bishop's letter, I thought readers would get the wrong impression if they thought Bonafulla had used the word Christian to describe the revolutionaries on the first page of his book. Obviously, he is not saying the revolutionaries were religious—their movement was anticlerical—but I think what he was actually saying was that they were *more Christian* than the Christians, which is one way to look at the word *benigno.*

In the end, I decided to translate *benignidad* as "human decency," while *malignidad revolucionaria* became "cynical revolutionaries with no human decency."

I chose the word cynical here because the definition of "always thinking the worst" is similar to the following definition of cynical from Merriam-Webster: "contemptuously distrustful of human nature and motives." The bishop repeats this thought several times. In a previous paragraph he writes that the revolutionaries were "thirsty for evidence of supposed torture for crimes that only ever existed in the imaginations of these wicked instigators of the fires." Using the words "human decency" here covers the second part of *malignidad* and also connects this to Bonafulla's use of *benignidad*. And finally, I hoped that by using two words, "human decency" rather than simply "decency," it would make this connection stick out more to readers.

I would also like to point out here that cynical/*cínico* is yet another example of false friends with some overlap. Both words can refer to the Cynics of Ancient Greece. But some definitions of *cínico* include shameless and obscene. So for example a man who catcalls to a woman in an obscene way would be called *cínico*—and this is totally different than cynical. If you're a student of Spanish or translation, I hope all this doesn't make you too bitter (and by the way, bitter and *amargo* both refer to the same flavor, but while bitter means resentful, *amargo* is more sad or sorrowful).

Anyways, these primary documents that Bonafulla provides in his book, such as the reactions from various religious authorities, reveal the irreconcilable differences in Barcelonan society. The clergy simply could not understand why the revolutionaries were against them. They saw themselves as do-gooders, helping the poor, teaching, spreading religion, etc. It was painful to see their world crumbling around them, and they apparently could not understand why. But the revolutionaries saw them as oppressors, criminals holding back progress, modern inquisitors and torturers. In the end, of course, not only did Catholicism survive, but, along with government authorities, they took their revenge.

Bonafulla describes the repression that followed the July events, beginning with the military tribunals and executions. In one chapter, he tells the story of a young, illiterate boy, Ramón Clemente García, who was falsely accused of rebellion and executed. In another chapter, he describes the exiles who were banished from Barcelona. Teresa Claramunt, a well-known anarchist who was Bonafulla's companion for a time, was one of these exiles.

Finally, Bonafulla describes what could be called the show trial of his close friend Francisco Ferrer and his eventual execution.

In 1886, Ferrer supported an attempted *pronunciamiento* by General Manuel Villacampa. This is an interesting word, too. It's not that there is a false friend, it's that this concept doesn't exist in English at all. There is a distinction in Spanish between a coup d'état (*golpe de estado*), which is a sudden, violent takeover of the government, and a *pronunciamiento,* in which the government is infiltrated slowly by individuals supporting the new regime. Once all the pieces are in place, all that is needed for the coup to be consummated is for a new government to be "pronounced" or "proclaimed." Throughout this book, Ferrer is accused of "proclaiming the Republic," which actually means "leading this type of coup against the Monarchy."

After this *pronunciamiento,* Ferrer was exiled to Paris with his family. His relationship with his wife was strained, however, and in 1893, they were separated. During an argument they had in 1894, she shot him, but it was not fatal, and he did not press charges against her. In 1899, he married a different woman, a freethinker whom he loved very much, and they traveled Europe together. Her name, Leopoldine Bonnard, was oddly similar to the one chosen by Joan Baptiste Esteve to be his pen name: Leopoldo Bonafulla. We can only guess why he might have chosen this name, but one thing is for certain—Bonafulla loved Ferrer dearly, and when he was finally executed, it broke his heart.

Included in the book are primary documents from the trial, including a description of the examining magistrate's report, which to my knowledge, is not currently available anywhere else in English. Reading these documents makes it clear that Ferrer was innocent of the crime he was accused of. In fact, he may have had a peripheral role during the July events, although this is debatable.

One of the themes of *The Revolution of 1909* is: What is logical and what isn't? Some people may have said that things got out of hand during that first antiwar protest at the pier. Bonafulla would answer that it made perfect sense historically. Others might ask: did workers lose their minds when they destroyed property during the general strike that followed? Or when they began burning

convents and friaries? Again, Bonafulla says society is crazy, not
the revolutionaries; look to the Church if you want someone to
blame. And during Ferrer's trial, the prosecutor claimed that he
was dispassionate, looking only at the facts. He said the revolutionaries had lost their minds, and Ferrer was their leader. But
Bonafulla was attempting to demonstrate that the trial was a
sham. It was quite the contrary—the authorities were passionate
and zealous for revenge.

The year 1909 was during the late-modern period. Everywhere
around the world, people were asking questions about progress,
but outmoded ways of thinking and living coexisted stubbornly
with very new ideas. The first Russian revolution of 1905 had
recently created a constitutional monarchy, but this was before
World War I and the revolutions of 1917. Freud had recently published *The Interpretation of Dreams* (1900), sending shockwaves
throughout the world of psychology and philosophy, but Karl
Jung had not yet coined the term "collective unconscious." (In this
book, readers will encounter the term "the universal consciousness.") In recent decades, painters experimented with perspective.
Picasso was just beginning his cubist period, and musicians like
Arnold Schoenberg were just beginning to experiment with ato-
nality. It was a time of great change, but even bigger changes were
close at hand.

While progress is both beautiful and historically necessary,
Bonafulla contends that "progressive trends must break through in
the midst of violent tumult." He also reminds us that it is painful
when friends die. But all movements must continue. My challenge
as a translator was to try to convey this mindset and this zeitgeist.

Chapter 1

Causes and Background. The Morroccan Mines • War in the Rif • Embarkation of the Reservists • Upheaval and Protests • Government Repression • Disturbances and Prisons in Madrid and Barcelona. Declaration of a General Strike

In the life of a nation, as in the life of an individual, there is a marvelous law that we might call immanent justice, by virtue of which one reaps, sooner or later, what one sows. We are offered a magnificent example of this in the destructive consequences for contemporary nations, particularly Spain—of capitalist egoism, the depressing dominance of governments, and the moral degeneracy of the clergy.[1]

We could deduce at this point that the events we will study, which have so moved the universal consciousness, do not arise from what the powers that be are aiming to stamp out, nor from the causes ascribed by many political enemies of those powers, but rather, as we have said, they are a logical consequence when people are unwilling to let go of their fanaticism, their hypocrisy, and their spirit of domination, all of which has been engendered by the current regime.

It would be useful to reconstruct the historical truth of the events of July, distorted as it has been by the insolent assertions

---

1. These three forces—capitalism, the state, and the church—form the traditional anarchist critique of power, distinct from orthodox Marxism in Spain which viewed capital as the sole source of oppression. At times they were referred to collectively as the "nefarious trilogy" of authority. See Lily Litvak, *Musa libertaria: Arte, literatura y vida cultural del anarquismo español (1890-1913)* (Madrid: Fundación de Estudios Libertarios Anselmo Lorenzo, 2001), 69-99, and Ackelsberg, *Free Women of Spain*, 37-38.

that traditionalists of all stripe have dared to proffer in statements and protests, even more useful if we consider the fact that history has never recorded such a powerful revolutionary movement in which the revolutionaries had put such sentiments of human decency into practice. Maybe such decency was its own punishment. The truth is that they proceeded with human decency, and that must be noted.

The working class, convinced that the war in Morocco was a bourgeois war, began expressing its discontent as soon as it learned that the government was attempting to mobilize reservists.[2] Although imperfectly cultivated due to a lack of education, the awareness by the proletariat of its own social character led to its demonstrating that the era of propping up political tyrannies and boosting capitalists' coffers with the sweat of its brow was over, and the war in the Rif, despite government concealment of its causes, was the result of a ruinous association of professional politicians and the banking elite, a combination that the modern spirit rejects decisively.[3]

It makes a painful impression to watch flocks of negotiators supported in their adventures by armies of obliged workers swooping down on these nations, exploiting them in the name of civilization. This was the cause of the war with the Riffians, and the people wanted to protest the enormity of it.

In their defense, governments cite their contractual obligations under the Act of Algeciras.[4] But keeping in mind that this diplo-

---

2. This call-up was the immediate cause of the Tragic Week. On the background to Spanish imperialism in Morocco see Sebastian Balfour, *Deadly Embrace: Morocco and the Road To the Spanish Civil War* (Oxford: Oxford University Press, 2002), 3–30.

3. This was a common trope of anarchist writing in Spain at this time: the proletariat "lacked education" to see the truth of anarchism, thus the route to revolution lay in more education and a "raising of culture," exactly the project that Francisco Ferrer saw himself as fulfilling. See the Introduction.

In anarchist writing of the period "modern" was often used synonymously with "anarchist," "rational" and "true."

4. A reference to the Algeciras Conference of 1906, which aimed to settle disputes between Germany and France over Moroccan territory. The main results of this agreement were that Morocco should remain open to international trade and its Sultan remain ultimate sovereign of the region, backed by the French and Spanish in their zones of control. See Balfour, *Deadly Embrace*, 7.

matic convention has been described as a masterpiece of imbecility, and at the same time remembering the trickery to which the people had so often been victim—it was enough to make them unwilling to once again become cannon fodder for their oligarchs. And further, to confirm this judgment, it would be enough to repeat what has been said and written both in and outside of Spain, that is, that it is still not known who had the proper constitutional authority to grant the protection of the Spanish state to the mining firms who, at the expense of the Spanish people, have opened up the mother lode of costs, bloodshed, and unease at the foot of the Citadel of Selouane.[5]

To avoid having to go back to this point, take a look at what the French magazine *Côte de la Bourse et de la Banque* has to say about the Moroccan mines[6]:

> The Act of Algeciras has, to the exclusion of all other Powers, recognized France's privileged position in the Algeria-Morocco border zone; it has granted Spain an equivalent advantage in the Region of Melilla and Ceuta, that is, in the Rif; and it has conferred special rights to France and Spain in the western part of Morocco, with the express condition that they must keep international interests in mind and practice what was called the "open door" policy. It follows that the Act of Algeciras has to a certain extent divided Morocco into three spheres of influence: one region that is solely French, one region that is solely Spanish, and one international region within which France and Spain nevertheless enjoy a certain priority. Article 112 of the General Act of the conference stipulates: "The Sherifian firman shall determine the conditions of the concessions and the working of mines and quarries. In the composition of this firman, the Sherifian Government shall be guided by foreign laws relating to such matters." This regulation, for which the French

---

5. A fortified town close to the Spanish-controlled Mellilla in northern Morocco.
6. Translated excerpt from « La question minière au Maroc » by M. Ernest Vincent reprinted in the biweekly newspaper *L'Écho des mines et de la métallurgie*, August 2, 1909.

engineer Porché is currently bringing together the necessary elements in Fez, has not yet been enacted.

The question of mining in the Algeria-Morocco zone has not yet been set forth. We can therefore only study it in the Rif, that is, the Spanish zone, as well as in Souss, El Goundafi, and Atlas, in other words, the international zone.

Given the lack of legislation regarding the matter and given that the most complete disorder reigns throughout the empire, it is not possible to specify which of the diverse groups (currently) disputing over Moroccan subsoil has a more legitimate claim to rights.[7] Some, if we are talking about the Rif, assert that their concessions are from Bou Hmara, pretender to the Moroccan throne. Others declare that they have contracts signed by Sultan Abdelaziz in their possession or written promises from pretender to the throne Mulai Abdelhafid. Each one works in the shadow, with utmost secrecy, scheming in close proximity to the Sultan of Taza or the Sultan of Fez, and waging war with their rivals.

We can observe the strange and sometimes amusing spectacle of certain shareholders of one group warring against a different group, all the while their associates are "playing both sides," concluding agreements with their supposed enemies.

It is very difficult to obtain exact information about one or another group, or their financial standing, especially concerning El Goundafi, Atlas, and Souss. It is almost impossible to get clear data on their centers of operation. On the other hand, while the exploitation of mines has commenced in the Spanish zone, mines in the international zone are nothing more than annotations made on a map with a blue pencil. The interested parties are awaiting better times.[8]

---

7. [Translator's note] The original French article used the term "l'anarchie." Bonafulla translated this into Spanish as "desorden."

8. [Translator's note] The original says: ". . . les intéressés attendent pour commencer les travaux des temps meilleurs, c'est-à-dire la fin de l'anarchie et une réglementation précise." Bonafulla omitted the last part of this sentence, which should read: "The interested parties are awaiting better times before beginning the work, that is, the end of the anarchy and a more precise set of regulations." Evidently he did not agree with their use of the term "anarchy" to mean chaos.

Three main groups have been established in the Rif region: *Compañía Norte Africana*, *Sociedad Clemente Fernández y Compañía*, and *Sociedad Española de Minas del Rif*.

Compañía Norte Africana, whose registered office is in Madrid, has a capital stock of ten million francs. Two or three hundred thousand francs were paid to the pretender for concession rights.

Ex-minister García Alix and several Spanish politicians have a stake in this business. In Paris, French engineer M. Massenet exercises the function of financial director, and M. Alex Baillé negotiated the enterprise. The company employs two land surveyors, a mine foreman, and two workers, who are French, as well as 200 native workers whose wage is approximately two Spanish pesetas per day. Starting a short while ago the company has begun using rudimentary procedures to exploit lead, which is rich and abundant near the surface or at a very shallow depth. The deposits are located in the tribal area of Beni-Bu Ifrur, which is at an altitude of 700 meters and is five hours away from Melilla. *Norte Africana* seems less mixed-up in the intrigues of the various groups, and of all the mining companies in the region, its work is the most advanced.

Now we will turn to the most turbulent of the corporations, whose scheming is infinite. From the Spanish firm Figueroa, which plays a central role in Moroccan mining matters, the Count of Romanones comes into view.[9] *Sociedad Clemente Fernández y Compañía*, whose registered address is in Madrid, was formed by the union of two entities, *Romanones* and *Clemente Fernández*. David Charvid, a French Jew from Melilla, served as intermediary. Aside from the Count of Romanones, the important figures in this group are don Clemente Fernández, don Enrique Macpherson, metallurgist, Ruíz Pastor, financial director, and the engineers del Valle and Moreno. We don't know what its capital stock is, but the company, which is exploiting a rich deposit of ferrous oxide (Fe_2O_3) near the surface

---

9. An important landowner, capitalist, newspaper proprietor, and Liberal politician in Restoration Spain, who would later twice serve as Prime Minister (1912–13 and 1918–19).

25 kilometers from Melilla, in the region of Guelaya, obtained its concession at a price of 400,000 pesetas and the allocation of 25 percent of its shares to the pretender.[10]

Sociedad Española de Minas del Rif is made up of four groups: first, the Figueroa group, which is made up of three brothers, the Count of Romanones, the Count of Mejorada and the Duke of Tovar; the second group is made up of the Marquis of Comillas and his nephew Güell; the last two are the Macpherson group and the Fernández group, which are also part of *Sociedad Clemente Fernández y Compañía*, as we have just seen. This company, with a capital stock of six million pesetas, is a study syndicate constituted to determine the value of the existing agreements between Señor Macpherson and the pretender.

Up to now, we have seen that the Spanish financial groups have been motivated by the perfectly legitimate desire to preponderate in the Rif and to obtain the greatest possible economic development in Melilla. France has no reason to complain about this attitude, given that the Rif is located in the Spanish zone. On the other hand, the Count of Romanones has declared, in the name of the Riffian mines, that while foreign collaboration will not be admitted within the Spanish zone, the "open door" principle should be recognized in international Morocco. But the situation gets complicated—at least one of the Romanones brothers (of the Figueroa firm), the Duke of Tovar, has joined the German Mannesmann Group, which is attempting with all its clout to deal a death-blow to the international thesis represented by the *Union des Mines Marocaines*.[11]

The four Mannesmann brothers, who call themselves "industrialists" in Rhemscheid, near Düsseldorf, possess a large

---

10. Balfour again provides the most thorough discussion of Spanish business interests in Morocco and the escalation of conflict, see above. In the view of anarchists such as Bonafulla (and a large sector of public opinion), Morocco exemplified the entanglement of capitalism, government, the military, and the Church that had brought enormous damage to Spain in recent decades.

11. [Author's note] Romanones stated in *España Nueva* that the Spanish shareholders declined to accept the pact offered by the Germans.

fortune and have had a longtime relationship with Mulai Abdelhafid. In the period when the current Sultan had not yet risen to the throne, they supported him with their money, and just a few days before the Casablanca murders, they played an unequivocal role, delivering large amounts of arms to Chaouia, under the guise of giving gifts. Mulai Abdelhafid granted them considerable mining concessions before their recognition in Europe. In March of this year, the sultan was unable to pay back a loan of 300,000 pesetas, which was then due. He conferred mining privileges to the brothers, disregarding the "open door" principle proclaimed by the Conference of Algeciras, and before the famous mining regulation could see the light of day, the Mannesmann brothers, wanting only to resell the Sherifian firman at a good price, made a proposal to cede all their rights to the *Union des Mines Marocaines* through a 50 percent stake in the international Syndicate. The *Union* declined their offer.

The Mannesmann brothers, realizing then that their "splendid isolation" could start to be bothersome, began seeking a financial and diplomatic backer in Spain. And they found it in the Duke of Tovar, who is connected, if not himself then through his brothers, to the *Union des Mines*. We have here the intricate spectacle of two rival groups, and the same personalities are involved in both, either personally or by proxy (*Dépêche Marocaine*, May 6, 1909).

Inasmuch as the Mannesmann brothers are joining forces with the Duke of Tovar to exploit certain mineral deposits that were not supposed to be international (ignoring the Act of Algeciras) they are making an alliance with Spanish groups of the Rif, and in February of that year they constitute *Mannesmann Rif CS*, a limited liability company formed for the purpose of purchasing land and mines in Morocco, and entering into loan agreements with the sultan, the Sherifian Government and the Berber tribes. Its capital stock was provisionally set at 300,000 marks. This study syndicate appears to be backed by the *Deutsch-Österreichische Mannesmannröhren-Werke*, a powerful group backed by representatives from Deutsche Bank, Wiener Bankwesen, and Société Siemens, et cetera.

So the Spaniards, having declared their rejection of all foreign interference in the Rif, are accepting German capital for the exploitation of the region as well as the technical collaboration of groups that have always stood out for their hostility to French influence in Morocco.

International diplomacy does not remain indifferent to these transactions. On the one hand, the Spanish minister, who is in agreement with his French and English colleagues, surely lodged a protest with the Sherifian Government last April against the concession granted by Mulai Abdelhafid to the German Mannesmann brand. On the other hand, despite international agreements, the Spanish Government withdrew its support of the Spanish companies that had decided to associate with the German enterprise. A Reuter telegram from April 13th declared that the German Government "was giving no support whatsoever to the Mannesmann House, regardless of the attitude of certain Moroccan officials." In fact, the only individual who, for the benefit of his compatriots, had obtained confirmation of previous commitments from Mulai Abdelhafid was M. Vassel, the German Consul in Fez. Despite these declarations, the underhanded scheming continued against those representing the international thesis, the *Union des Mines Marocaines*.

What is the *Union des Mines Marocaines*? It is an international study syndicate with a capital stock of only 500,000 francs (given the current state of affairs, there is no need for large capital sums) and constituted according to the spirit of the Act of Algeciras. It unites the principal European metallurgical companies (granting France a privileged position among them) for the possible exploitation of mineral deposits which are neither in the Rif, nor within the Algeria-Morocco region. Adhering to this union are: for France, *Schneider et Co., Societé d'Agadir, Mokta-el Hadid, Compagnie Marocaine, Châtillon-Commentry,* etc.; for Germany, *Krupp und Co.,* the *Thyssen* factories, and *Metalgesellschaft*; for England, *Wickers-Maxim;* for Spain, *Casa Figueroa* (Count of Romanones and Duke of Tovar); for Belgium, *Societé John-Cockerill,* et cetera.

Undoubtedly this formidable group is assured in every way of its technical and financial strength. The principle of absolute respect for acquired rights and the favorable reception to all (proportional to their value) who have done mining in Morocco or have committed to becoming consumers of ore, was applied from its founding—otherwise small companies might be apprehensive. The group also ensures the performance of Franco-German contracts regarding joint efforts and partnership capital for these two powers in Morocco. Until further notice, the international syndicate has adopted the only possible attitude: wait and complete all the data and information-gathering work. It does not negotiate with the sultan, and negotiation is unlikely until he decrees the necessary laws pursuant to the Act of Algeciras, after having consulted the foreign Legations in Tangier. How long will this take? Without a doubt, as long as this disorder reigns in Morocco. One of our Tangier correspondents who is familiar with the matter puts it very well: "The handling of that shapeless thing that is called Moroccan diplomacy eternally begins again."

Nevertheless, it seems we can foresee the following solution to the question of mining in Morocco: the Spanish Government should petition for and obtain confirmation of the mining concessions received by Spanish companies from the pretender. In the rest of Morocco it is not likely for any company to obtain a monopoly in their favor. If, convinced by the logic of coin, the always-needy sultan or, perhaps, his next successor, agrees to a monopolistic concession, something that is quite possible in this country, then the sultan will retain the money for his expenses, but the concessionaire will not be able to exploit the land. Chaos will ensue, and when it is over, it may be that the sultan's promises could become worthless.

The transparent greed and egoism above resulted in massive conflicts that have turned the precious deposits existing in the bowels of Mount Gurugú into something horrifying, a painful and angry hell.

We can clearly conclude that the popular protest was absolutely just.[12] Not attempting to stop this horrible picture from becoming reality, not proudly and enthusiastically protesting to hold back the greed and monstrosities of all manner of businessmen, would have been contemptible. The resistance seemed so justified that not even the leadership of the democratic political parties tried to contain it, managing only, as we might have guessed, to calm passions that might have shaken that principle of authority which is indispensable for the functioning of its organs.

Rallies were organized all over Catalonia in which the people denounced war.[13] These demonstrations did not manage to garner any respect from the government, although—despite the difficulties they had in mobilizing its troops and sending them off—it ordered both the New Castilian and Catalonian Huntsmen Brigade to Melilla during the month of July.

This imprudent manner of inflaming public opinion, which was only willing to approve of those fighting for their own independence, provoked serious upheaval in Madrid and Barcelona. Under the pretext of fearing more extreme repercussions of the protest, Madrid authorities were able to quell the disturbances by arresting several anarchists in their homes as well as many others voicing their protest at the Mediodía Railway Station.[14] Authorities in Barcelona, however, could not repress the protest despite having likewise put people in jail and arrested several journalists.

The demonstrations of general dissatisfaction multiplied, taking on alarming proportions due to the embarkation of troops set for Sunday the 18th.

All the reservists were scheduled to embark that day. It was not true that they themselves had deserted or that they had proposed flouting their military duties, as certain journalists who are

---

12. This view reflects anarchist thinking of the time that all protest was justified and commendable. This view was not always shared by Spain's socialist movement, which frequently chastised spontaneous protests and "imprudent" strike activity, preferring to "direct" the working class itself.

13. On the protests see Joan Connelly Ullman, *The Tragic Week: A Study of Anticlericalism in Spain* (Cambridge, MA: Harvard University Press, 1968), 129–140.

14. In Madrid the main antiwar protests were led by the socialist movement, reflecting their strength in the city.

not really in keeping with the truth have proclaimed. Not a single reservist disobeyed the order to regroup. They left their barracks to head to the pier in the most proper formation.

The truth must not be understated. Not the slightest idea to resist the mobilization order developed among the reserve troops; nor did it occur within the households of anyone called up to serve.[15] Wives, mothers, sisters, and friends felt a great seething indignation against the law's inequalities and against a government that was leading them to ruin. They had been conscripted six years ago, completed their service four years ago, and, with the proper authorization from the Captain General, they were married three years previously—but some of them were on their way to die in Africa. Children were left without fathers in the majority of the reservists' households, and elderly parents without a son to take care of them; these families, in the end, were destined for hunger, poverty, and desperation.[16] Meanwhile, twenty-year-old young men stayed home, not only the rich, but anyone who had had the luck of not having to serve active duty. The most recent replacement troops were all home, while those who had last served six years ago were marching to fight the Moroccans. The dualism that leads some to want suffering to fall on the shoulders of others is sad, but objections to the current state of things was logical, and resistance was only human.

A huge crowd came to the piers right when the order was given for the troops to embark. A rally was not planned at all. They were thinking of nothing other than saying goodbye to their children, their husbands, their brothers.

If there was any sobbing or shouting, it was because the most awful sorrow came over the enormous mass of the reservists' friends. This shared misfortune produced a huge influx of people.

---

15. Bonafulla here reflects the tendency within the anarchist movement to refuse to condemn the actions of conscripted soldiers, who they regarded as fellow workers (unlike the Civil Guard). During the Tragic Week protestors tried numerous times to convince soldiers to refuse orders and join with them in their common cause against the state and army officials.

16. The role of women in the anti-war protests is widely documented and seen as key to the escalation of protest in July 1909. On this subject see Temma Kaplan, "Female consciousness and collective action: The case of Barcelona, 1910–1918," *Signs* 7:3 (1982): 545–566.

Why would anyone invent agendas that never existed, when the situation in itself was enough to justify what would occur?[17] This was what an eyewitness wrote.

So stunning was that assemblage of soldiers' mothers, wives, and children demonstrating such urgency for a final embrace with the hapless men being sent off to war, that the authorities themselves understood it was necessary to proceed energetically against the crowd. When it comes to marching in proper formation, discipline is not very effective if the troops see their own wives walking next to them holding their little one in their arms.

The bravest soldier, who marches dauntlessly towards the enemy, steps out of line, hugs his wife, plants a thousand kisses on the little face that he may never kiss again, and for a moment he forgets he is wearing the uniform, thinking only about the fact that he is abandoning his wife and family.

Accompanying the troops were groups of tearful, desperate people. Hundreds of women, with their children in their arms, were running alongside the battalions. The music stopped because the musicians were unable to play. The troops broke stride. Even officers stepped to the side so the men of their companies could hug their children and console their wives.

Soon all you could see along La Rambla was an enormous swarm walking towards the port. Many uniforms could be seen among the crowd. More than one soldier was carrying a child in his arms while walking. Meanwhile their wives were carrying their rifles or hugging and kissing them desperately, frantically. There were tears in their eyes and sorrow in their hearts.

A colonel of the Luchana Regiment gave the order for the soldiers to disperse the crowd. It was necessary to put the troops in formation, but there was no room. The crowd invaded everything.

The operation was difficult. The families did not want to let go of the reservists who they were gripping tightly in their arms. Their last moments together had come, and everyone wanted to prolong their impassioned goodbyes.

---

17. One of many points in which Bonafulla stresses the spontaneous nature of the protests and the Tragic Week that followed. See the Introduction for more on this subject.

The same colonel ordered a bugler to call the troops to attention. The bugler obeyed the officer, but no one moved. The soldiers were covering the edge of the pier, the only place where there was enough room to line up.

A second order to call the troops to attention was given, but the bugler lacked the enthusiasm to play the notes. The people were yelling. Once the women were separated from the reservists, they began speaking in unmeasured shouts. They raised their babies over their heads so they could wave one last time to their fathers. In this moment of extraordinary commotion, some insulted the officers. Many women incited their relatives to rebellion. "Throw down your rifles! Resist the embarkation order! Either everyone or no one! Let the rich go! Return home!"[18] Such were the cries coming from the tightly-packed mass of people.

The colonel gave the order for the third time to call attention; the shouting increases. The people ask the bugler not to play, to have compassion for the wives. They tell him about their families. The bugler hesitates, and then suspends the battle song. The colonel demands that he follow the order. The soldier cannot do it and throws his instrument into the sea. Standing at attention before his superior, disciplined and upright, with resolve, he exclaims:

"My colonel, shoot me if you want; I will not play!"

He does not rise in rebellion, but he does not obey.

This sets off an indescribable uproar. The desperation, the hurt, the grief of the bugler has infected everyone. The women are shouting. They are no longer soldier's wives but wild animals defending their children's bread, their husbands' lives, the sanctity of their hearth and home. They hurl themselves at the rows of soldiers with more spirit than the men. The officers give the order to fix the bayonets. The soldiers obey, but they don't point them at the crowds. The screams are deafening. The order is given to open fire, but no one takes a shot and military formation is broken.

Every soldier has four or five people holding them by the arm. Despite everything, they struggle through to the ships, with tears

---

18. One of the most hated aspects of the conscription system was the potential for wealthy young men to buy their way out of service, see Ullman, *The Tragic Week*, 24–26.

in their eyes, fighting their wives, their parents, their siblings, and their fiancées to obey the command of their superiors.

Sure, many rifles fell into the water. The women must undoubtedly have thrown them. A few reservists were dragged to the dinghies to be taken on board foreign ships. A French steamboat that was weighing anchor received two of them on board. They were walking with five women and eight men. True prisoners of war, they were carried off by their own families.

It was impossible for there not to be a few cases of open insubordination. How could there not be? Two soldiers fled on a foreign steamship that was leaving for Mallorca. As soon as they made it on board, Civil Guards followed to take the deserters. The captain was unwilling to hand them over.

On the same boat which they had taken to Melilla, a corporal and several soldiers mutinied. They were placed in irons, in sight of their shipmates. But these shipmates seemed stupefied. They were not paying attention to anything except the shouts of their people who were still in port.

From this moment on, who could deny that Barcelona was in a state of open insurrection? In every home, in every family, people were preaching rebellion against the government's orders. At every turn, there were shouts of "Down with war!" shouts that reverberated along central streets, as many protesters were jailed after intense confrontations.

The firestorm was about to erupt, and Governor Ossorio, clumsy and imprudent, only added fuel to the fire with the publication of a decree in which provocations were followed by threats.

This decree characterized those protesting the war as professional agitators and scandalmongers, threatening to use the most severe measures against anyone making a public display of their feelings. Such temerity coincided with the disturbing news from France and England of the misfortunes of Spanish soldiers in Morocco, which spoke to the sterility of their sacrifice.[19]

---

19. On 19 July news reached Spain of heavy casualties amongst the Spanish forces in Morocco, further intensifying the anti-war protests. See Angel Smith, *Anarchism, Revolution and Reaction: Catalan Labour and the Crisis of the Spanish State, 1898–1923* (New York: Berghahn, 2007), 176.

In these circumstances, the Executive Board of *Solidaridad Obrera* convened a General Assembly for Friday, July 23rd, which the Civil Governor roundly declined to permit, and worse, the individual who had duly notified the proper authorities was kept in detention for the space of two hours.[20]

In that moment, the idea of a general strike emerged as the only way to make it known that the militant proletariat would not blindly obey a man who described them to other people as enemies, and that the despotism of the times was intolerable.

On the 22nd, 23rd, and 24th, there was an exchange of views among syndicalists, socialists, anarchists, republicans, nationalists, and radicals. Representation on the strike committee was affirmed by the first three groups, and for the record, almost the totality of workers who are active among the republicans, despite their misgivings, endorsed the movement as well, putting all means at their disposal into action, even sacrificing their lives, and ignoring the voices of order and the thousand excuses given by some leaders of that party.[21]

Workers went through the outer neighborhoods all day Sunday notifying people about the general strike agreed to for the following day. A few also headed for various surrounding towns with the same purpose.

---

20. *Solidaridad Obrera* was the syndicalist federation of the Catalan region, founded in 1907. Although officially politically "neutral" and at times claiming the support of socialists and radical republicans, anarchists formed the majority of the federation and controlled its periodical (also named *Solidaridad Obrera*). This organization was transformed in 1910–11 into the Confederación Nacional del Trabajo (CNT), a nationwide anarcho-syndicalist confederation which became the largest of its kind in world history by 1919, with a membership of around 800,000.

21. On the composition of the strike committee over this weekend see Ullman, *The Tragic Week*, 141–163.

Chapter 2

The Popular Protest is Generalized • Bloody Clashes and Resistance •
Barcelona Under Martial Law • Revolutionaries at the Barricades •
Convents, Friaries, and Churches Set Ablaze • Constitutional Rights
Suspended all Over Spain • Military Reinforcements Arrive. Last
Efforts of the Rebels • Bloody Epilogue • Injuries and Deaths

On Monday at the break of dawn, groups of strikers were circulating in every neighborhood inviting anyone headed to work to join the protest. Shortly before eight o'clock, the number of strikers had grown considerably, and they were greeted with applause when they visited workshops and factories that were still operating to encourage them to stop. This was verified at the time.

The strike was generalized within a few minutes, with the exception of carriages for hire and streetcars, whose resistance soured the protesters' mood.[1]

But given the motive for the popular protest, the noble sentiment that gave it impetus, this resistance seemed very strange—no one would have suspected that the streetcar personnel, starting with the director, would be opposed to it.

The governor did not think about the fact that maybe a warning from him to the director of the streetcar company would calm the mood, and he could have prevented some regrettable conflagrations.

It was around nine o'clock when groups of women arrived from El Poblenou wearing white ribbons across their chest and flying

---

1. The streetcar workers in Barcelona were generally seen as blacklegs, following the replacement of the old pro-anarchist union in 1904. See Smith, *Anarchism, Revolution and Reaction*, 177.

white banners inscribed with large black letters saying: "Down with war!"

Under the pretext of defending the freedom to work, the police intervened brutally, using their sabers in some cases. Another line of mounted police ended up on a certain street where they tried to disperse the assembly. The people offered some resistance, and the police fired their rifles at them, causing three injuries and the death of a young girl.

Violence began to crop up, and the men gathered there made use of whatever weapons they had at their disposal.

Throughout the morning, there was shouting, rock throwing, and clashes with the Civil Guards, who were ordered to protect streetcar circulation.[2] Shortly before noon, groups of people that were scattered in Paral-lel, Gran Via, Diagonal, Clot, and Gracia began losing patience. In the presence of the same police forces and Civil Guards that had been harassing them just a short while ago, they took apart rails on several lines, knocked a few carriages over, and set others on fire, destroying whatever material they could.

All streetcars ceased circulating by three in the afternoon, and with the suspension of all newspapers adding to its impact, the strike was fully generalized.

It was said that the protest against the war in Morocco would be peaceful and that it would be over twenty-four hours after it began. That version of the story was groundless. Besides the fact that no one who took part in the protest could have agreed to such a thing, the duration and character of demonstrations like these is dictated by the attitude of people towards their rulers, which in most cases, is one of loathing.

Accustomed as governments and their representatives are to ignoring the masses, any opinions of theirs are treated with exceptional disdain or marked hostility. This being the state of things, violence is only a stone's throw away.

---

2.   Spain's quasi-military police force, founded to stop the flow of contraband in rural areas in the early nineteenth century but increasingly used to crush urban revolts and strikes, as in Barcelona in 1902. As a result, the Civil Guard were particularly loathed by the working class.

The authorities judged the events that were unfolding with such bias, and when they received news of those who would surely react to the resistance of the streetcars—resulting in some places in shootouts between the Civil Guards and the people—they believed that declaring martial law throughout the province of Barcelona would greatly influence the public's mood.

Consequently, the Captain General issued the following decree:

DON LUIS DE SANTIAGO MANESCAU, Lieutenant General of the Spanish Armies and Captain General of the Fourth Region,

LET IT BE KNOWN THAT:

The Civil Authority having resigned command of this province; the formalities of the law on Public Order having been completed; and, making use of the functions conferred upon me by the Royal Ordinances and the Code of Military Justice,

I ORDER AND COMMAND:

Article 1: Martial Law is declared in the province of Barcelona.

Art. 2: All public assemblies are ordered to disperse immediately, with the knowledge that if they fail to do so, they will be dispersed by force.

Art. 3: Any crimes affecting the public order, whether social or political in nature, will remain within the purview of my authority, and their perpetrators may be subject to summary trial.

Art. 4: Any individual publishing news or opinions that could in any way cause military discipline to be violated, or undermine the right to work, cause damage to railroads, streetcars, telegraph or telephone lines, electrical wires, pipes, and water or gas tanks will be considered guilty of sedition.

Art. 5: All printed materials, whether produced by means of a printing press or other mechanical means, will be subject to prior censorship, for which purpose two copies of each publication must be forwarded, sufficiently in advance, in Barcelona, to the Captain General's Staff Office, and in other towns, to local military commanders, or in the absence of these, to their respective mayors. These publications may not be published until one copy is returned with the proper stamp affixed, with the knowledge that any printed section, drawing, or etching that has been crossed out must be deleted.

Art. 6: Reservists and individuals who have been granted indefinite leave from the army will be considered on active duty and subject to the Code of Military Justice for any crimes covered by this decree.

Art. 7: Civilian authorities and courts will continue to have jurisdiction wherever it does not conflict with the above.

Citizens of Barcelona:

Having assumed command of this province for the first time, I am resolved that nothing will upset the public order in this province, or in this beautiful capital city, and I am expecting your good sense and judgment in cooperating to that end, with the knowledge that I will repress any disturbance energetically and with the utmost severity. When the use of force becomes necessary, I exhort peaceful citizens to withdraw from public places, unless they wish to suffer the painful, but inevitable, consequences.

Barcelona, July 20, 1909.

Captain General Luis de Santiago.

Shortly after the authorities had their meeting, the Governor told journalists that Martial Law had been declared in spite of his vote against it.

At around three o'clock in the afternoon, several squads of dragoon regiments from Santiago, Montesa, and Numancia, as well as one infantry company from Vergara and another from Alcántara, left their respective barracks and reported for duty to Brigadier General Germán Brandéis.

Captain General Luis de Santiago, Military Governor Enrique Cortés, and Chief of Staff Francisco Rodríguez, and their respective aides-de-camp, several senior officials and other officers left the Captaincy heavily guarded, walked a few stretches, and returned after a brief while.

Naturally, this decree was not well received—at night, immediately after units of soldiers would put copies of the decree up at corners, they were torn up. With everything that had happened during the day, spirits were still running high among the people after nightfall.

The anti-war protest movement was seconded in Sabadell, Badalona, Granollers, Vilanova i la Geltrú, Tarrasa, Olesa, and Canet de Mar, where the revolutionaries interrupted rail circulation and telegraph lines. In Sabadell and Granollers, the revolution could claim victory from the beginning. Local authorities were forced to relinquish their powers to the revolutionary committees that were constituted.

In reality, no other result could be expected. When a nation is sick and tired of warring corporations whose aim is not to defend their own independence or foster progress in the moral evolution of a people, corporations which are the very picture of primitive savagery, then repressing people's grievances by force or compulsion produces a situation in which all the reprisals and provocations only upset the peaceful order of things. In the context of their everyday existence, in the exact moment when they find themselves intensely moved by a great misfortune whose unjust cause they have condemned with all their energy, each individual learns the extent of their indignation and desperation which is caused by the brutal repressions of despotism, and so, no one should be surprised by these events that are necessarily, inevitably doomed to unfold.[3]

***

By early in the morning on Tuesday the 27th, although women were still able to get supplies at the markets, the city looked sad, and there was tension reflected on every face.

An infantry column, subdivided into smaller groups, went along La Rambla, El Paral-lel and adjacent streets. Their presence caused numerous civilians to occupy the Old Town. They removed sections of pavement and formed barricades at many street corners.

---

3. Again, Bonafulla stresses that the Tragic Week was not planned, or directed, but rather the product of social conflict, inequality, and desperation, a view common to anarchist analyses of popular unrest.

The same thing happened in Gracia, El Clot, and other suburbs where Civil Guards were patrolling. There was some gunfire, causing curious onlookers—who had been filling the streets since the day before in search of excitement, which always happens—to take refuge in their neighborhoods, or rather, in their houses.

Confusing reports were coming in from certain towns in Catalonia, but all were in agreement that the movement had also spread to Igualada and Caldas, and had taken on a violent character in many towns in Girona, namely Palamós, Palafrugell, Cassà de la Selva, Anglés, Calonge, Amer, Banyoles, Figueres, as well as several points in the province of Tarragona, where it was learned that train cars with troops on their way to Melilla, and roads in Les Borjes del Camp, Esplugues de Llobregat, Montblanc, and Selva, were destroyed.

The suspension of the newspapers and the obstruction of the railroads did not prevent conscious revolutionaries from learning what was going on in the rest of Catalonia, especially since some people had gone to the above towns the previous Sunday to get them to endorse the movement in Barcelona.

At the first gunshots of the morning, two squadrons from Montesa came out to support the Civil Guards, marching in formation towards El Poblenou, where revolutionaries, taking a stand against the armed forces, burned down a building occupied by the Marist Brothers. At the same time, the local parish church in this neighborhood was on fire.

There were many incidents that occurred. We will not describe them, although to refute the false stories that interested parties were persistently inserting into certain local newspapers, and which were being echoed by many provincial papers, it would be necessary. We do not want to resort to commonplace fanaticism or have bad intentions. Nonetheless, we can make things clear now to avoid constant annoying repetition as we proceed in our report. It would be appropriate, in such turbulent times, to examine the attitude with which the revolutionaries acted.

Also, once a fight is established—is it any less painful when a victim falls at the hands of the police or military? During the revolt that occurred in El Poblenou, a Marist prior and a parish priest were killed, and I believe three or four law enforcement officers were injured. Among the revolutionaries, there was also one death, a twenty-year-old youth, and twelve wounded. The acts that can be truly called theft or murder were isolated cases committed by the vile scum spawned by a perverse society in which decadence and sloth are venerated, scum which lives from street crime most easily in large cities.

The same people that have so denigrated the revolutionaries also say: won't the unprecedented abuses committed at eleven in the morning, which we will describe, give way to the most extreme violence and desperation?

A sizeable infantry detachment was walking along La Rambla surrounded by an enormous crowd that was shouting "Down with war!" The soldiers continued on their way while the people were accompanying them, applauding continuously.

People were applauding and waving to their commanding officer, General Brandéis, with smiling faces.

When they arrived at the Passeig de Colom, the detachment penetrated the Captaincy General, and at that very instant, a squadron of cops appearing at the edge of the avenue fired at the unarmed crowd of people, who escaped in any way they could.[4] This brutal assault caused three deaths and many injuries, including several women. The news of what happened here and in El Poblenou spread quickly, and there was a remarkable amount of movement in El Paral-lel and Ronda Sant Pau, where many civilians seized as many weapons as they could find in an armory one block away at Príncep de Viana Street. Notable among these groups, some men, women, and children headed to the Piarist Friary and began dousing the heavy double doors of the great building with petroleum, setting them on fire. The fire barely burned, though, and with nothing else available to them, they threw a thick mat over to one of the doors, and to the other door, they threw a wooden streetcar kiosk and window blinds from the nearby Sant Antoni Market.

---

4. The contrast Bonafulla makes between the soldiers, applauded by the people, and the murderous "cops" is stark. In this instance the "cops" refer to the urban police, rather than the Civil Guard (the former being generally regarded slightly more favorably than the latter by the city's working class).

Bravely, a few people managed to penetrate to the living quarters, scaling the walls.

In these circumstances, the Captain General appeared with his retinue. His presence did not disturb the groups already stationed there.

The first military authority, seeing that it was powerless to put a stop to the conflict, withdrew, and the Piarist Priests hurried to safety.

Those who had penetrated the building immediately began throwing objects to the street which were used to start an enormous bonfire: tables, pictures, chairs, beds, cloaks, cassocks, images, chalices, books, medals, prints, iron cash boxes, shotguns, dies that the public believed were for making coins (although according to the Priests they were used for making medals), and lastly, a few bills from the Bank of Spain that were determined to be forged (the Priests also made every effort to make it known that they were used by their pupils to learn commerce). All of it fed the fire.

At the same time, another event just like the one we have described was unfolding at the Sant Pau del Camp Parish Church, where the building was set on fire and anything that could be found inside was destroyed.

Without wasting time, the groups split up, with some going to El Poble-sec, where, in less time than would be necessary to recount the details, they set fire to both the old and new Parish of Santa Madrona, the Franciscan convents, Handmaids of the Sacred Heart, Little Sisters of the Assumption, the School of Our Lady of Carme, the Catholic Workers Center of Santa Madrona, and the Asylum of the Sisters of Sant Vicenç de Paúl, on Aldana Street. Other groups headed towards the Church of Sant Antoni Abat, and after setting it on fire, went on to see that the same thing had happened at the Parish Church of Carme, and the convent of the Hieronymites.

Despite their clashes with the armed forces, the groups that were still operating in the Poblenou neighborhood, who, as we have previously seen, had initiated the idea early in the morning of burning the churches, convents, and friaries, set fire to the religious convent of the Franciscan Sisters of the Immaculate Conception, then moved on to the Pequín neighborhood, where they did the same thing to the church of Sant Pere Pescador and the Catholic Club. What was occurring during this same time in the district of Gracia? Real battles were unfolding. On Carrer Gran de Gràcia, the Civil Guards were trying to prevent barricades from being raised, and heavy shooting broke out between them and the revolutionaries. The yellows needed help from the cavalry forces who were stationed at Passeig de Gràcia.[5] These forces were received with applause and shouts of "Viva," but their lieutenant ordered them to undo the barricades, which the people opposed. Facing resistance, the armed forces withdrew from that location to take a position at the end of the street, where the lieutenant, placing himself at the rear of the Civil Guards, ordered them to fire indiscriminately into the crowd, resulting in one dead and several wounded. The gunfight continued, with less intensity, until well into the afternoon. Another gunfight was taking place between some civilians and Civil Guards stationed at the Electric substation at Travesera. These civilians were able to face law enforcement attacks by requesting arms at loan institutions and attacking the armory at Carrer Torrent de l'Olla, where one civilian managed to contain Civil Guards who were attempting to take over the barricade, and was seriously injured in the process.

While these events were unfolding, the Oratory of Sant Felip Neri was set ablaze, followed by the Parish Church of Sant Joan and the Convent of Barefoot Carmelites. Along with the raucous bell tolling of the high tower at Plaza de Oriente, where the civilians were sounding an alarm, this produced the most intense impression.

The Sant Pere district in Barcelona, away from the coast, seemed no less shaken. Large groups set fire to the Marcús Chapel, the Parish of Saint Cucuphas, the Church of Our Lady of Help, and the Church of the Ministers of the Infirm. The presence of troops at six in the evening saved the Sant Pere de les Puelles Parish Church from going up in smoke as well, but by nine at night, all three sections of that building were burning brightly.

5. [Translator's note] "Yellow union" [*amarillos*] is another term for company union, or a union of workers created by employers.

Groups moving throughout the city spread through Esquerra de l'Eixample, while others did the same along the top part of El Clot, Camp de l'Arpa, and the neighborhood of Grassot. In Esquerra de l'Eixample, the devastating arson destroyed the following convents and asylums: the Mission of the Penitents, Sisters of Charity, Sisters Adorers, Magdalene Sisters, Missionaries of Saint Vincent de Paul, Servants of Mary, and continued into the night with the Conceptionist Sisters and the Missionaries of the Sacred Heart.

In El Clot, another area that was mentioned, the convent of the Little Sisters of the Sacred Family and the parish church were also destroyed during the same hours. There were many skirmishes between revolutionaries in this neighborhood and the military and law enforcement, resulting in several casualties.

After nightfall, groups managed to burn down the Piarist Convent, located in El Camp de l'Arpa, and, situated in the Grassot neighborhood, the religious establishments belonging to the Missionaries of the Sacred Heart of Mary, the orphanage of Sant Josep and the Dominican Blesseds were also devoured by flames.

Finally, the burning of the convent of the Capuchins (Camp d'en Galvany), the Salesian Friary (Hostafrancs), and the Salesian Convent on Carrer Sepulveda completed the day's devastation.

It would be impossible to describe the grim appearance of the colossal flames simultaneously engulfing so many of the buildings that burned that night. There were thick columns of white smoke over here, over there, to the right and to the left, from one end of town to the other. The people were venting their collective hatred, contained until this day, towards governments and repulsive institutions. As the Red Cross passed through the streets, all of them dark, with their stretchers lit by torches, the crimes of a murderous regime were exposed, the seed of new hates and curses, the bloody destruction among people of the same caste who were always born to be each other's brother and sister.

The red night seemed as if it still hadn't ended. There was no rest. The destruction of houses of worship and convents continued without interruption.

***

At one o'clock in the morning on Wednesday the 28th, with the fires turning the burned buildings to ash, their glow was still lighting up rooftops, and a fire was started at the Convent of Saint Teresa of Jesus (neighborhood of Camp d'en Grassot).

In the Les Corts neighborhood, fires were raging at the School of Nen Jesús and the convents of Our Lady of Loreto and Discalced Carmelites. At the same time, the Santa Maria de Valdonzella Royal Monastery and the friary of the Marist Brothers of San Andres de Palomar were being devoured by fire. It was also learned that the friary of the Minim Brothers, located in the vicinity of Horta, had been burned the day before.

There was news from the outside of new repercussions. The movement had spread to other towns. Indeed, in Reus, Sant Feliu de Guíxols, Olot, Monistrol de Montserrat, La Bisbal, and Cassà de la Selva, the protest was spirited. Also, taking advantage of the embarkation of troops that took place there, the protest was reproduced in Mahon.

For two hours, from seven to nine o'clock in the morning, neighbors were able to breathe the air outside, although naturally, they were somewhat shaken by the idea that the fight was not yet over. Provisions were becoming scarce. There was no meat, and vegetables were expensive.

The Captain General had some more troops available to him—they had just arrived from different points around Spain—and he ordered them to cover areas that were threatened, posting the following decree:

DON LUIS DE SANTIAGO MANESCAU, Lieutenant General of the Spanish Armies and Captain General of the Fourth Region.

In view of the attitude of the groups impeding movement along public roadways and preventing a return to normalcy in this community,

I ORDER AND COMMAND:

Article 1: Whoever is occupying the streets of this city is ordered to disband and withdraw to their homes, with the knowledge that if they fail to do so, they will be fired upon with no warning whatsoever, regardless of any shouts they offer, including shouts of Long Live the Army or the like.

Art. 2: Remaining on balconies, terraces, and rooftops is likewise prohibited to the public, along with any shouting as mentioned in the previous article. Public areas must remain entirely clear, and any groups impeding movement will be fired upon.

Art. 3: Any renters of houses from which the Army is antagonized, or from which any type of shouting is heard, will be held accountable.

Art. 4: This decree will govern as of nine o'clock a.m., today.

Luis de Santiago Manescau.

Barcelona, July 28, 1909.

In no case did this second decree have its intended effect, either—divided into groups, the revolutionaries restarted fires at houses of worship and convents where the destruction was not yet complete.

Soldiers arrived at some of these points, firing heavily throughout the day along Les Rondes, Paral·lel, Poblenou, Clot, and central Gracia. A few cannons were placed at one end of Carrer Sant Pau, and at the entry to Clot and Poblenou to disperse the revolutionaries, who answered the artillery fire with tenacious resistance at houses where they had dug in. A deluge of grapeshot was spewed out by the cannons. Many were killed or wounded and were picked up by Red Cross workers.

At nightfall, the Captain General ordered this new decree to be put up:

DON LUIS DE SANTIAGO MANESCAU, Lieutenant General of the Spanish Armies and Captain General of the Fourth Region,

LET IT BE KNOWN THAT:

His Majesty's Government has issued the following Decree:

Sire: As a result of the serious attacks perpetrated yesterday in the province of Barcelona at the same time that our soldiers are fighting for their nation's cause in Africa, Martial Law was declared in the capital of the Principality. In such extraordinary circumstances, these attacks demand the proper repressive action, and, to be effective, it is, of course, necessary to extend this action to the bordering provinces of Girona and Tarragona.

Pursuant to Article 17 of the Constitution of the Monarchy, the Council of Ministers considers it appropriate and has the honor of submitting the following Royal Decree for Your Majesty's approval:

San Sebastian, July 27, 1909.

Sire, at the Royal Feet of Your Majesty, Antoni Maura Montaner.[6]

ROYAL DECREE:

At the proposal of my Council of Ministers, and in use of the powers vested in me by article 17 of the Constitution of the Monarchy, I do decree the following:

Article 1: The guarantees expressed in articles 4, 5, 6, and 9, and paragraphs 1, 2, and 3 of article 13 of the Constitution are temporarily suspended in the provinces of Barcelona, Girona, and Tarragona.

Article 2: The Government will provide due notice of this Royal Decree to the Cortes.[7]

Issued in San Sebastian, July 27, 1909.

Alfonso.— President of the Council of Ministers, Antoni Maura Montaner.

This decree is hereby made public so that it may be known to all.

Luis de Santiago Manescau.

Barcelona, July 28, 1909.

The shooting was more and more vigorous and generalized, and Barcelona was becoming a battlefield.

---

6. A reformist conservative who was Prime Minister of Spain from 1907 until the Tragic Week. Maura was loathed by the anarchist movement for his role in the repression of the movement during his first term as Prime Minister from 1903–1904. On 12 April 1904 the anarchist Joaquín Miguel Artal attempted to assassinate Maura, leaving him badly wounded.

7. The Cortes Generales is the Spanish parliament.

The troops, who were steadily taking stronger positions and decimating the revolutionaries, could not prevent some groups from spreading out to the NW of the capital and setting the religious houses of the Brethren of the Christian Schools and the Franciscans of Our Lady of Jerusalem on fire, while other groups beyond Sant Martí, did the same thing to the Catholic Workers Center of Sant Pere Claver (La Sagrera) and the Sant Andreu parish church.

Physical strength has its limits. Human nature is very poor. More so than the infantry and cavalry's charges and discharges, drowsiness and fatigue were what sunk that pack of unknown heroes, those children of the people, who, during the three days we have recounted so far, knocked down walls with their bare hands, destroyed great buildings with a few cans of petroleum, and, lacking weapons to fight with, used their own bodies fiercely, endlessly watering the streets of the big city with their blood, without any hope of victory and without even the respect of those who, after having fostered enthusiasm among the people, after having called their sacrifice for a just and honorable cause generous, stirred up those dregs that give birth to failure in the heat of the battle, in the critical hours, that is, the pessimism that chops down great works.

The situation of the revolutionaries was difficult at times. By now the military authorities had at their disposal the forces they needed to quickly subdue the population. Several political personalities consulted the day before did not demonstrate their willingness to facilitate a solution, despite having used their respective organs of the press to encourage the revolutionary protest at first. They claimed that what had happened was unforeseen and they did not believe they were authorized to resolve the situation. And the city was still in full-out revolution.

Two hundred forty-seven barricades were put in the troops' way, but without vigorous reinforcement, the movement had to die of exhaustion. How could they ensure that the enormous sacrifices they made would be compensated? What was to be done?

Was it better to be riddled with bullets at the foot of the barricades or shot to death in the moats of Montjuïc? There was no choice but to persist in the fight. And in the meantime, things were becoming more serious. The clashes became more intense, the skirmishes bloodier. The revolutionaries had to continuously defend their lives—there was no time for other considerations.

***

In this state of affairs, we come to Thursday. Like the other days, the morning began seemingly peacefully. In some neighborhoods, people were discussing the news that the movement had also been seconded in Manresa and Valls, and in the first of these two towns, the revolutionaries burned down some churches and convents. They did the same thing in Sabadell, Granollers, Palamós, and other points. It was learned that day that a few cases of rebellion were recorded in other towns like Hospitalet, Calella, Malgrat, Ripoll, and Villafranca. Towns in Alcoy, Mequinenza, Calahorra, and several towns in Aragon bordering the province of Lleida participated alongside the popular movement in Catalonia.

We have dispensed with sensationalist news stories that were believed by gullible, simple individuals or that unscrupulous people have taken advantage of to perpetuate false alarms. We have only reported those stories that, for many reasons, we had grounds to believe and were later able to confirm. We have undertaken to put forth only the truth, and our story is laid out on this basis.

Groceries were hard to come by, and meat—impossible. For those that were well off, it was ham or preserves. For the poor, codfish and vegetables, and even that with some difficulty because some stores in working-class neighborhoods appeared to be closed.

From early on, in the neighborhoods of Santa Caterina, an extremely vigorous exchange of gunfire announced that things would continue as on previous days. In these neighborhoods, the revolutionaries abandoned the barricades and occupied the terraces. The troops wanted to sweep them out of there. The gunfire lasted a long time and caused some injuries on both sides.

Taking advantage of the element of surprise, civilians ran to the network of alleyways surrounding La Reforma, continuing the fight almost all morning.

In the area of Barcelona's Old Town along Carrer de Sant Pau and Carrer de l'Hospital, there was more intense gunfire. The revolutionaries resisted desperately, and the soldiers were shooting so heavily that even the peaceful neighbors did not think they were safe in their homes—Mauser bullets penetrated into some of them. As if participating in a planned maneuver, the revolutionaries abandoned this area, resisting the troops in their pursuit, and, taking advantage of this, other groups from nearby streets assaulted a Barracks House on Sadurní Street which was used by veterans. Without causing injury to any guards or neighbors in adjacent houses (despite their having resisted), they seized 290 rifles and a few thousand cartridges of ammunition that had been deposited there.

New battles began immediately along those streets, but the fight became more and more unsustainable since the captain general had numerous new reinforcements available to him. The Mahon, Aragon, Lealtad, Constitución, Mallorca, Asia, and Luchana Infantry Regiments; the Almansa, Alcántara, Castillejos, and Treviño Cavalry Regiments; a company of Sappers; roughly one thousand Civil Guards; and siege artillery were operating at his command.

Nonetheless, the resistance continued steadfast in a few points in Paral-lel, Clot, and Poblenou. There were light skirmishes at night in Gracia.

The revolutionaries did not want to surrender, although they were obliged to withdraw from populated areas.

Many people were injured in all these scuffles, and several deaths had to be recorded. A considerable number of prisoners were taken to the jails and the Shipyard barracks.

***

Friday began apparently more calmly. In central neighborhoods, it looked as if the rebellion was coming to a close. Some agitation was noted only in the furthest suburbs, where smaller crowds were fighting off their pursuers.

By the end of the previous day, the movement had lost its character of resistance. For different reasons that we have pointed out in the course of our story, those who were the heart and soul of this revolutionary movement until its final hours, who never gauged the dangers, sought refuge at the French border and in a few ships at the port. It would have been crazy to expect complete triumph of the revolution. They didn't expect that. But having lost any hope of backing from those who, at the beginning of the protest, had declared themselves to be supporters, their sacrifice at this point would have been sterile.

The fighting in the streets was over, and the troops were able to occupy the most important points and all public roads.

In the afternoon on this same day, on the street where the University is located, heavy gunfire was heard against four boys who were attempting to set fire to the Seminary. Two of them, when they were surprised, escaped to the Plaça del Doctor Letamendi, and were pursued by troops firing streams of lead at them. They were mortally wounded a bit further down, near Carrer d'Arragó. They were completely unarmed.

Those who claimed that people were still fighting the troops and the Civil Guards on that day and the following Saturday were knowingly lying.

The popular protest was not yet over only in the town of Sant Andreu de Palomar, where the friary of the Fathers of the Sacred Family and the convent of the Religious of Jesus and Mary were set on fire, and in the town of Horta, where groups coming from Sant Andreu torched the parish church and later the friary of the Third Order of Saint Dominic.

During these last fires, troops arrived, and sustained gunfire left one dead and two wounded. The lieutenant in command of the soldiers was also taken away injured.

✷✷✷

Saturday began peacefully and continued that way. Not one shot was heard, and those people giving life to the streets were railing against what had happened as if wanting to get even for the anxiety and the silence that had been forced on them by the recent state of things, which had just ended. Everywhere they went, they stumbled upon patrols of soldiers, Civil Guards, and police officers.

Aiming to calm the passions and prevent any new incidents from once again disturbing the newly imposed sense of normalcy, the largest manufacturers and industrialists agreed to pay anyone who showed up to work on Monday their regular wages.

The first military authority hastily issued the following decree:

> DON LUIS DE SANTIAGO MANESCAU, Lieutenant General of the Spanish Armies and Captain General of the Fourth Region,
>   LET IT BE KNOWN THAT:
>   In light of this period of calm beginning, I invite all neighbors to contribute to achieving total peace by proceeding to open all manner of establishments, also keeping in mind that circulation on the street is permitted at all times, while knowing full well that assembling in groups remains fully prohibited in accordance with my previous decree; assemblies will be dispersed and punished as set forth there.
>   *Luis de Santiago Manescau.*
>   Barcelona, July 31, 1909.

As the people marveled that it was all over and, naturally, lamented their sufferings, rifle shots once again silenced everyone.

What happened? The shots seemed to be coming from somewhere between Avinguda Diagonal, Carrer de Córcega, and Passeig de Sant Joan. Recently opened doors were closed thunderously. A sense of alarm spread through the neighborhoods like electricity, and no one could explain what was happening.

We will accurately relate what happened. Once it was over, the curiosity to see the effects of the revolt brought many people out to visit the burned churches, friaries, and convents. Enormous crowds of curious onlookers were everywhere. Many people had penetrated into the convent of the Blesseds convinced that, just like at other places they visited, nothing would happen to them.

Well, what did happen there was atrocious, horrifying. As men, women, and children were nosing about among the ruins, a tremendous discharge produced the most frightening bewilderment, and they fled the scene in a frenzy, desperately. The screams of the women and children were gut-wrenching, but they were still being fired at as they pushed their way out to the street. Civil Guards who were lined up in a deep firing squad around the convent released a deluge of bullets from their Mausers, causing ten or twelve deaths and many more injuries among the peaceful, but curious people.

That same day, the tragic epilogue to the week's events was crowned, sadly, by the spectacle of forty onlookers who had escaped the barrage of lead from the Mausers, shackled and led to Montjuïc. All of them were released twenty days later after the military judges ruled that they had committed no crimes.

This brings the number casualties that occurred on all sides during these bloody days to sixty-five. Verifying the number of wounded was not possible. We are referring to official statistics.

We believe that the number of deaths was somewhat higher, and with respect to the number of wounded, we estimate about 350.

Chapter 3

Heinous Acts of Capital's Powerful and the False Messengers
of God • Manifesto of the Regionalist Deputies and Senators •
Message of the Committee of Social Defense • Document
of the Prelate of this Diocese • Agreements of the Diocesan
Board • Endorsement of The Parish Churches of Barcelona •
Declaration of Pope Pius X. The Extremely Timely Reply

It should not be surprising that the cruel brutality of medieval
times is still venerated today by certain classes that do not see, and
cannot see, the progressive current that is the driving force of nations in the present era.[1] But today, induced by the events of July,
we find ourselves obliged to take a look at the messages and protests in opposition to these events sent to the government by our
modern inquisitors, represented by the moneyed classes, with their
hefty appetites, and the clergy. We will lay bare the stark reality
of their shameful, ignoble, disastrous work, more inquisitorial, if
that is possible, than during the times when the agony of barbaric
passions touched even the children of the children of the torture
victims.

Fanaticism and class hatred pervert the most delicate sentiments and deprive human beings of their ability to achieve
progress quickly. Because of this, progressive trends must break
through in the midst of violent tumult. Those who lay blame, jeer,

---

1. References to Spain's medieval past (in particular the Inquisition) was
common trope in anarchist critiques of the Spanish state and its heavy-handed repression. This also plays into the European-wide notion of the "Black Legend" of
Spain, which held that the country had never fully rid itself of its violent past. See
Mary Vincent, *Spain, 1833–2002: People and State* (Oxford: Oxford University Press,
2007), 79–87.

and hurl epithets at this protest movement, the most honorable and humane that we can remember, are unwilling to respect this law of history.

In these ignoble messages and complaints, they request vengeance and they say that liberal and progressive affiliation is evidence of criminality. Instead it would be more appropriate and correct to call for justice.

Muddying the turbulent waters of society's passions to fish for the satisfaction of their vengeance and the annihilation of their adversaries will always be despicable work, the inevitable consequences of which will fall, sooner or later, to those same people who so basely inspire it.

It is sad to confess that the most powerful representatives of capital and the false messengers of God have put into practice the most wretched and base arts, which, while always repugnant, are monstrous and abominable when their adversaries find themselves with their hands and feet tied. Rosas Samaniego, Canon Tristany, [Pasqual] Cucala, Bishop Caixal, Cura Santa Cruz, and [Ramón] Cabrera were more honorable and less brutal, despite falling into disgrace as a horrible breed of inquisitors.[2]

There was profound social upheaval and many bloody battles as we went from an absolutist regime to a liberal one. Why? Because those who defended the old, absolutist ideas wanted to oppose the overwhelming tide of liberal ideas.[3]

The events in Barcelona were a turbulent, angry manifestation, as such things are when a people finds itself compelled to declare a protest, an aspiration, a tendency, a current. If the signers of the aforementioned messages and complaints persist in proclaiming everywhere, as they have done with such bad faith, that the causes of the July events were due to the vicious propaganda of lawbreakers directing the people and the rationalist lay schools' work of moral perversion, then their deception and error will subsist, and

---

2. A reference to the leaders of the Carlist factions during the three Carlist Wars (1833-1840; 1846-49; 1872-1876). Carlists supported an alternative line to the Spanish monarchy, and by the twentieth century they were associated with absolutism and ultra-reactionary Catholicism. See Vincent, *Spain*, 9-13.

3. A further reference to the Carlist wars, see above.

the consequences of this deception and error will be tremendously painful. If it continues this way, if the spirit of our times is not given satisfaction, a spirit that is bigger than any individual desire, then without a doubt, new clashes and fights will bring inevitable misfortunes.

We should agree that when, in the bosom of a nation, a movement is produced that comes to paralyze all commercial, manufacturing, and industrial activity, which cuts off all communication, causes unrest everywhere, and convulses the universal consciousness, then there is a great, powerful motive for it, and behind this movement there beats a legitimate desire, a noble aspiration that compels us to recognize and serve it in all its intensity.

Nonetheless, because they are more powerful, (and in power we find all the treachery of Spanish politicians), no matter how much they purport to be guided by reason and philosophy, the demagoguery of the white gloves and tailcoats, or, to be clear, of the ruling classes, found its inspiration in the terrible threat proffered by the Gallic chieftain on one solemn occasion: "Vae Victis!"[4]

And what do they want when they proffer this threat? Do they want to stifle thought? Every sect of fierce despotism tried and could not do it. Do they want to ban ideas? History would laugh at such designs. Do they want these ideas to die, to disappear, since they believe them to be antisocial and enemies of everything that is proper? Faced with the Christian ideal, and later, the Reformation, members of the old regimes had this very aim, and even so, the Christian ideal survived its agony, and in its day, the Reformation saw its faith deposited in the most powerful and cultured of nations. And in rebuke of those pitiful individuals who tortured Galileo, the *E pur si muove* still makes the rounds in intellectual spaces.[5]

---

4. [Translator's note] Latin for "Woe to the vanquished!" In 390 BC, Brennus led the Gauls to victory over Rome and demanded 1,000 pounds of gold from the conquered Romans. When they complained that the weights were inaccurate, Brennus reportedly threw his sword onto the pile, forcing them to pay even more gold. He shouted "Vae Victis," meaning there will be no fairness here—you have been defeated!
5. Italian for "And yet it moves." Said to be Galileo's response when he was forced to retract his claim that the earth moves around the sun. In other words, it is

Bloody acts are never inspired by propaganda of the truth. Falsity is what misleads and confuses. It is true that both truth and falsehood may spring from the human mind, but can we therefore say that the maxims of Christ or the apostle Paul incited Christians in 1468 to whip up their hatred of the Jews in Sepúlveda, Segovia, Toledo, Jaén, Córdoba, Seville, Andújar, lighting on fire, killing over twelve thousand creatures of God, and in Jaén, dragging away Constable Iranzo because he tried to prevent such horrible carnage?[6] Can we likewise assume that from 1833 to 1840, and from 1873 to 1876, such maxims were what incited crowds of fanatics to lay waste to the fields of Catalonia, Valencia, and Aragon, and spatter the mountains of Vizcaya and Navarre with blood?[7] Who would dare assert that the elevation of the human mind, which occurred when the darkness of obscurantism was dispelled, could cause a state of moral confusion in the heart of a people?

Now, to ensure that the criminal arrogance of those ceaseless instigators of popular conflagrations is judged forevermore, we should compile their manifestations of hypocritical indignation and their dogmatic declarations, imbued with false mercy, and we should always continue to compile and remember them because who else but they, the signers of such craven documents, preach peace and gentleness while simultaneously maintaining confusion everywhere among all sectors of life.

The time has come to be completely blunt. The Asturian Republicans advocated the same thing, rightfully so, in a notable article in *El Progreso*:

> We must speak clearly. Plunge to the depths of evil, and examine the causes of the mournful events we all lament, which,

---

true regardless of what anyone says or believes.

References to thinkers that had been persecuted by the Catholic Church (such as Galileo, Michael Servetus, Giodarno Bruno, and Copernicus) were common in anarchist discussions of "science" and "education." After his execution Francisco Ferrer's name was often included in this lineage.

6. References to the persecution of Jews during the *Reconquista* period, which culminated in their expulsion in 1492.

7. Dates corresponding to the first and third Carlist wars.

however plausible or implausible they may be, are undoubtedly true.

But it was retrograde individuals, not the lay schools, who widely distributed the leaflet inciting Catholics and Carlists in Valencia to take action against the liberals during the procession of Saint Bertrand.

The blood of liberals ran in Mataró during a Carlist celebration. In Zumarraga, supporters of the pretender to the throne did whatever they felt like for their spirit's expansion. In Begoña, they donkeyed around however much they wanted; in Olot, they blustered to their heart's content, and in Manresa, Somorrostro, Tarragona, Girona, and Canet de Mar, they ranted at their pleasure, dragging don Jaime every which way, hither and thither, making him pass through the same places through which don Alfonso was to pass, and finishing off their revelry with an anti-dynastic demonstration, like the one that took place in the Madrid Nurseries.[8]

Later, the focus shifted to the so-called culture budget. The Ultramontanists[9] opposed it. Social and political passions and their concomitant rancor was inflamed. A trail of powder was set. They patted Sanllehy on the back and cheered, they coddled Ossorio, they protested Moret and his Zaragoza speech, they won the match and paved the way for the explosion.

The war in Melilla, the protest of the radicals, and the call-up of the reservists—these produced the spark that caught fire and burned down Barcelona's convents and friaries.

We will reproduce the documents they dared to publish, since lessons can be gleaned from reading them, lessons that we can certainly use.

---

8. Jaime, Duke of Madrid, the rightful heir to the Spanish throne according to the Carlists.

Alfonso XIII, King of Spain from 1886 to 1931.

9. A term used interchangeably with Carlists in Spain in this period, signifying ultraconservative Catholicism.

Manifesto of the Regionalist Deputies and Senators[10]

OUR PROTEST:

The events that have disturbed Barcelona and Catalonia are events that rouse our conscience as human beings, our spirit as Catalonians. The beautiful city, which had given so many examples of its lofty sense of civic duty, the land of Catalonia, which had dignified popular suffrage and had made it the weapon par excellence of our political fights, has become the victim of unspeakable brutalities, of unseemly attacks, of repugnant violence. And not the charters governing human life; nor the sanctity of the conscience; nor the respect held in all parts of the world for schools, libraries, works of art, and the glorious memories of the past; nor the majesty of death and burials; nor love of the city whose interests have been damaged, whose renown as a cultured capital city has been offended and degraded—nothing has held back the arm of the stirred-up mobs; nothing has broken the criminal leadership that has inspired them.

Life does not stop its forward movement even for an instant. While the ruins are still hot, it will resume its progressive course, albeit with somewhat weakened energy, but if all the elements that make up our society limit themselves to verbal protest, if the lesson they receive becomes a lesson lost on them, then the evil will remain locked up inside; it will continue to gnaw at our people's open sores, until one day the circumstances are favorable, and it will explode furiously. A generation that has burned down convents, friaries, and places of worship one day, will burn down factories, banks, houses, and stores tomorrow because what persists in human beings is the temperament towards either violence or tolerance, and what changes and varies easily is the ideal, the direction in whose service these temperaments place themselves.

---

10. At this point Catalan regionalism was generally regarded as a bourgeoise project. Very few within the anarchist movement considered themselves "Catalanists," and only one of hundreds of anarchist periodicals published in this period used the Catalan language. See Smith, *Anarchism, Revolution and Reaction*, 163–173.

AFFIRMATIONS:

The magnitude of the evil that has been caused does make us lose hope for the splendorous future that we had dreamed of for our city and our country, that splendorous future that has been the sole driving force behind our engagement in political life.

Nonetheless, this evil, though it is extremely serious, is not irreparable. For the causes that produced it to disappear forever—that depends mainly on us Catalans; changing the atmosphere around which our people's collective life has revolved, and replacing it with an atmosphere of normalcy, of good acts and fecundity, of a healthy and generous tolerance that puts an end to all attempts at violence and disturbance and forever cures us of our pessimism and mistrust, which belong only to the realms of powerlessness and egoism—that depends on us *exclusively*.

That is why, standing face to face with this radicalism that hates the present and denies the past, against this radicalism which abhors the present and the future, we affirm the continuity of our social life, respect for the past, adherence to all the substantial elements of our present society, faith in the future, to which we will go with resolve, with a heart open to all the generous innovations, all the advances, all the improvements that the future holds for us.

Against radicalism and intransigence, with their attendant hatred, violence, and spirit of destruction, we affirm justice, the desire to realize our ideals, and, to use the present reality as a starting point, we respect that reality, allowing all that live to take advantage of it, replacing all that dies in the people's consciousness, transforming the present reality, gently and progressively bringing it closer to those ideals, following behind the successive transformations of society's spirit and our national aspirations.

Against radicalism, which advocates rebellion and revolt, guided by the convenience of individual feelings, of egoism, we affirm the urgent need for social discipline based on the fulfillment of civic duties.

Against radicalism, which fosters the fetishism of idealistic programs, legislative formulas, and government regulations, presuming that good and evil, wellbeing and misfortune, abjectness and grandeur, depend on the government, we affirm the necessity of persistent, conscious, ordered effort from the citizenry, collaborating alongside the persistent, conscious, and ordered efforts of the public authorities.

The education they began at school was completed as they listened to orators at demonstrations who best embodied the radical sentiment, as they rested in their workshops and political party halls, and as they read their press, and they prepared themselves to receive the gospel of barbarism from their idol, the dogma of destruction. Stopping not even at tombstones or altars, they received the order to sack our civilization, to burn property records, to assault the convents and friaries, to rob, to burn, to kill, and to die.

Enchanted by words, then enchanted by events, their radical education continued further; then came the general strike, the assaults of the Catalanist and Republican centers and newspapers, the disturbances of the demonstrations, the burial of Sr. Juli, the mob attacking attendees of the demonstration at Las Arenas, the assault at Hostafrancs.

And if there were any doubts in their mind, any hesitation as to the truth of these doctrines, the legitimacy of these actions, they were erased immediately upon seeing that those who were feeding them this spiritual sustenance, those who were enacting these programs were grouping together—sometimes permanently in political organizations, sometimes temporarily for the most consequential occasions in civic life—the clergy, the military, judges, industrialists, and potentates in such eloquent plebiscite, so much more eloquent, so much more indisputable when it is freely, spontaneously formed against their own interests.

Is it any wonder that as soon as a favorable moment presented itself, with Barcelona and other cities undefended; with the authorities' resources weakened; with conservatives paralyzed because of the pacifist sentiment against the war in

Melilla aroused by the radical dailies throughout Spain, and especially in Catalonia; with soldiers and workers painted as victims of private interests; and so many constituents thrilled by the hope of a supposed lack of military discipline (although that was incited)—is it any wonder, with so many hands helping set the charge, that the dynamite would explode?

CONSEQUENCES:
The damage caused to Barcelona and Catalonia by these latest events was immense.

The economic crisis, which has brought with it the emigration of thousands of workers, has impeded the usual, progressive wage increases for those that have stayed here, and this will inevitably continue because of the withdrawal of capital that always follows any disturbance of a nation's normal existence. Barcelona's prestige as a cultivated and civilized city has suffered a terrible blow in the eyes of the entire world, one from which it will take a long time to recover: today Barcelona stands before the world like a Balkan city or a Turkish one, convulsing like an epileptic, presaging the ultimate death to which an ordinary, strong people condemn cities and races that demonstrate their inability to adapt to modern life, and Catalonia, which not long ago inspired admiration and envy as a strong and vigorous people destined to inspire and bring Spain along the path of progress and a new life, is presenting itself today before all Spain given to the vain, sterile convulsions that undermined Spain in the nineteenth century.

Against radicalism, which, judging the current regime through the lens of an absolutist program of fixed formulas, systematically declares that the laws are unjust, that the institutions fighting against their ideals are outdated, denying the former the power to compel and denying the latter the authority to demand adherence and obedience, we affirm respect for the established institutions, whatever the opinions of each one may be, and we affirm obedience to the laws as long as they remain such (which is not incompatible with legitimate efforts to change them, bringing them closer to our ideal). Against radicalism, which unmasks its sterility and impotence the moment it expects its ideal to be implemented not by convincing the citizenry, but through an act of violence, a revolution, a mutiny, a military uprising, we affirm our faith in the potential of popular suffrage and adherence to legal processes to make our aspirations triumph.

Against radicalism, which advises Catalans that to achieve Catalonia's collective ideals, they must abstain from the government until they see the resolution of a preliminary matter of government or dynastic legitimacy or some other matter, we affirm the duty of all citizens to actively intervene in the nation's government, not tomorrow if the Republic triumphs or if the Sovereign is replaced, but today, and not only in certain spheres, but in any way that befits our society.

And in formulating these declarations, we do not believe ourselves to be formulating a group program, raising the banner of a party because today, more than ever, banners and programs, groups and parties must subordinate themselves to Catalonia's interests and future.

As a point of utmost patriotic unity, Catalonia's interests and its future demand that today, all Catalans and all those who, not being children of Catalonia, have found hospitality there, people of all classes, political parties, and creeds must from now on establish the rule of law and normalcy in the development of our collective life so that our people can move forward in an atmosphere of active and fecund peace, of respectful tolerance in the face of whatever separates us, and of effusive brotherhood in the face of what unites us—only thus will Catalonia attain its grandeur and accomplish its mission, to be the foundation for the grandeur of a new Spain.

Raymundo de Abadal, senator for Barcelona; Marquis of Alella, senator for Barcelona; Marquis de Camp, representing the Barcelona Economic Society in the Senate; Manuel Farguell, senator for Girona; Sebastián Torres, senator for Girona; Francisco Cambó, deputy for Barcelona; José Puig y Cadafalch, deputy for Barcelona; Ramon Albó, deputy for Barcelona; Luis Ferrer-Vidal, deputy for Castellterçol; Ignacio Girona, deputy for Granollers; Federico Rahola, deputy for

Igualada; Leoncio Soler y March, deputy for Manresa; Trinidad Rius y Torres, deputy for Mataró; José Bertrán y Musitu, deputy for Vilanova i la Geltrú; Eusebio Bertrand y Serra, deputy for Puigcerdà; Juan Ventosa y Calvell, deputy for Santa Coloma de Farners; Juan Garriga y Massó, deputy for La Seu d'Urgell; Manuel Raventós, deputy for Valls; Pedro Milá y Camps, deputy for Solsona.

The Committee of Social Defense

The same bad faith that is repugnant in the previous manifesto of the Regionalist Senators and Deputies can also be seen in the extensive document published by this entity.

After emptying the most venomous hatred into this document and characterizing their despicable treachery as a mission to bring morality to society, proving thereby that they are worthy successors of Arbués and Torquemada, the Governing Board of this association proposed adoption of the following determinations.[11]

If the revolution was satanic, the reaction to it must be divine, and for that we must turn to God to remedy the offenses that have been done to Him and appeal for mercy through private acts of prayer and sacrifice and public acts of repentance and supplication. And still it would be beneficial, if circumstances permit, to organize a great pilgrimage or procession, which would be a solemn testimony to the sentiments of the Catholics of Barcelona towards the crimes that have been committed in their presence.

Turning then to those means dictated by earthly prudence, we must solicit the public authorities to punish all attacks against religion, authority, family, and property, whether it is done in newspapers or books, in schools or at public meetings, amending, to that end, the Penal Code and other laws related to publishing, teaching, and public assembly.

11. Arbués and Torquemada were leading officials in the Spanish Inquisition, notorious for their brutality.

Of course, all associations must be prohibited which in any way conspire against the above fundamental principles of social order, and they must be placed under the utmost surveillance to prevent even those associations that have been constituted with seemingly commendable ends from committing acts in opposition to these principles.

We must loyally help the authorities fulfill whatever is asked of them, and applaud their efforts to this end.

We must establish organized intelligence among all entities and individuals that have essentially subordinated their aspirations to the glory of God and the good of the homeland.

We must rebuild parishes, churches, chapels, convents, friaries, schools, and centers that were set on fire, to that effect soliciting aid from the State and private and public companies.

We must see to the creation of a defense body for churches and religious institutions.

In all political and administrative elections, we must grant suffrage to those who will most sincerely ensure the defense of our supreme social interests.

We must engage in active and constant propaganda, both written and oral, in and outside of Barcelona, in defense of our interests, and combat the sophistry with which these interests are attacked.

Wherever they do not exist, we must develop and implement social works of both an instructive and economic character in benefit of the working classes.

Once the above groundwork is laid for the program that is required by circumstances today, the Committee of Social Defense, whose existence and activity has once again been justified by recent events, will do nothing other than continue the mission it has been carrying out. The work of its Legal section, Press and Graphic Arts section, Teaching section, Politics section, and Social Questions and Propaganda section have proclaimed loudly that since its founding, it has devoted all of its efforts to combating all enemies of the social order, in whose attacks it foresaw that the first revolution that would break out in Barcelona would have an anti-religious character, an opinion which was at odds with those who proclaimed that the fight for our principles was over for good.

The events of last July oblige all good citizens to participate in this fight if they do not want their person or their interests to fall victim to the Revolution, whose deepest causes have not yet gone away. For the glory of God and the salvation of the homeland and its legitimate interests, we look forward to the adherence of all to the above program.

The Governing Board of the Committee of Social Defense.

Barcelona, September 8, 1909, Feast of the Nativity of Our Lady.

The Prelate of this Diocese

Doctor don Ricardo Cortés, bishop of Eudoxia and vicar capitular, sede vacante of this diocese, published the following documents:

The horrors of the revolution that has broken out these past weeks has wrested an energetic cry of indignation and protest from every upright soul.

In this city of work and progress, which was proud of its culture and Christianity, lawless mobs have burned close to forty churches and religious houses, vilely ejecting defenseless citizens from their peaceful dwellings, citizens who committed no crime other than being devoted, in observance of divine and earthly laws, to prayer and the care for our people's orphans and helpless children. They have destroyed venerated, precious art, and valued archives and libraries, heritage of past generations. They have destroyed twelve parish churches of this diocese (one of them stained with the innocent blood of a parish priest), sacrilegiously profaning the Eucharist and the Sanctuary's sacred images and cups, and, without respect for even the resting of the dead, they have plucked corpses of nuns from their tombs to turn them into a source of mockery and derision for the mob. Later, in an unhinged orgy of concupiscence, they passed through the ruins of the convents and friaries, thirsty for evidence of supposed torture for crimes that only ever existed in the imaginations of these wicked instigators of the fires.

We would not be doing our duty if we remained silent in the face of such a day of blood and indignity. With our hearts ripped apart at the sight of such heinous excesses, after having represented the magnitude of the wrong to the public authorities, we protest before God and man with all our strength, in the name of the Church that has been vilified and persecuted by demagogic crowds that must not be allowed to represent Barcelona, against the shameful abuses of the physical order and especially the moral order which have been committed these past days, abuses that are condemned not only by Christian law, but also by natural law.

The religious houses—we can proudly say—the convents and friaries, have never been, as some have led the people to believe, criminals' lairs or dens of secret violence, and only a sectarian spirit could inspire this shadowy legend of crimes and disruptions, which have no other basis than the infernal aim of ripping any remaining Christian faith from the hearts of our people, faith which is a source of celestial virtue, never a motive for senseless passions.[12]

We repeat, the religious houses are houses of contemplation and prayer, always open to mercy and peace, always accessible to the ecclesiastical and civil courts, for whom we have on every occasion facilitated the clarification of the supposed crimes. It has been said that our cemeteries are clandestine, but these burials are authorized by the laws of the kingdom.

It would be endless and perhaps useless at this time to insist on the enormous effort to repudiate all the slander and fantasies circulated by the cynical revolutionaries with no human decency, latching on to appearances interpreted in a twisted manner by the mob.

Our Lord God who will judge all people, have compassion on the unfortunates who, in evil hour, raised the assassin's hand

---

12. [Author's note] Emphasis added by us as a matter to be corrected. May History shed light on the prelate.

against Christ and his Church, and though we will undertake the appropriate measures as soon as possible to raise fervent intercessions of atonement to your Divine Majesty, we hope that without prejudice to that, any citizens who value the good name of Barcelona at all will join our protest, while the prayer of the poor victims will intercede before the God of vengeance to beg He not spill the cup of His ire on our beloved city.

To the religious communities of this diocese that were damaged during recent events.

Our heart is deeply saddened by the heinous events that have recently occurred in this city and in several other towns of this diocese, in which religious communities, both of men and women, both under our ordinary jurisdiction and exempt, have suffered so much harm, and we believe ourselves obliged to direct a few words of consolation to them. At the same time, may these words be a sincere expression of the profound pain with which we will accompany you in times of such great calamity.

The zeal and diligence with which you promote the glory of God and the sanctification of souls in this city through the spiritual ministries to which you are consecrated; and the Christian education that you pass on to all sectors of our society, from the highest aristocracy to the lowest classes; and the charitable establishments, which you have sustained at the cost of enormous sacrifice, looking after helpless orphans, aiding the needy, caring for the sick, and remedying the countless and various miseries that present themselves in our capital city; and the spirit of fervor with which you raise your prayers to heaven, praying for those who do not pray, beseeching God's mercy for those who need it most and will not beg for it themselves, holding back the arm of Divine Justice countless times, and attracting the Lord's blessings to this city—everything, everything you have done demands that our venerable secular clergy and our beloved diocesan priests of Barcelona consider your misfortunes to be our own, and to consider ourselves and our interests to have suffered the violent persecution and the criminal dispossession that you have suffered in these sad days.

There has been exhaustive proof showing that what motivates these frequent attacks of the mob's slander, insults, and abuses is not the supposed unpopularity of the religious orders, but rather the satanic hatred of God and all that is done in His holy name, hatred that indistinctly envelops the asylums and parish churches in an infernal anathema, asylums where the Lord's angels in human flesh reach out to the poor orphans with their virginal arms, and churches where newborns become the regenerated children of God, where the divine blessing descends upon husbands and wives who unite until death in the sacred bond of Christian matrimony.

Even so, console us, venerable nuns and friars, console all of us who have suffered persecution for the sacramental character that the Holy Spirit has imprinted on our souls, and I say, let those meaningful words of our Savior console us (Matthew 10:24): "The student is not above the teacher, nor a servant above his master." And if we esteem ourselves to be hardworking disciples of Christ, who was reviled, persecuted, and tormented until his death on the cross, we should delight and rejoice at our own persecution because, as it says elsewhere (Luke 6:23): "Your reward is great in heaven."

Let us pray for God's grace to illuminate so many minds who have lost their way and soften so many hearts hardened in evil and encourage the good people to work with renewed vigor, united with one heart and one soul in the restoration and defense of our sacrosanct Religion.

The Diocesan Board

The Diocesan Board has met in extraordinary session for the defense of Catholic interests. In addition to renewing the protest raised by the executive committee to the President of the Council of Ministers and stating for the record its sentiments regarding the death of innocent victims during recent events and the innumerable damages caused to the convents, friaries, churches, and Catholic associations of this diocese, including several associations which are part of the Diocesan Federation (which, it was agreed, would speak for the other associations), it was agreed, notwithstanding any agreements not listed below, to execute the following:

Reply to the deputies and senators from the traditionalist minority expressing our vigorous thanks for the assistance offered to the Diocesan Board in claiming compensation for the innumerable damages to the parish and other churches, convents, friaries, and Catholic clubs.

Petition for the same assistance from other deputies and senators throughout Catalonia who presumably condemn, justly, the vandalism that occurred during the last week of July.

Reply to the Catholic societies outside of Barcelona which have telegraphed protesting recent events, thanking them for their sentiments.

Take active part in the process that is taking shape to find out exactly what has happened, along with the specific details and circumstances, in order to be able to aid the courts in their undertakings and to learn exactly what damages have been caused. It was agreed to order the various associations to look after the work of clarification of whatever events occurred within their respective boundaries, also requesting that anyone having information on the burned-down churches, convents, friaries, and centers, to communicate it to the secretary of the Board, located in the Catholic Youth Academy (Portaferrissa, 13, main entrance).

Promote, in accordance with the supreme ecclesiastical authority of this diocese and its reverend parish priests, numerous solemn gatherings of atonement for the excesses and sacrilege committed in Barcelona and its diocese.

Take up a collection throughout Spain to satisfy the pressing and extremely urgent needs of worshippers, communities, etc., resulting from the work of anarchic devastation that took place during the last week of July.

Contribute 500 pesetas for the individuals of the armed forces and the families of those who died while fulfilling their duty during recent events.

The Parish Priests of Barcelona

To his Excellency the President of the Council of Ministers:

The College of Parish Priest of Barcelona endorses the protest raised by its honorable prelate on the 9th of this month. For now we will not say anything more, Your Excellency. The College of Parish Priests of Catalonia's capital, which has seen eleven of its parish churches ignited along with its archives with no cause whatsoever, not even some excuse, while we who live far from political contests, who have dedicated ourselves to spreading works of charity and teaching for the material relief of the needy classes and the promotion of their moral and intellectual culture, we who today find ourselves parishes without a church, citizens without a home, seeing all parochial life disorganized, our protest should be a cry of indignation. We will make a heroic sacrifice, stifling that cry in the depths of our bosom, we the parish priests of Barcelona, because while we are eager to fulfill all our duties, including our civic duties, we might fail in that duty that today is paramount to all others: the complete pacification of Barcelona.

When this has been achieved, then those of us who were not able to defend our churches will, in this country which still calls itself Catholic, defend our dignity and our right to fulfill our mission to educate and impart morals in accordance with the law and the dictates of our public authorities. Then the time will have come to state the facts—in our capacity as citizens with the right to intervene in our country's public affairs, and as residents of Barcelona, which, it seems, there is an evil desire to destroy (and if the title of citizen will not suffice, we will use another which we consider more sacred, that of victim); therefore, please allow us to reveal the causes of the evil as we see it, to point out some ways it can be remedied, and with the numerous ruins as our starting point, we will indicate new directions for the political and social order which will safeguard our mission of peace, love, and the illumination of the Christian conscience, which is the basis of our moral and social conscience.[13]

---

13. [Author's note] We have highlighted this statement in order to offer it for the consideration of all those who work towards social progress. The tenacity

Because, Your Excellency, if we continue stoking the flames of the brutal hatred that is closing in on the walls of our temples, our religious works, our works of charity and teaching, even ourselves, then logically, the flames of these fierce passions might once again become real flames, and it would be better not to rebuild our churches if they would only be used as lightning rods for other interests. So our ministry's work of pacification and the imparting of morals becomes very difficult, if not impossible, and instead of continuing in this state of moral and social disorganization, it would be better to follow the advice of Jesus Christ: "Shake the dust from your feet and leave that place."

Pope Pius X

Rome, August 12th, 1909

Most illustrious and reverend Monsignor Ricardo Cortés, titular bishop of Eudoxia, vicar capitular of the Diocese of Barcelona.

Most illustrious and reverend sir:

When with true anguish and a heart filled with compassion, I was going to send your most illustrious and reverend lordship humble and affectionate words of consolation, and through Him, I wanted to greet the most noble victims of recent attacks with the reverence and love they deserve, our most generous father and supreme pastor Pius X was so kind as to communicate to me how much he suffers thinking of the tribulations of so many priests, friars, and nuns persecuted by soulless crowds, and I saw to it that some words of encouragement from his august name would be sent to your lordship as an ordinary prelate of the city and diocese that has most cruelly experienced the horrors of cosmopolitan impiety. And in the person of your

---

they reveal conflicts with the needs of the populace, which they persist in stifling. If they are incapable of redeeming themselves, which can be deduced from their own words, what right do they have to claim they can redeem humanity? What utter lack of morals!

lordship, these words of encouragement would be forwarded to all the diocesan prelates and religious superiors, and their respective subjects who have been persecuted, adding deserved praise for those people who have so generously taken in nuns and friars, and also communicating certain extraordinary powers that His Holiness was so kind as to grant the Ordinary of Barcelona and the other ordinaries in Catalonia, who need them in such exceptional circumstances.

***

Do not forget these chosen souls, for whom their present tribulations better serve to purify them of the defects of human weakness and sanctify them ever more. Hear this advice of Saint Augustine: "Child, if you cry, and it is your father who makes you cry, do not allow tears of indignation and pride to run down your cheek; he makes you suffer not to cause pain, but to cure you, not to condemn you, but to correct you." Above all, this humility in persecution makes us see in our persecutors the hordes of the demon, who has them so wretchedly deceived and so frightfully blinded that they do not see the horror of their criminal, sacrilegious attacks on human beings, the churches, and the holy dwellings consecrated to God. In the words of Saint John Chrysostom: "Whenever someone persecutes you, do not pay attention to him, but rather the demon that instigates him. Calm your indignation; pity him instead, that he has been incited to such a point by the devil, who is the origin of the lie and even more so, the unjust ire."[14]

Those who are persecuted do not admire the incredible malice of the heart of the impious. Pope Saint Gregory said of them: "For men of God, human hearts become like those of beasts, and the hearts of beasts like those of man."

And although good priests and religious people who are

---

14. [Author's note] Indeed, following the advice of Saint Augustine and the words of Saint John Chrysostom, they correct and they pity, but in their own way, sealing their temple doors and arming themselves, stoking the fires of hatred and resentment, undoubtedly to make God the world's enemy.

faithful to their vocation are rightfully counted among the most eminent benefactors of humanity and the most sincere and heroic friends of the people, they do not become indignant when they see such ingratitude in return for their constant work and their constant sacrifice in favor of their very persecutors and their own children, for whose temporal and eternal good they have made all possible efforts, with so many works of apostolate, teaching, and beneficence. This ingratitude is nothing new, and the abovementioned Saint Gregory was already saying in his day: "With execrable perversity, evil men often persecute and torment the just who try to save them." They are not perturbed when they see themselves scorned and treated like vile slaves even by those children of the people who owe them the most favors. Saint John Chrysostom also warns us about this, saying: "We see there are many who, after having received charity, scorn their benefactors, treating them like slaves and swelling up with arrogance against them."

The victims of the recent attacks generously forgive and sincerely pity their enemies, and they are more tormented by the horrible sins that these poor blind men have committed than by the bad treatment, slander, and injustice they have suffered; this is proof of the love they profess towards their enemies, in accordance with this advice from our Seraphic Father Saint Francis: "A man truly loves his enemy when he is not offended by the injury done to himself, but he feels sorrow for the sin committed and proves his love in a practical way." With ever more charity, wish these poor deceived men well, and when they and their children come to the doors of your homes or places of worship to beseech material, intellectual, and moral aid, be generous and even heroic in their favor, to win them over for heaven, fulfilling this lesson from Saint Augustine: "Desire for your enemies to be at your side in eternal life; desire to make them your brothers: you don't love in your enemies what they are, but what you would have them become through your prayers." "Let the victims' forgiveness, love, and prayer be their holy vengeance for the evils done to them, and if they should have preferences in this sublime charity, let it be to love most those who hate them most and who have done them the most evil; let them pray with more fervor for their conversion and eternal salvation."[15]

Amid the horrors of these past days committed by crowds who have no religion and no homeland, one thing has been very comforting, and that is the spectacle of genuine Barcelonans and Catalans, heirs to the Christian patriotism and the ardent faith of our superiors, giving generous hospitality—without fear of the satanic fury of the impious arsonists—to clergy who were deprived of their holy residences, and to the parish priests and other priests who were persecuted. The promptness, spontaneity, and Christian nobility of their hospitality will become a badge of glory for Barcelona and Catalonia, and the cause for many blessings for our people. With holy pride, our Saint Isidore, Archbishop of Seville, has certainly seen his advice taken to heart in our land: "Guests should be received gladly and with promptness; be assured that there will be a reward on the last day. And although you should graciously give the favor of hospitality to all, pray for the great honor to take in a monk as your guest."

So that they can promptly give the assistance that is required by current circumstances, Our Holy Father has been so kind as to grant the following powers to the Ordinary of Barcelona, and any ordinaries in Catalonia that may need them:

Authorize priests belonging to a religious order, who for some reason are unable to celebrate religious observances in their convents, friaries, or other churches, the use of a portable altar in a decent place; authorize secular and regular priests to celebrate mass using a portable altar in a decent place in houses where religious priests and three students are taking refuge,

---

15.   [Author's note] After reading this last paragraph, one can't be sure whether or not it was written to praise the actions of the revolutionaries, who brought to light the lack of evangelical sentiments of the clergy whom Saint Augustine is addressing—because it is known that the revolutionaries were not beset by this vengeance; meanwhile forgiveness, love, prayer, and sublime charity did not at all enter into the hearts of the pious victims, who acted as informers, confidentially pointing out the anti-religious so that they could convert, if converted at all, to cold, inert bodies.

fulfilling the precept that both those who are taken in and those who offer this charity should hear mass.

Allow the Most Blessed Sacrament to be stowed in oratories that have already been erected or which an authorized ordinary erects for that purpose:

a) in houses where at least three religious priests are taking refuge;

b) in houses where at least three cloistered nuns are living together;

c) in houses where at least six religious brothers, or six religious sisters who have taken simple vows, or at least three of each, or three with four people who lived in their religious communities as pupils or refugees.

Pope Pius X goes on for another three paragraphs establishing various rules for religious practices and exhorting all not to abandon their commitment and charity towards their enemy; instead, they should undertake to do their holy work—the greater the people's spiritual need and the more tenacious the efforts of the devil to destroy their admirable works, the greater their passion should be.

Cloistered nuns forced by these present circumstances to live outside the walls of their convents should be treated by the faithful with special charity, so that they may one day be able to meet again in their cloister and continue being the privileged souls, who, with their holy, withdrawn lives full of sacrifices unknown to the world, can more effectively ward off the rays of God's justice when He is so irritated by the sins of men.

I conclude by recommending that Your Lordship make this letter public as soon as possible and send a copy of it to the Venerable Metropolitan Bishop and the other prelates of Catalonia.

Having finished the commission with which His Holiness has been kind enough to honor me, I beg my kindest respects to your most illustrious and reverend lordship, your most devoted servant and brother, Friar J.C. Cardenal Vives.

There were various other messages and protests, which, without rhyme or reason, the Vaticanists and other retrograde individuals from different points in Spain sent to the public authorities. We will not reproduce all of them here since the ones we have compiled in this chapter summarize the character of the rest.

After reading this, one doesn't know what to condemn more, the tendentious exaggerations in connection with the revolutionary acts or the stupid diatribes and slander hurled at certain political and pedagogical entities. This is the extent of their moral dislocation.

Despite the clumsy maneuvers of the press intended to compromise any journalistic entities that didn't want to contribute to the chorus of false stories, they were caught off guard by a distinguished ex-deputy, Sr. Francisco Pi y Arsuaga,[16] who calmly and bravely contributed a most timely response to one of these chorus leaders, *El Universo*, which we will provide for the all the signers of the above protests as a correction to their outlandish conclusions.

There is no prohibition against honorable people protesting honorably against the criminal events that occurred in Barcelona. This is clear: there is no prohibition against partaking in common decency and expressing unconditional indignation over what occurred in Barcelona. Explaining, arguing, assessing, reducing these events to their natural proportions—that is one thing. We must limit ourselves to condemnation. To those who think like this newspaper does, that is what is important.

Well fine, we'll make them happy this time; we democrats, republicans, and revolutionaries protest the acts of violence

---

16. Son of Francisco Pi y Margall, the federalist politician and President of the First Spanish Republic in 1873. A number of anarchists had close ties to the federalist party and a great respect for Pi y Margall, who was one of the few politicians to stand against the repression of the movement in the 1890s. Pi y Arsuaga succeeded his father as leader of the federalist party in 1901.

that occurred in Barcelona and a good part of the rest of Catalonia during a week that has rightfully been called bloody.

As democrats, proponents of a regime based on political equality, we do not want for others what we do not want for ourselves, so we cannot stand by and applaud when someone's house is burned down or broken into, just as we would not want ours to be broken into.

As republicans and federalists, we aspire to a system of government that ensures the rule of justice and liberty as the basis of all laws and which represses all reckless behavior.

As revolutionaries, we only justify the use of force and violence against the violence and force of tyranny and despotism.

We will always be democrats and federalist republicans unless progress imposes upon us (and it is unlikely to do so within the short space of one lifetime) the most complete and perfect method for governing nations. We aspire to stop being revolutionaries. While we unconditionally submit to what is for us the obvious effectiveness of our democratic, republican, and federalist convictions, we long for the day when revolution can be called a crime and when we can scorn that which we today consider honorable.

Is the colleague satisfied?

But let us allow ourselves, after this public self-examination, to provide a more complete response to the insinuations that *El Universo* has thrown at the radical newspapers for what they believe are their tepid condemnations of the events in Barcelona.

We are not pessimists. We do not believe that human cruelty is inherent; on the contrary, we believe people to be innately good. Why is it, if they are good, that they do evil things? Because they are spoiled by their environment. Because a series of prejudices that the egoism of lesser individuals imposes on them offers an eternal example of an endless chain of misfortunes and cruelty. Because, disdaining the advice of reason, they begin what is called a fight for their lives, which is only justified, if it exists, in places where reason is not strong enough to organize life in conditions of strict equity.

Clambering thus over one another, one side fights to maintain their hegemony while the other side to supplant it or at least destroy it, and suddenly on both sides, the morals that each side claims are superior are dispensed with.

Truncated morals, illogical morals—it is a puzzle that perturbs the universal consciousness: it is a triumph of immorality.

Violence is condemned, but only halfway. I, the State, the Nation can exercise it without any restrictions whatsoever. Confiscation and harming individuals is not forbidden to me.

I, the State, will eliminate a person whenever it is to my benefit; whenever I feel strong, I, the Nation, will invade places where the people are weak. Spreading civilization is a pretext; I will enter foreign territories and devastate them. If the local residents dare resist, I will gun them down, annihilate them.

Their lands and their treasures will belong to me. Do they have mines? I will not teach them how to exploit them; they will learn by watching how I exploit them for my exclusive benefit. Do they have natural ports? They will learn how to use them when, in my possession, I enable them to operate for my profit.

So the future dispossessed will be unable to resist me, I will count how many of them there are and station twice their number of forces, I will sharpen my weapons so they cut more than theirs, I will create and perfect methods of destruction that they will have no knowledge of, I will thoroughly study their territory to learn where it is more accessible and less dangerous for my business, and if I can, I will catch them unawares. And when my superiority seems to me to be indisputable, I will warn them that if they do not surrender they will be eliminated.

And all of this is moral. And all of this, which is described in the Penal Code and is sanctioned, not in written form, but in practice, in the International Code of Law, is legal, moral. It is called development; it is called civilization, law.

And these morals are practiced by the light of day, out loud, without any qualms whatsoever, without euphemism, without pretense, and nations are pushed into the contest and stirred up. And those who kill or are killed are called heroes, and the extermination of men and cities is celebrated with bells, and bows and arrows, and volley shots.

Woe to those who dare oppose the killing, and woe to those who call for reason and duty to humanity! They will be cursed, loathed as unpatriotic and cowardly.

When the concept of quiet, well-governed valor is replaced by delirium and cruelty, what do you expect but that the force used to achieve all this will not seem to be legal, a usual, every-day process?

Thou shalt not kill, say the Ten Commandments, and during the course of centuries, the State has found no other way to correct wrongdoing except by killing.

Thou shalt not kill, but thou shalt go to that town that thou dost not hate and layeth it waste. Sacrificeth thine own life if that is necessary; but winneth for me territories, with which, after their conquest, I will not know what to do.

The way of the world still rests in the secret of force. Whoever is stronger is better.

And with this clear example of morality, how do you expect to pluck that idea, the call to violence and crime, from the human mind?

Yes, the events in Barcelona were abominable, but let us coolly examine the news that was allowed by the censors.

To protest the war, the Socialist Party agreed to a general strike. Did it seem to members of one of the parties that the moment had come to transform the strike into a revolution? Well, they raised barricades, and the insubstantial character of the events changed. Without bosses, the rebels had to find an immediate object of their activity, and the idea emerged (a very popular one, we can even say traditional) to set fire to the convents and friaries.

And why was this idea popular?

The people see the friar with profound antipathy. In general, the friar is one of the greatest enemies of religion and the Church. He is seen as someone who procures inheritances at the bedside of the dying or who seeks alms small or large. The friar does not allow himself to be seen except when begging.

Distanced from parish services because of his condition, the friar appears only to take. He makes a vow of humility, and quite often, his arrogance is heard in sermons and discussions; he makes a vow of poverty and he is seen gorged and fat living in sumptuous buildings, usually located in the best locations; and in his friary's treasury one finds all manner of stock certificates.

Ordinarily there is more compassion for nuns, since they are women and since their cloister seems stricter.

Nuns and friars sometimes do charitable work and teach, but do not trust the science they impart, since, because it does not challenge religious mysteries and legends, it can be no less than mediocre, especially when they must give preference to exercises that require long hours.

It is also assumed that their teaching, while dedicated to the poor, is just a pretext—anyone can see that while the private institutions are living precariously, the religious communities are flourishing. In their hands, isn't instruction a weapon used to perpetuate, for future generations, prejudices and traditions that are at odds with the progress of the times? And also, both in teaching and in industry, their communist organization gives them a destructive competitive advantage against private establishments.

For a long time, they have been exempt from payment of all charges. They have taken advantage of their pupils and their guests more than a few times to do their work, resolving the issue of their wage and hours of labor in ways only they know.

Meanwhile, they are shrouded in mystery: nuns and friars are secluded in religious houses which even the authorities cannot penetrate without difficulty. They live separated from society, with their own church leaders who punish them when they commit crimes. They bury their dead secretly in their cloisters.

The enclosed religious orders cannot break their cloister unless the authorities intervene.

No wonder legend has it (and it is not always legend) that they have hidden more than few unsavory characters. They are often accused of harboring criminals.

Deadly bomb explosions have been striking Barcelona for years.

The authorities have been able to search every home. The jails are filled with workers who were unjustly accused.

The city is searching in vain for the perpetrators of such barbaric attacks. Sections of the public have wondered if the reactionaries who were given shelter by the friars may have used these means to affirm and strengthen their existence. The secrecy of monastic life has favored evil thinking.

If the friars and nuns lived in the open, without their shutters and locks, in communication with the people, and if the mystery, in whose shadow anything is possible, were gone, all the suspicions of criminal activity would dissipate.

With people who live with their constitutional guarantees always suspended, and who have even renounced their natural rights, anything can be believed.

It has been repeated ad nauseam that graves have been profaned. They have been profaned if we consider that some of them have been opened and the bodies exhibited. People talk of the torture of nuns and friars held prisoner. The desire to know makes them want to verify this; it is not to mock the remains of the martyrs, but to prove the crime.

The first inquiries appear to have confirmed this as bodies have been found with their feet tied. It is said that this was the practice in certain communities. That may be, but undeniably, the mistakes of those whose intention was to vindicate the martyrs were not so blameworthy considering that the practice was unknown. Another disadvantage to the secrecy in which the cloistered live and die.

But it wasn't just friaries and convents that burned down—some churches did, too.

The Church is also hated by a large section of the population. The Church had a beautiful mission to fulfill. The Church has played a sublime role in modern societies. First, it should have concerned itself with its reputation. If its hierarchies were proper, they could be preserved, but they should stand out for their great virtues, not for their great ostentation.

The people see two churches: one uncared for and poor (and in more than a few cases, ignorant and vulgar), the other illustrious and rich.

The one that rides in coaches and wears silks serves princes and rubs elbows at their tables.

The vulgar and poor one with mended clothes is not its equal. To baptize, marry, or bury a poor person, one clergyman will suffice; to baptize, marry, or bury a prince, a bishop is sometimes not enough.

This arrogance, this insolence, this inequality lowers the prestige of the lowly clergyman and does not raise the prestige of the lofty one.

The lofty clergyman corrupts the lowly one with his bad example, and both lowly and lofty with their temporal desires, live life and prosper more than they win souls for the supposed heaven.

How different the fate of the Church would be, regardless of the contradictions of their dogma, if they had managed to be Christian more than just in name and if they had always been found at the side of the needy and distressed!

If only their temples were modest and their priests were humble! At hospitals, in jails, in neighborhoods beaten down by misery—*that* is where their ministries should be, always counseling the poor.

They should always shelter the weak and defend them against injustice. They should always have a merciful word for the criminal and seek their pardon before the authorities. They should preach peace and anathematize war.

The people see the clergyman fighting in a party, with a blunderbuss in his hand. They see him suing their debtors before the courts, filing complaints against their slanderers, whether that slander is real or imagined, and they see him given to all the base passions.

Standing at the side of those who are condemned to die, the clergyman can be seen pretending to help them. We know of only one case where a priest stood before the firing squad in the place of a prisoner.

That should have been the conduct of all of them, protesting that iniquitous penalty, defending the laws of their God who gives life and reserves the right to take it.

Of course, such protest would not have won in the moment, but what better reward than to see oneself persecuted for being unable to sanction iniquity with one's presence.

But the Church is a friend to the meek in appearance only. It is unyielding, and the only thing that matters to it is outside appearances. It takes in the false Christian if he claims to be a friend. It rejects and ridicules the true Christian if he challenges dogmas. It is greedy. It hoards. It is decorated with images of gold and precious stones and deigns to allow the poor and defenseless to be seen at its temple door. It is cruel to its enemies and adulates those who are important, for whom it reserves its benevolence. It is hypocritical, humble only with the powers that be when seeking new privileges and gifts.

Is it too much for friars and clergymen to be equals in the eyes of the people?

We do not want to get into the details of the events because we are writing only to respond to *El Universo* and explain the tepidity, which they may not have noticed in us since we are a modest paper, but which they definitely have in other more flashy radical newspapers. They can explain themselves on their own; we do not intend to do it for them, but for ourselves only since we want justice for all.

Petty crime, which plagues all large cities and represents the biggest danger for all rebellions, has cropped up during the events in Barcelona. Therefore, looting and robbery has been recorded.

Doubtlessly, if the movement had persisted, it would not have taken long for the traditional, gruesome pattern of all revolutions to reappear: "Death penalty for thieves."

The rebels, the revolutionaries burned down convents, friaries, and churches, not friars, nuns, or priests. We do not have news of any more than one death, and that was someone who suffocated from the smoke. And it is known that there was a wad of banknotes found on the unfortunate man's body (which was thrown into the bonfire).[17] Those who did it wanted to show once again that man shall not live on bread alone. Surely they are not capitalists, and nevertheless, their action benefited capital, since the ashes of those notes represent a profit for the Bank of Spain.

Yes, some friars were persecuted, but there was no lack of protectors among the revolutionaries who would save their lives.

The miseries of an asylum for consumptive children served as a shield for their guardians.

The police, the security forces, and especially the rebels themselves have provided the greatest number of victims.

The police victims, we suspect, were the result of personal vengeance. The revolt in Barcelona was a long time coming!

The military victims seem to be the consequence of the same repression they were entrusted to carry out. Fortunately, there were a small number of them.

Casualties were most numerous among the revolutionaries. The tally is 200 deaths.

Respectfully, we find ourselves before this pile of corpses in which friends and enemies, equal in death, have had their passions and their hatreds extinguished.

El Universo knows this already—that we condemn the rule of violence and we condemn it in all its forms.

We vigorously desire for it to disappear from the world.

Without it, our ideals would rule, ideals that one day we will impose without calls to revolution.

Our Republic, a work of legality, was toppled by the swords of Pavía and Martínez Campos, who did not realize when they brandished them that two wars would beleaguer the homeland: the Carlist War and the war with Cuba.

With his harsh and impartial judgment, Mr. Pi y Arsuaga has managed to prove the causes that induce the people to hate the religious and monastic centers, and at the same time, he vindicates the revolutionaries before their slanderers.

---

17. A reflection of the general tendency to destroy, rather than loot Church assets during the Tragic Week, which was also evident during the anti-clerical violence at the outbreak of the Spanish Civil War in 1936.

It is incumbent upon us to vindicate them, too, neutralizing certain smears.

The revolutionaries were accused of being cowards and traitors because of the fact that in the first few days, they received the troops with applause, continuing their work of destruction as soon as they went away. We will simply say that this accusation has no merit.

When the protest began, the people did not imagine that they would be impelled to welcome the army. They were vociferously angry at the Civil Guards and cops, and that is why, without diminishing their protest, they were inclined to fraternize with the soldiers and not be hostile to them. This is strictly the truth.

Accusations were thrown around regarding the shots fired at soldiers from hiding places on certain rooftops and the accompanying lack of necessary resistance. This was not the work of revolutionaries.

"The men of the terraced rooftops" were a mystery at first. Later, some were discovered participating in several incidents, which gave us the affiliation of these hidden diabolical figures who shot at soldiers to inflame their anger against the revolutionaries.

One such madman was arrested in El Poble-sec. He was dressed as a stonemason, and his pants and shirt had large mortar stains on them. But when he was detained, it became apparent that his hands were cared for in a way that was unusual for a scaffold worker. The weapon he shot from the roof was a high-priced Browning pistol. He was searched, and a Russian leather wallet with one thousand pesetas worth of banknotes was confiscated . . . along with a membership card to a Catholic club!

On another rooftop on a different street, a priest disguised as a worker was killed by the troops.

From the rooftop of one house on the corner of Carrer de Ferlandina and Carrer de la Lluna, troops were attacked in the same way, and one of their shots injured a woman inside her house. Two municipal officers found out about this, and then nothing more was heard.

Fourteen clergymen were arrested during the above events and led to Montjuïc as prisoners. There is only one case in which the public knows what the authorities know regarding the arrested priests. He was captured holding a revolver and a knife of regular dimensions, and the Public Order laws were applied to him—he was jailed for fifteen days. Regarding the others, not even this is known.

We believe we have said enough to prove the correct, measured—all too measured—actions of the revolutionaries. They could also have taken possession of enormous amounts of money that the friars and priests were piously safeguarding as evidence of their contempt for worldly things. Nonetheless, it has been proven that the majority of these stacks of banknotes were salvaged by their owners, though some were burned.

Finally, we will add that the regionalist senators and deputies, the informers of the Committee of Social Defense, the Prelate, the Diocesan Board, the parish priests, Pius X, and the adulators of the Ultramontanist press are denying that the revolutionaries found instruments of torture, dungeons, and abused corpses in the convents and friaries, but why don't they show the public the monastic regulations dealing with the application of torture and the circumstances in which they are to be applied?[18]

In these penal treatises, as Friar Gerund calls them, in these same regulations approved by the Church, the practice of torture has been prescribed since the time of the Flood in places where the screams of the tormented could not be heard by the people and without authorization from the civil authorities.

The mere existence of these regulations and the privilege to bury those who die in their communities in their own convents and friaries justifies the honorable spirit that motivated the revolutionaries, and at the same time, it reveals the infamies and the atrocities that have been tolerated even by nations that claim to be civilizing the Riffians.

---

18. Here Bonafulla reflects the widespread belief in the nefarious, secretive practices of the Church, which can be viewed as one of the causes of the burnings and ransacking of the Tragic Week, with crowds opening up the "darkness" of religious buildings to the "light" of truth.

Chapter 4

Government Brutality. Anomalies of the Military Courts • Lack of
Internal Struggle • There was no Compassion, Purity • Drumhead
Courts-Martial Begin • Life Imprisonment • Sentenced to Death • First
Firing Squads • Ramón Clemente García • An Astounding Case

To find a period comparable to the one following the events
we have recounted, we would need to go back to the times of
Ferdinand VII, when obscurantism's assassins wanted to reestab-
lish the Inquisition, and those who were branded as liberals were
hanged.[1]

This period of reaction that we have suffered at the hands of
the priests and friars is the worst of the reactions.

The Jesuits have become the new masters, terrorizing the people from their refuge in the Committee of Social Defense, in the
brotherhoods, confraternities, and various other neo-political
entities, seeing to it that socialists, anarchists, freethinkers, and
republicans were put in jail. No one was safe in their homes.

This time, they didn't resort to regimes of hunger and thirst to
obtain confessions. Any police statement supported by witnesses
whose names were withheld was sufficient to plunge any individual
or family into desperation.

The government had already satisfied the desires for vengeance
of the hungry vultures by muzzling the press and responding to its

---

1. Ferdinand VII was overthrown by Napoleon in 1808 and became the head
of the counter-revolutionary forces in Spain. He returned to power in 1813, agree-
ing to rule according to the liberal Cádiz Constitution of 1812. Once in power he
rejected the Constitution, arresting its drafters, refusing to call parliament, and
banning the liberal press.

insinuations in the pages of the reactionary newspapers and in the manifestos that our readers are already familiar with.

Within a few days, the jails, the Atarazanas Barracks, the military prisons, several barracks belonging to the Civil Guards, and Montjuïc Castle were crowded with prisoners. The *razzia* was likewise spreading throughout every Catalonian town. Men, women, and children were seized from their homes whether or not they were the perpetrators of the events that were the result of government brutality. Espionage was the order of the day. There were well over two thousand prisoners.[2]

With this whole inquisitorial system of citizen informants, military tribunals began operating. The general sense of anxiety could not be greater, considering that sentences, which were handed down quickly in summary trials, were carried out the next day.

And increasing that sense of anxiety was the belief that, even in ordinary cases, the rights of the accused would not be sufficiently guaranteed—they would be restricted in their choice of attorney, and their attorney would be subject to evidentiary constraints.

On the subject of the natural anxiety that we have observed, *The War and Naval Law Gazette*, which we presume will not be labeled anti-militaristic, said that "today, in reality, everything depends on the benevolence of the tribunal," adding later:

> The worry and contemptuous prejudice with which the court views the defending attorney, denying him evidentiary means, cutting down the time he needs to study the case, and restricting the greatest possible number of powers at his disposal, can be clearly seen, to the point where, without fear of engaging in exaggeration, the defending attorney can be described as a decorative figure of the Tribunal, which patiently tolerates the reading of his arguments.

Also, in consideration of military command and discipline, the official defending attorney is not able to truly see from the

---

2.   The scale of repression is similar to that enacted upon the anarchist movement during the 1890s in the wake of terrorist attacks in Barcelona, where the infamous Montjuïc Castle became a symbol of the violence of the Spanish state.

perspective of the accused when he committed the act which the Code deems to be a crime.

We will leave the work of reforming the Code of Military Justice to others. We understand that anything that makes it a crime to resist, to work against everything that is antagonistic to the sentiments of each and every individual should be dispensed with.

The problem is that at present, within the military system of justice, certain anomalies are prevalent which are a terrible threat and weigh heavily on those who fall within its jurisdiction.

It should have been the government's responsibility to stop that bloodthirsty pack of clergy, which was hungry for new flesh, from using these anomalies to continuously seek victims.

Unfortunately, the lack of internal struggle among some individuals makes them unmoved by the whirlwinds of passions, or even by sublime true love. Their morality is perverse. Ardent love and sacrificing for others could never be the object of their reflections. In all the depravity of their surroundings, these people believe themselves to be superhuman and have no virtue whatsoever.

Their first and foremost code is the violent principle of authority, the instrument of the security forces. They say obedience is kindness, silence is order, destruction is expansion, and pretense is civilization. Their prestige is fruit of the ignorance of others.

These men with their dominating attitudes make themselves unbearable. Arrogant and haughty because of their successes, they believe that everything is of their own doing; they concede nothing to circumstances.

They have a propensity towards anger, which they dissimulate finely, that "foolish passion" as Charron defined it, "which puts us wholly out of ourselves, and in seeking the means to withstand the evil which threatens us, or that has already affected us, it makes our blood boil in our hearts, and raises a furious vapor in our spirits which blinds us, and casts us headlong into whatever may satisfy the desire we have for revenge."[3]

An inclination towards excess predominates in these men. The servile classes surrounding them certainly adulate this, but at the

---

3. [Translator's Note] From Charron, Pierre, *A Treatise on Wisdom*, paraphrased by Myrtilla H.N. Daly, 1891.

helm of the state these inclinations take on a refined cruelty, and the inevitable popular storms threaten the next shipwreck.

This is what has occurred again and again, with more or less intensity, in this or that circumstance, in every capitalist regime. There was no compassion. The system of repression that followed, we repeat, was unyielding and draconian, not to deter crime, but to satisfy the predominating inclinations of government ministers and the refined cruelty of those who instigated them. We have already said that military tribunals began.[4]

The first one was constituted at the Atarazanas Barracks the day after the events were over, and on August 2nd, Ramón Báldera Azuara was sentenced to life imprisonment for involvement in the rebellion.

Four days later, a second drumhead court-martial was held, and Antonio Capdevila Marqués was given the same penalty for the same crime.

The third court-martial began at ten o'clock at night on the 9th and was over by six thirty the next morning. Thirteen residents of Monistrol were put on trial in this short space of time for the crimes of rebellion, setting fire to streetcars at the station in Sant Vincenç de Castellet, and damaging rails as well as telegraph and telephone lines. All of them were sentenced to life in prison, except one minor, Rafael Falio Curt, who was given a prison sentence of seventeen years and six months.

The fourth court-martial was held on the 11th. The defendant, Antonio Malet Pujol, was accused of leading the rebellion in Sant Adrià de Besós. The military judicial authority dissented from the tribunal's decision to impose the death penalty, and sent the case to the Supreme Court of War and Navy.

The fifth court-martial took place on the night of the 14th. The case against José Miquel Baró was heard and a judgment rendered. The news that came through the military censor was that "the vast majority of witnesses who spoke, including some defense witnesses, accused the defendant of having captained revolutionaries in Sant Andreu de Palomar, who set fire to the parish church of the

---

4. For further information on the trials see Ullman, *The Tragic Week*, 283–297.

Religious of Jesus and Mary. He was also accused of attacking the barracks of the Civil Guards, constructing barricades, and seizing weapons from the municipal customs office." He was sentenced to death.

We can confirm this story, which the Barcelona newspaper *La Publicidad* published later without prior censorship. Here are some interesting notes on the story:

He was forty-three-years old. He had been active in the Republican Party for a long time, being a member of the Autonomist Republican Center of Sant Andreu since the age of sixteen. He was affiliated with several workers' organizations, including the Workers' Artistic Center of Sant Andreu.

He occupied a position as a worker at Town Hall, later switching to the role of security guard at the Deputy Mayor's Office in Sant Andreu, a post which he held at the time of his arrest.

José Miquel was given a summary trial. Nothing was known of these proceedings, until on August 16th at ten o'clock at night a waiter from an establishment on la Rambla de Santa Mónica paid us a visit. This waiter delivered a box of matches to us. Mysteriously, as he was serving his meal in one of the jail cells of the Atarazanas Barracks, Miquel Baró handed it to him and asked him to pass it along to us.

Inside the box of matches there was a letter penciled on the back of a used envelope.

Here is the text of the letter:

"I don't know how to spel. Dear frends. The day befor yesterday, the gards came with some fals witnesses. They told me at 8 I had a court marshal at 3 they told the witnesses I was disoriented till That time I didn't know why they Arested me of what they accused me of I'm ignosent becaus the witnesses de clared aganst me very badly they gave me the deth penalty I'm inosent I did not shot even one bulet or set fire no where, I mean it's stranje and it was good for the gards when they taked with 'som frends.' Frends defend my sad situation Protest To D. Francisco

Esteban—don't abandon me.—I'm inocent.—don't dezert me. José Miquel. To lapublicidad."

This was the letter we received from Miquel Baró, along with another piece of paper written in pencil, which we were unable to decipher.

In this dangerous situation, we were immediately able to interest several personalities in soliciting clemency for the unfortunate man who was condemned to die.

Deputies Corominas, Hurtdado, and Rodés made efforts to obtain the clemency. It was already too late. Although it was being processed, José Miquel Baró had already faced the firing squad in the moats of Montjuïc.

Immediately after writing his letter, he was transferred at night from Atarazanas to the Castle, and executed on the morning of August 17th.

He left behind a wife and children, penniless.

José Miquel Baró was a man of feeling. After he was taken to the castle, he spent six hours in the chapel. He heard mass indifferently and declined to sign the sentence.

Upon arrival at the moat at Santa Amalia Bastion, he stood tall before the execution squad.

The day after this execution, it was announced that from that point forward in cases presided by military judges, no drumhead court-martials would take place against the accused. That they would be tried by ordinary military tribunal, which would have the same powers anyway. What did this news mean? Was this about softening the alarm that we described earlier? Since the military tribunals continued giving out terrible sentences (and although they may have been handed down in accordance with the written codes, that did not mean the victims were safe from the bloodthirsty clergy, whose system of confidential informants hindered the defense of the accused), what was the purpose of this? Fast sentences handed down in summary trial and carried out twenty-four hours later are terrifying, but nothing compares to the unimaginable torment and horror caused by slow proceedings that kill or throw a person into prison without any hope of salvation.

A new spasm of pain made clear that there would be another execution.

At ten thirty at night on the 27th, a short man wearing a mechanic's suit was headed through El Paral-lel to Monjuïc. He was in the custody of two Civil Guards on horseback and eight on foot. It was Antonio Malet, supposed leader of the revolutionaries in Sant Adrià de Besós, who was sentenced to death during the court-martial held on the 11th, whose case we have already described.

At two o'clock in the morning on the 28th, the Brothers of Peace and Charity arrived. At four o'clock a cavalry section came, followed a short while later by infantry forces.

Sentinels at the fort ordered the innumerable individuals there to withdraw from the vicinity of the moats.

At fifteen minutes before eight o'clock, forty-three cavalry soldiers, two lieutenants, and their captain, who had been stationed to the right of the castle's main entrance, took a position next to the moats.

When the fort's clock struck eight, the prisoner walked out of the chapel, and five minutes later, a volley of shots was heard, followed by a sepulchral silence indicating that the sentence had been carried out. The execution took place in the same location where Baró was shot, at the southwest glacis.

The people believed no one else would be sentenced to death. They tried to console themselves, hoping in vain. They still cannot conceive of the perversity of a hyena that covers its claws with perfumed gloves and chooses the victims it will devour in carpeted salons.

On September 5th, in the Hall of Justice of the Roger of Lauria Barracks, a trial began against two security guards accused of rebellion, Eugenio del Hoyo and C. Carrillo.

According to the testimony, Del Hoyo, hidden behind a curtain in his house, fired at the army several times on July 27th.

Without actually specifying the accused, all of the statements of the officers and the troops who arrested Del Hoyo agreed that shots were fired at them from his balcony.

Carrillo appears as an accomplice who covered up his associate's crime.

The prosecutor asked for the death penalty for the former and twenty years in prison for the latter.

The defense attorney argued that there was no material evidence, asserting the theory that such serious penalties should only be imposed in cases of absolute proof.

The defendants' conduct was exemplary and they had the benefit of having an honest background.

The tribunal sentenced according to the prosecutor's wishes.

And on the 13th, there in the moats of Montjuïc, for the third time, the firing squad carried out the fateful death sentence.

The security guard Eugenio del Hoyo fell to the ground, horribly disfigured.

At nine o'clock in the morning on September 9th, in the Hall of Justice of the Roger of Lauria Barracks, an ordinary military tribunal was constituted against the civilians Ramón Clemente García, Agustín Redó Castells, Juan Espelleta Torres, José Basagañes Pujol, and Leandro Espelleta Torres, with Infantry Captain Luis Franco Cuadras as examining magistrate. The first defendant was accused of rebellion and profaning of corpses, while the others were accused of rebellion only.

The chief colonel of the first dragoon regiment of Numancia, Cesáreo Caravaca Urtiagu was the presiding judge, while captains Vicente Martorell Portas, Joaquín Jiménez Frontín, Sebastián Pozas Perca, Juan del Solar Martínez, Víctor Enseñat Martínez, and Sebastián Clares Octavio sat as members of the panel. Their alternates were Eugenio Rovira Terry and Patricio San Pedro y Ayinat.

First Lieutenant Nicolás Torio of the dragoon regiment of Montesa acted as prosecutor; Ensign Second Class Carlos de la Escosura Fuentes acted as an adviser; and the defense attorneys were Captain Jorge Cabanyes Mata and First Lieutenant Jorge Barrie, both from the ninth mounted artillery regiment.

The prosecutor asked for the death penalty and imprisonment for Clemente; life imprisonment for Redó, Juan Espolleta, and José Basagañes; and he withdrew the charges against Leandro Espolleta.

This astounding case, and the weight of such a terrible sentence, is supported only by the statement of a single police officer, Inspector Mercier, the sole witness for the prosecution, and the strange circumstances that led to the sacrifice of a young man condemned to death, Ramón Clemente García, have caused us to advance an alternative examination of the case, to show all impartial and honest people what his political and social ideas were, and to show the great evil sanctioned by the deputies, the senators, the Bishop, Corporations, the Committee of Social Defense, and the Regionalist League, who could have obtained a pardon if they had asked for it, and they did not do it!

Chapter 5

This alternative examination of the case will be impartial—we intend to corroborate the story with interesting opinions and documents that deserved the acceptance of anyone who learned of
them.

We simply want to relate a chapter of history.

The facts of the case occurred on the corner of Carrer de Carme
and Carrer d'En Roig, where a barricade was raised last July 27th.

The examining magistrate, Señor Franco Cuadras, read the
charges, from which, based on indirect testimony from Chief
of Police Felipe Mercier, it would appear that after the defendant helped raise a barricade, Ramón Clemente García, a coal
store clerk, then took the corpse of a Hieronymite nun, carried it
through the streets, danced with it mockingly, and tossed it away
on Carrer de les Egipcíaques.

The charging document also says that the other defendants
helped raise a barricade at an egg store on Carrer d'En Roig. In
that document, Officer Mercier said that the accused José Redó,
Ramón Clemente García, and others deserved full credit, although
he was unable to reveal his sources.

The defendant Agustín Redó denied his participation. Juan
Espelleta and José Basagañes affirmed that although they had
placed four or six stones on the barricade, they were obliged to do
so by two men who had pointed a revolver at them on their way

out of a tavern, which they had gone into to drink vermouth. They said the men threatened to kill them if they did not help, but they escaped to their houses as soon as they were freed of them.

Finally, Leandro Espelleta denied any involvement.

None of the defendants had a criminal record.

Ramón Clemente García was a volunteer bugler of the 14th Cavalry Regiment of Alcántara, and was later exempted from service because he did not fulfill the height requirements.

After the case was sent to a full session of the court, his defense lawyer requested that a doctor examine him, since he was convinced he was mentally degenerate and not criminally responsible. When the judge denied his request, he protested energetically.

Defense attorney Sr. Cabanys asked if Ramón Clemente García could enter the courtroom so the judges could see him and form their own judgment as to his criminal responsibility. The panel agreed that this would be done at the end of the session, and Sr. Cabanys pleaded his case, in which, after calling for exemplary punishment for any perpetrators of the infamies that Barcelona saw, he expounded on how hard it was for him to act on behalf of prisoners who were accused of having been involved in these events, which he sincerely condemned.

He expressed that the declarations appearing in the police statement could not be valid because by law these statements could only be made before a competent individual—the police could not be considered as such, and no one except a judge could be.

No one came to say they saw the defendant fire or even carry a weapon, so he could not be considered guilty of the crime of rebellion.

For this purpose he read the article on rebellion, and he deduced from it that it could not have occurred because the accused did not form a party or commit assault.

He denied that there was profanation of corpses. According to his defense lawyer, the sole aim of the accused, who was impelled by a humanitarian sentiment, was to bring the nun's body to City Hall, which he would have done had he not found the rightful owner of the body on Carrer de Egipcíaques, which obliged him to abandon the body there.

Once the ruling became known, neighbors from the streets of Carme and Roig sent Sr. Maura a telephone message soliciting clemency, which they then formalized with the following appeal:

Dear Sir:

The undersigned neighbors from the streets of Carme and Roig, Barcelona, sincerely declare:

That they were truly astonished to find out, in confidence, that as a result of the military tribunal held in the city of Barcelona on the ninth of the current month, Ramón Clemente García was to be given the capital punishment for the crimes of rebellion and profanation of corpses.

It was for this reason that they sent Your Excellency a telephone message beseeching your mercy for clemency for Clemente García.

Today, more calmly and peacefully, we are once again petitioning Your Excellency, and at the same time, we are confessing in all sincerity that we are to blame for the ruling since we were not able to go before the examining magistrate as defense witnesses for the unfortunate Clemente García.

The announcements for the court case did not come to our attention, and if we learned of the ruling, it was because we saw it reported on the front pages of every newspaper in Barcelona. Our conscience obliges us to confess this to Your Excellency, since if we had been able to make a statement, we would have testified that during those days that were so tragic for Barcelona, Clemente García possessed no weapons of any kind, and as such could not have taken up arms against the army or against anyone else, nor could he have promoted or incited rebellion because he is a somewhat simple boy, who is barely able to coordinate his sentences. And finally, the judgment on profanation of corpses should be reduced since some neighbors asked him to take the body, inside its coffin, to City Hall. The true profaners had left the body on top of the rocks of the barricade on Carrer del Carme.

Again, we are sending this statement to Your Excellency to obey the dictates of our conscience and to show the sense of humanity and justice that moves us to beseech your mercy for the clemency of the unfortunate Ramón Clemente García.

We declare that we are certain Your Excellency's kindness and patriotism will support our humanitarian petition. Your humble servants.

Barcelona, September 20th, 1909.

Pablo Valí, A. Malagrida, Joaquín González, Julián Gil, Miguel Cardona, José Sentadé, Jaime Ramoneda, Agustín Roca, A. Ribas Comas, Ramón Martí, José Dedem, Juan Vich, Salvador Rafols, José Herrada, José Rosell, Juan Roca, Leonor Concustell, Domingo Batllori, Ramón Soler, Andrés Puig, Manuel Regordosa, Enrique Massana, Alejandro Amigó, Caballero E. Molinas, Juan Vidal, Ramón Sardá, Francisco Subirats, José Lluhí, Francisco Balaguer, Jacinto Roca, Antonio Serra, José Martínez, José Riera, Ramón Castell Coll, Venancia Garafulla, José Zabia, Andrés Duro, Juan Arnau, José Riera, Rafael Rovira, Juan Trías, Ramón Castells, Eduardo Grant, Clemente Fuster, and Juan Domingo.

Your Excellency Sr. President of the Council of Ministers.

On Friday, October 1st, there was some surprising news—the superintendent of the women's jail had received an order to have the unfortunate Ramón Clemente García ready because Civil Guards would come pick him up at eight o'clock that night as soon as the Council of Ministers had approved the death sentence.

The superintendent, a feeling person, did not want the poor boy to get the impression that he would be leaving his jail cell at eight o'clock that night, and suddenly he would be faced with that entire security apparatus. One hour beforehand, he sent an officer to tell him that the judge would be calling at any moment for a necessary statement. The boy was singing about how he would be getting out. The message was received, and a short while later, the unsuspecting boy was taken down to where the security guard and other employees usually stand.

A while later, they pretended there was a telephone call, and they said the judge had informed them that he would not be able to come, and that he had ordered him to be taken to the Atarazanas

Barracks, where he would have a confrontation with other prisoners. Clemente did not suspect anything and was still cheerful.[1]

Afterwards, ten Civil Guards on horse and foot walked him to the Atarazanas Barracks with his hands tied. I saw him this way along El Paral-lel.

The owner of the coal store was at Atarazanas, and when he saw Clemente, he embraced him and kissed him, crying.

The boy then realized what was happening and became completely discouraged.

From Atarazanas, he was taken to Montjuïc with others who were facing life imprisonment. According to employees of the women's jail, the boy was so defeated he had to be carried by the guards.

This occurred on Friday night, and the day after he was put before the firing squad, the Barcelona press could barely express the sense of horror that was caused when the sentence was carried out, a sentence that was based solely on the indirect testimony of Inspector Mercier.

I have here some newspaper articles on the execution:

La Publicidad

This morning, the military tribunal's ruling against Ramón Clemente García was carried out. His clemency petition had been denied, and he was given the death penalty.

As reported earlier, Clemente was taken from the jail on Carrer de Amalia to Atarazanas Barracks on Friday, and after filling out some paperwork, he was transferred along with another prisoner to Montjuïc Castle. He was locked in a cell there until two o'clock in the afternoon, when he was taken to the chapel.

At four thirty in the afternoon, a car arrived at the fortress door with the Brothers of Peace and Charity and a priest, who immediately went into the chapel to cheer up the prisoner, since he was very depressed.

At five thirty this morning, fifty soldiers and two buglers from the dragoon regiment of Numancia, commanded by a

---

1. In a confrontation, or *careo*, two witnesses with conflicting statements meet face to face to determine who is correct.

captain and two lieutenants, began their climb up to the castle, along with a company of the Mallorca regiment.

At seven o'clock a carriage carrying a priest and four members of the Brotherhood of the Virgin of the Abandoned went inside the castle.

Forty minutes later, the horsemen from Numancia headed to the usual execution site, the moat at the bastion of Santa Amalia, where they took their positions.

The prisoner left the chapel at exactly eight o'clock in the morning, accompanied by the two priests. Five minutes later, the military tribunal's ruling was carried out.

A few moments after that, the Numancia soldiers abandoned their positions and went into the castle, but before they entered, the Mallorca Company, composed of the Mixed Engineer Regiment and the Artillery Command, both under the command of a captain, went outside. Later, two carriages exited, one with the Brothers of Peace and Charity and the other with the Brothers of the Abandoned.

A company from the Constitution Regiment was standing in formation.

The prisoner was twenty-two-years old.

Rest in peace.

El Diluvio

At eight o'clock in the morning in the moats of Montjuïc Castle, the hapless Ramón Clemente García was shot to death. His sentence had been upheld by the Supreme Court of War and Navy.

The convict, who was twenty-two-years old, was transferred to the castle last Friday night and then to the chapel at two o'clock in the afternoon yesterday.

During his last eighteen hours, Ramón Clemente was seized by a profound dejection and frequent nervous fits. Nevertheless, when the fateful hour arrived, he regained his composure and went to the site of the execution of his own volition.

Rest in peace!

El Diaro Mercantil adds these details:

The castle chaplain Sr. Eloy Hernández Vicente and two Brothers of Peace and Charity visited the prisoner.

At eight o'clock yesterday morning, after the prisoner heard mass, he was taken to the moat at the bastion of Santa Amalia, where the sentence was carried out by eight soldiers from the Constitution Infantry Regiment.

Brigadier General Manuel Bonet was present at the execution, along with a company from the Mallorca Infantry Regiment, a dragoon squadron from Numancia, and troops from the Artillery Command and the Fourth Mixed Engineer Regiment.

R.I.P.

El Liberal

The prisoner was transferred on Friday from the old jail where he was being held to the Atarazanas Barracks, and from there to Montjuïc Castle, where he was placed in a cell.

The day before yesterday at exactly two o'clock in the afternoon, he was notified of his sentence and then immediately taken to the chapel. The Brothers of Peace and Charity were then advised of this and went to the castle, arriving shortly thereafter, at four o'clock in the afternoon.

The fortress's chaplain came to give support to the prisoner, who was very downcast. The Brothers helped him in his charitable task, endeavoring to comfort the prisoner, who declined to eat or drink anything, or even smoke.

With great effort, they managed to serve him something to restore his strength, a cup of coffee with cognac and later some broth and an egg.

The Brothers of the Abandoned and a priest from the House of Mercy arrived just before sunrise with a coffin for the prisoner's mortal remains. Clemente had regained his composure somewhat; he heard mass, confessed, and took communion. He appeared more resigned to his fate, but lamented his sentence, saying that others who were guiltier than he was were free.

At five o'clock in the morning, troops from the Numancia Regiment went up to the castle, taking positions beside the moat and stopping anyone from getting near the place of execution. A company of the Mallorca Infantry Regiment was with them, as well as a section from the Mixed Engineer Regiment and another from the Artillery Regiment.

The prisoner left the chapel accompanied by the castle's chaplain, the priest from the House of Mercy, and the Brothers of Peace and Charity. Of the soldiers lined up from the Constitution Regiment, four soldiers stepped up at eight o'clock after the last bell of the castle clock rang. They carried out the fatal sentence and the prisoner ceased to exist.

R.I.P.

The troops from Mallorca and Numancia, the Engineers, and the Artillery troops left the castle to go back to where they were being housed, and then the brothers from the two brotherhoods who had visited the prisoner also left.

As is known, the prisoner was a twenty-two-year old young man with reddish-blond hair. He dressed like a poor man, dark pants and a striped shirt. At the age of fifteen, he served in an infantry unit, completing his commitment.

The day before the events leading to his court case took place, he had been working at a coal store on Carrer d'En Roig.

The other newspapers do not add anything else.

The news of this execution caused astonishment and indignation in every Spanish town and in some points outside Spain. The following day, this criticism appeared in an *El País* editorial:

There was neither compassion nor justice when Ramón Clemente García was executed.

Clemente García never killed anyone, and he has been executed! He never took up arms against the troops or the police, and he has been executed! He did not lead a mutiny and he was not the head of any rebel groups, and he was condemned as if he had been. He did not belong to any political parties or any workers associations; he was not a member of *La Casa del Pueblo* and it is unknown whether he even read *El Progreso*, and yet he met the same end as the leaders of a failed revolution. He never stole or looted or went searching among the ruins of the religious houses, and he has been executed! He never set any fires, profaned graves, took apart railways, or destroyed telegraph lines, and he has been executed!

What was Clemente García accused of? Why was he given yesterday's sentence? He was accused of having placed a cobblestone on a barricade on his street when requested to do so, or coerced, by the rebels. He was also accused of having taken the body of a nun into his arms, which some gravediggers had with them, and of having danced with it in a macabre manner.

And who is accusing him? What witnesses are there? What is the evidence? The accusation was made by no more than one indirect witness who was not present in court. This single witness for the prosecution was Inspector Mercier, whose background is Carlist and who is known for being cruel and despotic. The inspector did not see anything himself. His accusation is based on confidential information from several individuals who did not appear in court because the inspector refused to provide their names, reserving his right to professional confidentiality.

It is possible that this inspector is a personal enemy of Clemente García, or maybe he acted in good faith and was tricked by his anonymous informants. Has anyone forgotten that Juan Rull was the confidant of Barcelona's civil governor?[2]

Against Clemente García was the inspector's statement. In Clemente García's favor was the nature of the crimes attributed to him; his age; his lack of culture; his removal from politics;

---

2. A reference to a scandal in which the anarchist Rull was paid by the Barcelona police to "discover" bombs planted by his own gang (if not himself) across the city from 1905 to 1907. See Smith, *Anarchism, Revolution and Reaction*, 154 and Antoni Dalmau, *El cas Rull. Viure del terror a la Ciutat de les Bombes (1901–1908)* (Barcelona: Columna, 2008).

the deputies for Barcelona (other than the regionalists) who petitioned for clemency; the coal-workers' association, which also petitioned for clemency; and the neighbors from d'En Roig and del Carme (the scene of the events where presumably the shy Garcia participated) who appealed for clemency, more from a sense of justice than mercy.

Clemente García has been executed. The government, in its harshness, has had helpers in the higher and lower clergy of Barcelona (who routinely petition for clemency for those sentenced to death, regardless of how brutal the crime that brought the offender to the scaffold) as well as in the Regionalist League and the security forces, who in theory, are enemies of the violence they practice: they condemn it with words and they spread it with their deeds.

Nothing creates such an impression or an example as these extremely severe penalties applied belatedly. We understand when the troops were ruthless at Thiers to take control of the *Commune*.[3] We despise this cruelty, but we find it justifiable. Controlling an insurrection, a rebellion, a revolution, and harshly punishing the prisoners tends to be counterproductive, but, however merciless, it obeys logic. Espartero defeated the conspirators of 1841 and executed General León with swift cruelty, with the celerity of an avenging ray of thunder; Narváez crushed the revolution of May, 1848, and the moment it was over, he constituted a drumhead court-martial outside the Alcalá Gate, next to the walls of El Retiro, and executed anyone who was caught carrying arms. It was harsh and it was cruel, but not repugnant.

Later, O'Donnell had blood on his hands when he repressed the June 22, 1866 insurrection, and that blood tarnished his memory—it was not so much his innate cruelty, but his weak submission to cruelty that was alien to him. The

---

3. Adolphe Thiers was a key figure in both the 1830 and 1848 revolutions in France and an opponent of Louis Napoleon. Following the fall of the Second French Empire in 1871, Thiers was elected President of the new French Fourth Republic. His first task was the defeat and bloody repression of the Paris Commune.

numerous victims sacrificed at the end of June and the beginning of July were the prologue to the revolution of 1868, and did not even serve to affirm the odious O'Donnell's power. As Pedro Antonio de Alarcón said, the sergeants who faced the firing squad became the Baptists of the revolution.[4]

Now, two months after this tragic week, Sr. Maura, who filled the pages of *La Gaceta* this past Good Friday with clemencies for parricides, fratricides, thieves, murderers, arsonists, and even child-killers, has dispensed with normal legal processes and the requirement of quality evidence—to kill a man.

Four individuals were executed up to yesterday. Four executions one after the other: Baró, Malet, the security guard, and Clemente García. Justice described as swift proceeds at a slow pace. If the process that has been used continues, then within two years another unfortunate individual will be executed, accused by an inspector that heard some people say that he did such and such thing during the Tragic Week, and this inspector will keep their identity secret.

What is gained by this, but to inspire pity for the victims, slow the pacification of the people, give fodder to those that talk of an Inquisitorial Spain, and favor the campaign of the so-called "apaches" and tricksters for the most explosive ministerial posts?[5]

If there had been waves of bloodshed, bullets striking insurgents, and mass executions in the first few days of August, it would have horrified us less than this cold execution of an unfortunate whose death did not satisfy the dictates of retributive justice, but the private desires of the clergy, the Committee of Social Defense, and the Regionalist League, who asked for, and continue asking for examples to be made of certain people. Was the execution of Clemente García an example?

---

4. The previous sections are filled with references to *pronuncamientos* (coups) and repression during the nineteenth century. See Vincent, *Spain*, 9–44 for an overview.

5. "Les Apaches" were a violent, semi-organized underground gang in Belle-Epoque Paris.

Several municipal councils wanted to protest, for the record. The session of the Madrid City Council that took place four days after the execution deserves to be reproduced in these pages, as it assumed great importance:

> Having read the minutes of the previous session, Pablo Iglesias took the floor to protest on behalf of the Socialist minority that it was not allowed to manifest its opinion last Friday, when Señor Barranco asked for the Council to process the clemency petition of the unfortunate prisoner Clemente, who has already been executed.[6] With this in mind, he pointed out the arbitrariness with which the mayor has proceeded with the debate and he censured the continuous lack of consideration with which he has treated the radical minorities. He likewise stated for the record that with respect to the failed clemency petition, his vote was with that of the Republicans.
>
> The mayor responded evasively and briefly corrected Sr. Iglesias.
>
> Sr. Santillán spoke on behalf of the Republican minority, first endorsing what the Socialist leader had expressed, then asking that the protest of the Republicans on this point be added to the record.
>
> Sr. Santillán later said that it was necessary for the mayor to become aware of the motion made by the Council in favor of clemency for the prisoner from Barcelona and the government's reply. In his understanding, this being a matter of humanity and not policy, the motion should have been brought directly to the Committee, and maybe with the people's cooperation, which would surely not have been lacking, a man's life would have been saved, a man whose guilt has not been sufficiently demonstrated.
>
> He energetically condemned what occurred in Barcelona, and he reminded the Council that as this miserable prisoner was being put before the firing squad for having danced with the body of a dead nun, official protection measures were being

---

6. Iglesias was the founder and leader of both the Spanish Socialist Party (PSOE) and its national union (UGT).

issued in Melilla for Riffians who were called "friends" after having cruelly mutilated and profaned the dead bodies of the brave Spanish soldiers at Wolf's Ravine.

The mayor, nervously ringing the bell, prohibited Sr. Santillán from continuing to speak on these matters and he said that if he insisted on doing so, he would be asked to leave the floor. Santillán protested, and the bell ringing and calls to order began again.

Finally, the Republican speaker was able to make himself heard, and he affirmed that the reason he was speaking that way was that he feared that the executions would continue.

"We were headed toward a great horror," he said, "a period as tragic as the one in Barcelona from July 26th to the 31st. There are still two thousand pending cases, including an estimated one hundred in which the prosecutors are asking for the death penalty." (More bell ringing from the mayor.)

"This is the official truth . . ."

"But we cannot deal with anything other than municipal matters here."

"But faced with such horrors," Santillán said, "I forget that I am a councilmember and that I am a politician. I am a human being, nothing more."

He ended by insisting on his protest on behalf of the Republicans.

The mayor responded briefly without adding anything new other than what had already been expressed. He affirmed only that he had applied to the Minister of Grace and Justice for the clemency, and when any future cases presented themselves, he would act in accordance with his duty and conscience.

Sr. Abellán asked that the record show the sentiments of the Committee when they learned of the execution of the prisoner, but the mayor, interrupting him, prohibited him from continuing down this path.

We now see that the boy from the coal store on Carrer d'En Roig was neither republican, nor socialist, nor anarchist, nor anything else; we might say he was a good example of illiteracy and the failure of the Church as educator of the people.

Why was he killed? It is not enough to rely on the honor of the homeland and the army. He had been a bugler and was still attracted to the red uniform he wore. He admired the prevailing customs. He was not a member of any rebel faction.

The charges brought by Officer Mercier referred to events that he did not witness himself, and which he admitted he never saw. Their origin was indirect and based on information that was kept secret. Even if we accept the officer's statement as true, the punishment does not fit the crime.

Why, then, was he not granted clemency? It was appealed for by: the prisoner's mother, the owner of the coal store, the coalworkers' association of Barcelona, the neighbors from Carrer d'En Roig and Carme, several Catalonian deputies, *Hispana Nueva, El País, La Época,* and, through the beautiful initiative of Councilmember Barranco, the Madrid City Council. All in vain.

In the end, why was Ramón Clemente García sacrificed? It was because Sr. Maura's clericalist government was faced with the indignation of international multitudes shrieking before Spanish embassies to demand Ferrer's freedom, and he needed a show of force. They could not release their quarry; the higher and lower clergy demanded it.

Suggesting clemency for Clemente García meant they would have had to do the same for Ferrer, and the death of that apostle of rationalist teaching had already been decreed by the Vaticanists.

So we know that sacrificing this young man was not about order, the law, or to redress the damage and the offenses committed, but about responding to Europe's defiance with an even greater infamy. The execution of Ramón Clemente García.

Three days later, the military issued a public notice: on the 9th of this month, at eight o'clock in the morning, an ordinary military tribunal would be convened in the assembly hall of the Cellular Prison. The examining magistrate from this Captaincy, General Valerio Raso Negrini, was to hear and decide the case against the civilian Francisco Ferrer Guardia, who was accused of the crime of rebellion.

Chapter 6

The reactionaries who were rabidly persecuting anything even re-
motely smelling of liberal might have been momentarily satisfied,
except that today the old halls of power are devoid of humanity.
The executions were not enough to satisfy their vengeance,
nor was seeing the jail cells and barracks halls filled with honorable
people. "Clean up Barcelona!" they shouted furiously and haugh-
tily, and as they set to work, they closed innumerable radical centers, community centers, educational centers, and all the lay and
rationalist schools. They deported teachers and anyone they said
was listed as an anarchist in the police registers (although it wasn't
true), and there were many republicans among them.

And this arbitrary system did not only predominate in Catalonian provinces that were affected by sedition; it was also applied in
many other Spanish provinces where there wasn't even the slightest attempt at a general strike.

No one could explain all these irregularities, and regarding the
unjustified closures of schools and the indefinite deportations, it
was impossible to guess what grounds the government had for its
actions.

In relation to the deportees, if they were presumed guilty, if
Barcelona needed to be purified after some reprehensible act, the
logical thing would have been to process them or even imprison
them and put them on trial later. If they did not commit any

crimes, but the authorities feared that they might do so, they could be watched scrupulously, and it would be much easier to do so in a capital city that spends enormous sums on public security than in a hundred small towns scattered here and there with no express personnel for that purpose. If the deportees' preaching was what created suspicion, the only thing gained by deportation was to ensure that the seeds of the propaganda they aimed to repress were scattered more easily to the four corners of the earth.

In no way was it possible to understand, using logic, the why of the deportations.

And on top of all this, every town has the right to look after the peace, and this right was violated—when people saw shackled individuals enter their towns in the custody of pairs of Civil Guards, they felt a twinge of disgust and humiliation. They could never have imagined that the place where they lived would become another Fernando Poo.[1] Logically, the honest people of these towns objected. If the government considers them dangerous, why would they send them these guests?

Certainly, the spectacle could not be sadder or more humiliating for the deportees and for the townspeople who saw them arrive.

In general, the deportees were without means; as workers away from the places where they ordinarily lived, they were unable earn a living. One of the two—either the townspeople had to consent to allowing the victims of reaction to die right before their very eyes or they had to give them support to prevent this cruelty.

We do not want anyone to say that we have entered the field of speculation to maximize our attacks. Real life will show our readers what our pen still has not. The deportees of Cantavieja, who were later transferred to Alcira, will speak for us. Their odyssey causes one's fists to clench.

The arbitrary and violent measures of a despotic and reaction-

---

1. An island off the coast of Africa now called Bioko. Spain deported undesirable politicians and scholars there during the nineteenth century. This island is part of Equatorial Guinea, the only nation in Africa where Spanish is currently one of the official languages.

ary government against citizens who have committed no crime other than having progressive ideas, far from intimidating and humiliating us, give us strength to face the enemy and determination to endure this disgraceful persecution to the very end.

We have been seized from our homes, leaving our mothers, wives, and children in misery and poverty, and they will doubtlessly suffer our same fate, in other words, they will lack the proper food and shelter because they will lack us, their support. We have been brought here shackled and under arrest, exiled to Cantavieja, a sparsely populated town which is insulated to our principles and more suitable as a hiding place for Carlists than for six artisans seeking a life of honest work.

We should point out our treatment by those responsible for carrying out the order to transfer us from the "former Carlist headquarters" to Alcira. We were led through rough mountains in the province of Teruel, walking eleven-and-a-half hours per day in the intense sun and rain. Where the "magnanimity" of the mayors was at its finest, we were offered riding animals, which, considering the harsh terrain and how bad we were at riding, made us suffer greatly.

We spent the night in filthy jail cells, wretched hospitals, or in the barracks of the Civil Guards. As we walked through so many town centers, we were exhibited as if we were dangerous criminals, but in honor of the truth, we should confess that many of those country folk looked at us with eyes full of commiseration and sympathy; they did not see us as vicious and miserable like their clergy wanted them to.

Finally after so many calamities and misadventures, we found ourselves in Alcira, where in spite of the Mauras and the Ciervas,[2] we have been received with kindness and generosity by the neighbors.

We do not protest or complain about our treatment by the authorities; it is the expected reaction to those who yearn for a

---

2. Juan de la Cierva y Peñafiel served as Maura's Minister for the Interior, and was thus responsible for policing and repression. Like Maura, he was deeply unpopular with progressives, particularly anarchists.

better-organized society, the bread which feeds and strength-
ens our convictions.

Alcira, September 28, 1909.

Francisco Bernadas, Sebastián Curto, Vicente Jordana,
Gabriel Brías, Celestino Magí, José Benaiges.

The Teruel exiles expressed this to the press and the public:

The undersigned Barcelonans, exiled first to Alcañiz and then
to Teruel, reduced to a faraway place where it is impossible to
live, demand their right to life, which cannot be taken away by
suspending constitutional guarantees or by the laws of Public
Order.

We live in a house that is watched day and night by police
officers and pairs of Civil Guards. We cannot leave by ourselves; they do not even allow two of us to go to one place
and two or more somewhere else. If a salesperson comes to
the house, or even the postman, he is escorted by an officer.
We are not allowed to have visits. The only time was when
an acquaintance asked to visit one of us to do an errand. He
needed special permission from the governor, and the visit
was made two days after the petition and in the presence of
the required officer. The doors are locked at seven in the evening, and it is like a drawbridge closing at a fortress—no one
can leave. A neighbor from Teruel who was asked by some
friends from Reus to visit one of us came to our house, but an
officer forbade the meeting, declaring that there was an order
that we were not allowed to speak to anyone or even say hello
to anyone.

In this situation, we cannot look for work or work, and we
are unable to earn a peseta. Up to now, we have been living by
depriving our families of the few resources they have and also
from some donations from our friends. We are haunted by the
specter of hunger and abandonment.

Our condition as exiles proclaims our innocence. No
accusation weighs on our shoulders and we have not had a
trial. Nevertheless, a prisoner is given food and shelter and is

allowed to communicate, while for us, there will be no shelter, or clothing, or bread, or even a hello from a friend, or the essential compassion from a fellow human being.

Such a state cannot be sustained: if we are quiet about it, then hunger, cold, and hopelessness will kill us in no time, and faced with this danger, with the feeling and the conviction of immanent justice, we protest before public opinion, appealing to its organ, the press, and we trust they will fulfill their duty.

Teruel, September 1909.

José Casa-Sola, Anselmo Lorenzo, Francisca Concha, Mariana Lorenzo, Flora Lorenzo, Mariano Batllori, José Villafranca, José Robles.[3]

Now, reader, take a look at the Siétamo deportees:

We were arrested, our personal details were carefully taken at the police school, and they transferred us from Barcelona to this town without taking any statements and without any explanation. They only wrote in our passports that we were being exiled for reasons of public order, but they did not add the specific reasons for this. And here is a simple truism. They didn't specify the reasons because there were no reasons. On the contrary, aren't there more than enough judges to process and put us in prison just based on assumptions and inferences?

However, we were able to find out that our names had been in the police registers, and this, combined with the government's fears in cases like these, led us to believe that this was the cause of our exile.

And we arrived after twelve or thirteen hours of traveling, with our wrists cruelly shackled and without having eaten. Also, even worse, it was as if we were the dirtiest of criminals.

---

3. Anselmo Lorenzo was one of the most high-profile anarchists of the movement. Lorenzo had been present at the founding of the Spanish branch of the First International and had remained one its most important labour activists and publishers in the following decades. His part-memoir, part-history of the early movement, *El proletariado militante: Memorias de un internacionalista* is available online at: https://www.portaloaca.com/pensamiento-libertario/libros-anarquistas/4473-el -proletariado-militante-anselmo-lorenzo-libro.html.

So here we are in the noble and hospitable town of Siétamo, where the future is as uncertain as it is bleak for those that, like us, work in industries or do other labor found in big cities, which is completely unknown in places as small as this, where the people live—or maybe sometimes don't live—from agriculture.

The passports given to us in Barcelona show that we are exiled to a place that is more than 245 kilometers and less than 250 kilometers away, without setting a fixed point, so it is undeniable and clear that determining that is our option. Even so, our train tickets were purchased without telling us where we were going, and only when we set foot in Huesca did they tell us we were going to Siétamo.

Now, Siétamo is a small agricultural village high in the Aragonese mountains, where it would be impossible for us to stay permanently because there is no means of support for us, no way to earn a daily livelihood.

It seems that the government has the premeditated goal of making our exile abhorrent to us, bringing us to this town in shackles to make these simple folk suspicious of us, forcing us to die of starvation because though we cannot earn money, we have to spend it—our families are forced to sacrifice for us, thus compromising them. It seems that instead of pacifying and relieving the situation, the government wants to purposely find ways of making everyone agitated.

And luckily, reactionary anger has not been indirectly set off against us, like for the women exiled in Huesca who were forced to leave their house and take refuge with a friend. In any case, we know to fly our ideals high in our situation as exiles, and as much as these provocations of the government and the Jesuits have put us in a difficult situation, we know to remain strong in our thoughts and feelings.

But in the meanwhile, it is necessary to counter the flagrant contradictions of the administrators of the law.

We have been exiled for no purpose on account of the public order. We have not been given any stipend from the government, and we have been taken to a place where, to live, the people have to struggle with the barrenness of the land from sunrise to sunset.

Governments there do whatever they please. Secure in our ideals, we know what our path is, and we will follow it to the end, without letting any obstacles get in our way for even an instant. Exile, imprisonment, vicious accusations may cross our path, but there, far off at the end of it, we can see our supreme redemption. It is complete and absolute, and we are headed there.

Meanwhile, how will this matter be resolved? Is it reasonable, is it fair to exile people for no reason whatsoever to a place where subsistence is completely impossible?

Our passports do not specify a place. The government issues these passports and the government forces them on us. The government finds no reason to house us in a jail cell, but it does justify sentencing us to die of starvation in some far-off corner.

This is the heart of the matter.

Siétamo, September 10, 1909.

Luis Beltrán, Tomás Codina Gil, Miguel Serre, Jaime Sanroma, Fracisco Curto, Juan Bta. Esteve.[4]

Obviously, as barbaric as the resolution adopted by the government was, the perfidy and the cruelty with which it designated where the deportees would reside made it even more abominable. The government showed bad faith when it did not allow them to select a place where they could find work or friends, forcing the deportees to live in towns where, knowing that earning a livelihood would be impossible, it was also certain that they would be denied asylum and hospitality because of their ideas.

Of course, they were not this inhumane everywhere, but the odyssey of the Cantavieja deportees, read previously, was reproduced for those deported to Puebla de Híjar (Teruel). They were forced to move to Pina (Zaragoza), where they managed to get help from the local authorities.

---

4. Juan Baptista Esteve was Bonafulla's given name.

They, along with four Alcubierre deportees, and the deportees at Monzón (Huesca) and Sant Mateu (Castellón) fled these towns where they had no means of subsistence.

In contrast, it would not be fair of us to withhold our praise for the noble and gracious conduct of the people of Almudé-var, Ayerbe, and its capital, Huesca, not only for their hospitality towards the exiles, but also for their rebuke of the government's bad faith. And the best praise we can provide would be to gather the statements of the exiles in their own words.

This is what the Almudévar deportees said:

Attempting to transfer the painful scenes we witnessed on our forced pilgrimage to paper would be a chimera for us. Neither our good faith, nor the anguish and desperation produced by this government measure could properly be used to give the reader a true impression of reality. Better writers than us, more cultivated minds can do the work of teaching the people.

We are moved to take the pen only with the intention of letting the world know that the noble Aragonese people, or at least the majority of them, have a completely different concept of the exiles than the government. We have been driven out of Catalonia like dangerous animals. They tried to make people believe we are the scum of the earth, but common sense, the exclusive birthright of the governed, has raised a dam against the iniquity of those from on high, and we exiles have been given a good welcome. We should say this again, loudly: the people respect us. The liberal and progressive element finds reinforcement for the much broader propagation of their own doctrines, if that is possible. And those who are indifferent to social and political matters sympathize with our situation; they threaten that if they ever go to Madrid. . . . Soon enough, the crazed people there will learn of their excellent treatment of us.

But all this does not mean that those of us who have been persecuted for the sole crime of thinking are satisfied. Our moral satisfaction, our peace of mind, and the solidarity of these noble people towards us do not stop us from feeling the iron hands of our rulers striking at us, now more than ever. We have wives, we have parents, and we have children who are hungry for bread and justice, and because they are not by our side, they cannot take part in the moral satisfaction that gives us strength and encouragement; the material suffering of our families destroys our peace of mind, in part. We the undersigned do not have the words to give due praise for the hospitality, the righteousness, and the compassion with which the people of Almudévar have welcomed us, but far from here, in the Catalonian capital, there are people crying over our absence and cursing the causes of their misfortune. This, nothing else but this, is what distresses us now.

We ask nothing of those who treat us this way, we are too proud to beg for mercy, and we expect no compassion from the Maurists. There are kind-hearted people, and we go to them seeking justice. If we have committed a crime, there are jails, but if we are innocent, there are plenty of government procedures for that.

We are conscious of our own worth; therefore, before we humiliate ourselves, before we beg forgiveness for crimes we have not committed, we are going before the public, the only true judge of our case, so that it can sentence us more in accordance with human dignity. José Oran, Juan Usón, B. López, J. Guachola, R. Arbolí, T. O. A. Duch, M. Valls. Almudévar, November 23, 1909.

A declaration of gratitude from the Ayerbe deportees also deserves mention. They were rightfully received in the friendliest possible manner and they wrote this letter to the press, in which, after tactfully attacking the injustice done to them when they were iniquitously separated from their families and affirming their progressive ideals, they concluded with these feeling words:

> We most enthusiastically thank whoever has acted in solidarity on our behalf, including the people of this honorable town whose noble actions will be engraved in our memories.

We are deeply indebted to them, and if ever our society's ingratitude causes them to be in exceptional circumstances, which still weighs on us, we will reciprocate.

We wish them good health and a long life. Heriberto Caba, Magín Argelich, Baldomero Savans, Magín Fonoll, Abraham Caba, Ricardo Blasco, Esteban Bover, Mariano Anglés, Camilo Oriola, Agustín Casellas, and Joanquín Escalera.

The government could not ignore the advice of those sniffing out new victims and it was also getting ready to deport women and children.

The controversy that resulted from their deportation was tremendous—if their presence upset the regressive Carlists, it particularly delighted the liberals, who, despising the furor of the Ultramontanists (unfortunately there are many of them in Huesca), offered the warmest hospitality to the exiles.

A noteworthy article with a comforting spirit floating gently between its lines was published in *Diario de Huesca* and reproduced in Madrid's *El País*. We will concede the same space to it that we had reserved for the deportees' statements.

Could a more truthful and impartial perspective be contained in the pages of this article which the author Juan del Iriso sentimentally sketches out for us?

There was a bit of curiosity to meet the indefatigable propagandist Teresa Claramunt, and also there was something of that innate compassion which those who have been persecuted and suffered have always inspired in me, whatever the cause of their persecution and suffering—which led me to the boarding house yesterday afternoon where Teresa Claramunt was staying with her comrades in exile, Julia Iborra and María Villafranca.[5]

When I penetrated into the room, Teresa, pale-faced and

---

5. One of the earliest and most prominent anarchist-feminists in Spain. Claramunt had organized a women's textile-worker union in the 1880s, and became an important figure in anarchist publishing in the following decades. In 1901 she launched *El Productor* with Bonafulla, with whom she had a close relationship (see Introduction).

humble, was pacing back and forth, rocking a beautiful newborn child in her arms, Villafranca's daughter; she squeezed it against her bosom as she kissed the little exile's innocent, rosy countenance. That image, such caring and tenderness, made a deep impression upon me. I then remembered this strong, spirited woman's checkered life, a life of protests and rebellions, of fights, suffering, and persecution, well a life that would overwhelm another heart unlike hers which was so steely and manlike; and there she was in my presence, swaying the child so placidly and as calm as those exalted believers.[6] After saying hello to me, she left the little baby in the arms of its mother, and sat in a circle with her other friends, who like me, were moved by a noble impulse.

Teresa Claramunt began to speak, a woman who can be called a philosophical anarchist, who disseminates and defends her doctrines at demonstrations, in books, and in newspapers with the vehemence and tenacity of an apostle.

Nothing is as alluring and engaging as a conversation with this indomitable woman. Her accent is unhurried and calm; her manner of speaking is pure and correct. The words "humanity," "justice," "liberty," and "progress" flow from her lips like the bubbling of a clear spring, and in her eyes, in her dilated pupils, it seems as if thunderbolts are flashing, revealing the storms that quiver intensely in her spirit.

And in all of this, not one rude word, not one uncouth sentence, no irony, no complaining, as if none of her humiliations had left even a kernel of hatred or evil in her heart.

"For the past four days," she tells us, "we've been sleeping on the floor. They grabbed us and took us from our homes without even giving us time to say goodbye to our children. They take us to Huesca, and although it's terrible, what seemed like a punishment turned out to be a blessing because we've found what you can't find sometimes in towns that are known to be centers of culture: the noble, aristocratic hospitality that should always be given to foreigners, especially those who

---

6. Attributing "male" characteristics to anarchist women was common in this period (including by female activists such as Claramunt).

are in exile. Let people know our profound appreciation to Huesca," she begged me with a kind look as we said goodbye, "if you have the means to do that."

In truth, these words spoken in a sincere and effusive outburst from her thankful bosom, flattered my own sense of self respect; I once again felt proud to have been born on Aragonese land, this cradle of generosity, refuge of chivalry, but at the same time I left saddened by these social struggles that are gripping our nation. As reprehensible as they are, and as much as the excesses of the lower classes have been, it is no less true that the high born have not done a true examination of their conscience, weary as some of them undoubtedly are from their indulgence in delights and drunk with power and control.

The deportations continued en masse, over 200 individuals driven out by the state. The dragnet spread to other places in Spain where there was not even the slightest hint of protest. Constancio Romeo, illustrious professor from the lay school of Coruña, was exiled to Lugo after the school was unjustifiably shuttered. The honorable Torroella de Portbou brothers were deported, one to Fraga and the other to Boltaña. Their only crime was spreading their republican ideas. Samuel Torner, director of the school at Valencia, had to sail to Buenos Aires so that he would not die from malnourishment in a poor agricultural village.[7] The school was closed under reprehensible, false pretexts. José Torralvo, who was arrested and sentenced to deportation the very instant he returned from Panama, also petitioned to go to the Argentine capital. The anarchists Mateo Moscoso and Diego Martínez from Jerez, were deported with unheard-of brutality to the province of Málaga, as were so many others from various towns across the peninsula, who, as we have already said, barely had a chance to find out about the events of July.

The schools were shuttered just as unjustly. The number of closings in Barcelona was incalculable. The pettiest denunciation,

---

7. Torner was a follower of Ferrer and had established a Modern School in Valencia in 1907. He later reopened the school, which—despite being constantly targeted for repression—remained the most tangible example of Ferrer's program outside Catalonia until its final closure in 1926.

without any prior inspection and consultation, was enough. The obsession had no limits. Lay schools were closed same as workers schools, republican, anarchist, socialist schools, and even those with no political leanings whatsoever. The schools at Irún and Catarroja suffered the same fate.

It is true that none of these schools preached regicide like Juan de Mariana and other Jesuits; it is obvious that their benefactors have never set fire to any towns, violated any young women, or shot any children. What is certain is that no Vincent, exterminator of Jews, of industrious people, ever came from these lay or free schools, nor a Dominic, destroyer of Albigensians, as one celebrated writer ironically said, nor an Arbués, nor a Torquemada. Nor do these schools create rabid sectarians of the traditionalist caste who inform on people in a cowardly manner, who monopolize faith, and defraud the national treasury. But all this means nothing for the Azoríns with their mighty pens who see the crimes committed by these schools, crimes which according to these rabid Ultramontanists are that they show children books that are not so ridiculously juvenile, prudish, and repressive.[8]

And also, and this is the most horrifying part, much more so than what led to the closure of the school in Valencia and the deportation of its director—all these schools operated without the proper certificate from the parish priest.

And now the predominance of the Church has been reestablished. The civil authorities have been humiliated once again by sectarian fanaticism. Could it be true, as someone once said, that Spain is not a European nation?[9]

No, we must not believe in regression. The false Herculeses have flung off the howling beast: soon they will be attending their own funerals.

---

8. Azorín was the pen name of José Martínez Ruiz, a leading novelist and literary critic in Restoration Spain. In the 1890s he had been a political radical and appeared to support a range of anarchist ideas, though by 1909 he was a supporter of Maura's conservative "regenerationist" project.

9. A further reference to the "Black Legend" of Spain, one aspect of which is to deny that Spain was a "modern," "European" country, but rather a backwards, "semi-African" territory. The above comment may refer to the (almost certainly apocryphal) line attributed to Napoleon that "Europe ends at the Pyrenees."

Chapter 7

There Was No Leader • Sacristan Ugarte, Supreme Court Prosecutor •
Summons and Arrest Warrant Issued for Ferrer • The Arrest •
Letters from Ferrer and Soledad Villafranca • Police Circulars •
The Famous Lerroux Letter • The Defense Witnesses are Not Heard

The revolution in Catalonia did not have a leader; it was solely driven by the workers, and at the beginning of the protest against the war and the government, it was given encouragement, as I believe we have mentioned elsewhere, by republican, freethinking, syndicalist, and libertarian newspapers.

It is well known that the most important people in the movement were able to make it across the border to Paris and relay the details of it, the incidents, and the outrages of the general strike. Everyone knows that.

Also the false versions of the story that the reactionary newspapers and their acolytes made perfidious efforts to circulate have been rightly corrected. All these accounts lent the movement a degree of organization it did not have.

But how was it possible to do away with all of this without consequently understanding the causes of this now finished revolution and how it developed? Why insist on the idea that there was a conspiracy, when in reality the protest was spontaneous, a generalized expression of outrage?

Only at the behest of a fierce hatred, and in observance of a sinister plan can this spontaneity be denied. Also, while time goes by aimlessly for certain classes, that is not the case for the workers, especially for the workers of Barcelona, for whom the continuous revolts against government abuses and capitalist greed have been a university of rebellion and strategy, a means of providing the militant proletariat with simple, practical knowledge that puts it in the position to be able to act quickly and with precision, without the need for leaders.

We fear it would be irrelevant to delve deeper into this matter, and not because there is no more to say, given that nothing could stop the deep social upheaval.

A plan for revenge was put together, to which it seems Sr. Ugarte, sacristan and Supreme Court prosecutor, came to devote all his energies. In those days of his strange conduct, it coincided with the publication of the following edict:

> Mr. Vicente Llivina y Fernández, commander, examining magistrate of the Recruiting and Reserve Depot of Barcelona, number twenty-seven.
>
> Having left the administrative territory of Montgat, in this province, where he had been residing at his estate known as "Mas Germinal," Francisco Ferrer Guardia, fifty years of age, founder of the Modern School on Carrer de Bailén in this city, whose other personal details are unknown, will be prosecuted in the case in which, by order of the regional judiciary, I have been named the examining magistrate against the instigators, organizers, and directors of the events that occurred in contravention of the public order in this capital city last July twenty-sixth through the thirtieth.[1]
>
> In accordance with the jurisdiction granted to me by the Code of Military Justice, I hereby cite, call, and summon the aforementioned Ferrer Guardia to appear before this Court located in the Parque de Artillería for his charges to be heard twenty days from today, with the understanding that if he fails to do so in the above timeframe, he will be declared in rebellion, and all other rights to criminal prosecution against him will remain in effect.
>
> Also, in the name of His Majesty the King (may God pre-

---

1. "Germinal" was a term frequently used in both anarchist and republican circles in this period to signify nature and growth. Both movements were also admirers of Emile Zola's novel *Germinal*. See Litvak, *Musa libertaria*, 381–405.

serve him) I exhort and demand that all civilian and military authorities make efforts from this day forth in search of the above suspect, and if he is found, to transfer the prisoner using the appropriate security measures, and place him in my custody at this city's Cellular Prison.

And to ensure its due publicity, this summons will be printed in the *Gazette* of Madrid and the *Official Bulletin* of this province.

In Barcelona, August seventeenth, nineteen hundred and nine.—Vicente Llivina.

Three days later, Soledad Villafranca and José Ferrer, Francisco's brother, were deported early in the morning to Alcañiz (Teruel) and summarily interrogated.[2] They were accompanied by Anselmo Lorenzo, his wife and two daughters, Cristóbal Litrán, Mariano Batllori, and other colleagues from the Modern School.

The retaliation was beginning, and Francisco Ferrer, understanding what happens in Spain during periods of persecution, decided to stay in the country and wait for the dangerous atmosphere looming over his head (the work of the reactionary clergy) to dissipate. He knew that he had not participated in the events, and therefore, it was just a matter of avoiding what we unfortunately all know happens in the first moments of furious reaction.

On September 1st, we were surprised by the news that the day before, Ferrer had been arrested in Alella by a night watchman and two members of the citizen militia. He was transferred to the custody of the civilian government of Barcelona and then went to the Modelo Prison.

Readers who enjoy fantastic exaggerations will not see their novelistic cravings satisfied in our story. We believe that when faced with a firing squad, no human lips can utter an unserious word.

We must also be succinct to avoid repeating ideas and facts that appear in other parts of this book.

---

2. Soledad Villafranca was a former teacher at the Modern School, who accompanied Ferrer during his exile in 1907–09 and continued to promote his work after his execution.

Held incommunicado in the basement of the cell block number one, where it was cold, dark, and dirty, he described the 43 days he spent there before his military tribunal.

The following letter, written by Ferrer in his cell, will illustrate it better than the clumsy maneuvers of government agents.

Cellular Prison, Barcelona October 7, 1909.
To the director of *El País*.

Dear Sir: Yesterday, only six days after my incommunicado status was lifted, I was permitted to read the newspapers I had been requesting since my first day here, and upon discovering the enormities that were printed in reference to me, I rushed to write you this correction, begging you to do me the great favor of printing it in your esteemed newspaper.

I will begin by saying that it is not true that I participated in the events of the last week of July, not as a leader or in any other way. There have been no charges in the case-file against me.

And it is not that the examining magistrate has been idle all this time in search of evidence of my guilt. Firstly, he has had, by the looks of things, about three thousand prisoners interrogated in all of Catalonia, asking them if they knew me or if they had received any orders or money from me; none were able to answer affirmatively.

Later, a detailed investigation was made in the towns of Montgat, Masnou, and Premià, where it was said that I had turned everything upside down, and the authorities, the major taxpayers, and anyone else who was in a position to aid the investigation was asked about what part I may have played in these events—because the case file talks very much about an armed party, gunshots, dynamite, explosions, a tartana carriage that went continuously between Montgat and Premià, and some cyclists who constantly carried orders from Ferrer to the rebels. Everyone affirmed this, but nobody, not a single person could tell the magistrate that they actually saw the armed party, the tartana carriage, the cyclists, or heard the gunshots or explosions. Everyone said that they had heard it said.

Not finding, therefore, evidence against me, the magistrate ordered my house in Montgat to be searched again, despite the fact that it had already been done twice before. The first time was on August 11th by about two dozen police officers and Civil Guards (it lasted around twelve hours), and the other time, which lasted three days and two nights, was on the 27th, sixteen days later, by six police officers. According to the confession of one of the police officers, it was ordered by four hundred (400) telegrams from the minister. There will be much to say about that search, but this time the magistrate sent two officers and several soldiers from the honorable Engineers Corps, who spent two days probing the walls of the house and all the rooms, demolishing whatever they felt was necessary for their mission, drawing up plans for the house and the underground water pipes, but not finding the evidence they were looking for, just like in the two previous searches.

Not knowing at this point where to find this evidence, the happy occasion of addressing Mr. Ugarte presents itself. Since he was in Barcelona making a government-ordered legal inquiry, he asked the Supreme Court prosecutor how he chanced upon this propitious evidence, and he answered, so apologetically, that if he told a reporter that I had directed the whole thing it was because he was echoing a widespread rumor in Barcelona, in other words, like the people of Premià, he had heard it said. This was the magistrate's final diligence.

Mr. Director, what do you think about this?

Is this serious, worthy of Spain?

What won't be said of us?

I must also add a vehement protest against the conduct of the police. If three years ago, during my trial in Madrid, they behaved in an unacceptable manner, even falsifying documents in their eagerness to prejudice the case against me, this time they have done worse things, which will be revealed on the day of the hearing. I also protest that they have taken my clothes, everything from my socks to my hat. They have dressed me in other, humiliating clothes, forcing me to wear them before the examining magistrates (I have had two) and in front of the prison personnel. The last time I saw the magistrate, I requested, in vain, a suit of the kind I have in my house for the day of my hearing, and I was refused because my suits have also been confiscated. I could not even obtain a couple of handkerchiefs.

Another protest I have yet to make is that during my month of incommunicado detention, I was placed in a cell of the kind that is reserved for severe punishment, a cell that had such poor hygienic conditions that if it had not been for my robust health and my will that prevailed over all these human miseries, I would not have come out of it alive.

I conclude by imploring the directors of all the newspapers, not only the republican and liberal ones, but all those whose upright conscience and sense of justice is above all political and religious passions, to reproduce this correction and these protests in order to dispel, in part, this atmosphere which has been unjustly poisoned against me and to thus facilitate the work of my defense lawyer before the tribunal before which I will soon be judged.

Many thanks in advance to you, Sr. Director, and also to whoever will answer my plea. Sincerely,

F. Ferrer.

First, he was visited by the judge, Commander Llivina, and later, on the 6th, 9th, and 19th, by the new judge, Sr. Valerio Raso.

In his first statements, Ferrer was able to provide important details, now well known, that contradict his involvement in the July events, denying also that the circulars which the reactionary press talked about with such notorious bad faith belonged to him. It was said that the police had found them at Mas Germinal, Montgat, where the accused spent his summers.

Since these police circulars and the famous letter from Sr. Lerroux, written ten days earlier, were added to the case file as evidence for the prosecution, it would be good to gather them together in these pages so that some calm reflection and common sense will show they are actually rebuttal evidence.

CIRCULAR NUMBER 1[3]

Friends . . .

Friends in degradation, misery, and ignominy:

If you are men, listen: let the bourgeoisie calculate what abuses, what usury, what poison will be most lucrative.

Let professional politicians forge programs of all kinds—all of them lead to one thing, our exploitation.

Let the traders of the so-called *Unión*, false egoist saviors, be content with their hundreds of millions and promise to keep paying (at our expense) the clergy and the army, who enable their thievery and their fraud.

These traders, these politicians, all of the bourgeoisie are nothing more than a despicable minority. We are greater in number and better, but they exploit us, they sacrifice us, they kill us, and they dishonor us, because either we are not men, or we do not act like men. They think we are a vile flock of mangy sheep, and they are almost right because we have consented.

Fortunately, the time has come to demonstrate before the world that we will no longer be exploited.

Friends, be men!

The moment for rebellion is approaching. Rise above the shameful bourgeoisie and their ridiculous programs. Before building, we need to tear down the ruins. If there are any men among the politicians who are worthy of respect, a citizen who is popular, whether justly or unjustly, you will see how they will try to contain you in a critical moment, how, under the pretext of humanity and kind sentiments, they will put out the lit fuse. Well, don't pay attention to them. Kill them if necessary. By chance did they remember that kindness or humanity when Portas was torturing in Montjuïc or when Polavieja was killing in Manila, and Weyler was brutalizing defenseless victims when Cuba was burning?

---

3. Whoever did write this circular, its contents and tone were no more incendiary than material frequently published in the anarchist press of this period. As with Ferrer's trial in general, the main contentious issue should perhaps be whether publishing something like this should be given such weight in a tribunal for sedition in a country with a free press, rather than whether Ferrer wrote it or not (and he certainly wrote similar pieces over the preceding decade).

Let revolution come because it is as inevitable as bankruptcy. But do not leave it in the hands of a bourgeoisie that is as hateful as it is reactionary. And do not rest until you have taken the revolution as far as it will go. Without you, it would be as shameful as it would be sterile.

PROGRAM
Abolition of all existing laws.
Expulsion or extermination of the religious communities.
Dissolution of the Judiciary, the Army, and the Navy.
Demolition of the churches.
Expropriation of the Bank and the assets of all civilians and military members who have governed in Spain or its lost colonies.
Immediate imprisonment of all of them, until they can justify themselves or are executed.
Absolute prohibition against leaving the country, not even if naked, for anyone who has served in public office.
Expropriation of the railroads and the misnamed "credit" banks.
To carry out these first measures, a delegation will be constituted with three delegates or ministers: of the Treasury, the Interior, and Foreign Affairs. They will be elected by plebiscite; no lawyer can be elected, and they will jointly answer to the people.
Long live the Revolution!
Exterminate the exploiters!
Long live the Revolution!
Avenger of all injustices!

Note: Friends who wish to demonstrate that they are men, ask the person who gave you this for circular number 2.

Friends:
Before reading this second sheet, we remind you about the program contained in the first. Look for it if you have not read it. Let your comrades know about it. Have your children learn it by memory and distribute it as much as possible.

Ours is the only sincere, liberating, revolutionary program. Do not pay attention to those who say this is the work of the government, the police, or the enemies of the proletariat.

Do not fear that they will divide you. Only political-party programs full of gaps, hesitations, and bad intentions can do that. We cannot be any clearer. We need and want to destroy everything, and we say this with true candor. We would not lie even to our enemies.

Some will say that this is a negative program. True, but that is only because this is the first stage. The distribution of provisions and residences will come later, along with: the destruction and demolition of filthy neighborhoods—and even entire cities—that are anti-hygienic, anti-artistic, and supremely unhealthy; the distribution of land; and the popular acceptance of the revolutionary acts. These things are not accomplished by including them in previous programs, but through the supreme will of the people, through the joint efforts of the immense proletarian masses. This will be guided by the instinct for preservation—without these things, the Revolution will perish and set off a bloody reaction.

It would be natural for the thieving conservative classes to resist: what is incomprehensible is when the pariahs with their filthy frock coats and their dented hats resist, too, as if they were not also victims of the most irritating iniquity. These journalists, these employed workers, the unfortunates who stay up at night working to enrich others are more impoverished than we are, but they do not fight for their freedom. Let us fight for their redemption and for our own until they are convinced that militarism and clericalism are the two arms of capitalism, the executioners of men, the scourge of the people, and the great enemy of human redemption. Let us finish off the arms so later it will be easy to cut the head off the beast. Be ready, workers, for the hour is near.

The famous letter:

El Progreso, republican newspaper. Address: Montera, 51, main entrance, Box 126. Madrid, December 1, 1909

Dear Friend Ferrer: Since you know, albeit from afar, the bustle of my life and my struggles, and also, you'll remember the importance of your epistle, date October 11th, so my delay in responding should not surprise you, and you should not attribute my lengthy silence to disrespect or discourtesy.

It's a dog's life, dear friend, that awful struggle for survival, which consumes so much of our energies, and the great, noble struggle for our ideals, which is the breeding grounds for so much sorrow: these two struggles embitter my days. Please, therefore, forgive this slave to his daily bread and this miserable Sisyphus with his ideal.

I have read and reread your letter. No, I haven't forgotten; I still have a good, clear-thinking head on my shoulders.

No one knows better than I do what I am worth and what I can do, but you give me more credit than I deserve in reality, as is well known. I could never be a boss of anything or a political leader, and if it ever seems like I am the latter, it is because I go to the front, where the fighting is heaviest.

Aside from this, you have left out the true causes of republican impotence, which I will remind you of, though gently.

The party leaders have exhausted themselves, and their programs have become old; in consequence, the parties have broken up. Republican doctrines have not progressed in the work of making new molds. Everything has progressed around us, except these tenets. Analysis, science, and popular culture have produced ideas that are more in line with reality and the future. Republican leaders, in their quest for power, have succumbed to social tyranny and infamy; therefore, the people (by people I mean those who live through wage labor, without enough bread or education) have abandoned them. They, and every thinking person, know that the Republic in and of itself will not fundamentally improve the society we live in, except by accident. Well how do they plan to create the Republic without republicans? And the few that stay, officially, entertain themselves by debating if it's evolution, revolution, federal, or unitary! New molds, new programs, new ideals—that is what is missing. We seek out the people and we tell them: "Wage worker, the state, the rich, the priest, the soldier, and the idle judge live from you, robbing you of two thirds of the product of your labor, but we are going to end that. We want everyone to work, everyone to produce, no one to strike or live at the expense of another. Workers, we are like you: the moral equality preached by Christ is not enough for us, nor is the political equality preached by the French Revolution; social transformation—let us do it, and well, if we need a government, let it be the Republic, as liberal and radical as possible, but on whose flag, we will write this slogan: 'We will fight until people no longer need laws, governments, God, or masters.'"

There you have my opinion, and an outline of my ideals; above all, we must guarantee the right to life: let all work, and all can nourish their bodies and their minds.

I communicate this in writing and aloud, in newspapers and at demonstrations, every day and every hour. It would be easy for republicans to move forward in the work of winning public opinion. This is the focus of my efforts, and I am not asking for anyone's vote or a medal. Now, can I or should I launch manifestos? No, my friend, Ferrer.

I would be finished, ridiculed. A person who does not have financial independence, and who maybe has to rely on generosity to be able to survive and put out a newspaper, cannot raise a banner. I will not raise it.

On the other hand, the idea of a national subscription is very kind, but not very practical: in a year, I wouldn't be able to collect even one thousand pesetas. I know this country well, and I assure you of this.

What we must do is spread these ideas, using whatever pretext, better in the country than in the city; we must organize Committees, Commissions, Associations, Boards, whatever the case may be, and keep in contact with all of them, creating a sort of tacit Federation, and written agreement, of all the revolutionary forces. And one day, taking advantage of some situation, whatever shape it takes, to the streets.

Your good friend acts, thinks, and believes in this way. A warm hug, Lerroux.[4]

In the letter signed by Francisco Ferrer himself, we have seen the charges against him discredited with facts and reasons that leave no room for doubt. Now, readers, here is another letter from Soledad Villafranca on the police circulars.

Teruel September 15, 1909.
To the director of *El País*.

Dear Sir: After my release from prison and exile to Teruel in the company of José Ferrer and his wife, María Fontcuberta, I was astonished to read that certain documents were found during a search in Mas Germinal, one of them being a revolutionary manifesto that was published in its entirety by *El Diluvio* of Barcelona and *El País* of Madrid.

Present at the search conducted by Inspector Salaŝaray, which occurred on August 10th, was a Civil Guard lieutenant with twenty-one individuals at his command, including police officers and civilians, and the mayor and constable of Montgat, who spent thirteen hours scrutinizing, inspecting, examining, and moving everything around in the house and throughout the estate with the most painstaking scrutiny. After hearing the aforementioned inspector express his satisfaction with the work, which meant in his judgment the duty was fulfilled, I have the right to doubt the authenticity of the manifesto.

Confirming my doubt is the significant fact that a paper that should have been in possession of the magistrate and under an order of secrecy has been circulating freely in the press.

My duty is to tell the public about my legitimate doubts in order to counteract the effect on public opinion of what I believe to be an apocryphal document, clearing the way for truth and justice.

Sincerely,
Soledad Villafranca.

---

4. See the Introduction for more on Lerroux.

The days passed in agonizing silence for the accused, while the defeated clerical beast did not cease to slander and defame him in every nation, thus bearing witness to their Christian charity. Noting that the Teruel exiles who collaborated in the Modern School were not asked to be present in court, as they should have been, and since they had been led to believe that they would figure in the process as defense witnesses, they sent the following statement to the examining magistrate:

The undersigned Teruel exiles, finding it strange that so much time has gone by without us being called in as witnesses in the process initiated against Sr. Francisco Ferrer Guardia, and having been led to believe, when three of us were imprisoned in the Teruel jail for eight days, that we would be called, we are writing to you, the examining magistrate in this case, declaring that we know what the accused was doing during the time when the events in Barcelona were occurring, and we wish to contribute our testimony to clarify the truth and ensure the triumph of justice.

Trusting that our wish will be satisfied, and with sincere appreciation,

Teruel. September 28, 1909.

Soledad Villafranca, José Ferrer, Mariano Batllori, Alfredo Maseguer, Cristóbal Litrán

This was the state of things, and, while ignoring the defense witnesses, the government also schemed to hastily reward the individuals who arrested the accused, as if that would confirm his guilt before the magistrate could begin the proceedings, a repetition of what happened when the bomb went off at Carrer dels Canvis Nous and Cánovas established the law of repression against the anarchists before the judge could say who the perpetrators were.[5]

---

5. A reference to the bombing of the 1896 Corpus Cristi procession in Barcelona, which left 12 dead and 70 hospitalised. This attack brought severe repression against the anarchist movement in Spain and led to the infamous "Proceso de Montjuich."

The day arrived, October 8th, and it was announced publicly that the military tribunal would be held the next day.

As the tribunal was constituted, Soledad Villafranca, Anselmo Lorenzo, and Cristóbal Litrán reported the following information to the public:

1. Despite the fact that there has been an effort to accuse the Modern School of the tendency to commit antisocial crimes on the basis of its books, Ferrer's defense lawyer, who is persuaded of his client's innocence, has been denied a collection of these books.

2. It is important to understand and keep in mind that Ferrer was arrested because when he read the accusations in the Supreme Court prosecutor's report, he decided to give himself up to the examining magistrate of his case. If not for this, he would not have been arrested when he was, and the Alella night watchmen would not have received compensation for arresting someone who was headed to the train to turn himself in.

3. It should be known that before being sent to the magistrate, the prisoner was turned over to the governor and placed in a jail cell. His clothes were taken from him, and he was subjected to the detailed anthropometric measurements used for professional criminals, then given an inadequate, low-quality suit to make him appear disagreeable.

4. After he was taken to the prison, he was placed in a filthy cell, and 250 pesetas were taken from him, of which he requested that 50 be given to the prison management for his expenses. His petition was denied, and when his incommunicado status was lifted, he was not even able to send a telegram because he did not have the money, and there was no one to lend it to him. After being without outside contact for forty days having only prison food, some family members offered to bring him food, and this was denied. The prisoner was told that he should pay some nuns to serve him, but he did not agree to this. Also, he has been deprived the few conveniences allowed by prison regulations, having been placed under a regime of arbitrariness.

5. In their haste to find charges against the accused, numerous neighbors from Premià, Masnou, and Montgat have been interrogated as to whether he had taken part in any acts of rebellion or arson, all of them answering in the negative.

6. Prisoners throughout Barcelona have been asked if they had received orders or money from the accused, and all of them have answered in the negative, except for one individual who said he had heard of a certain Ferrer who was a politician.

7. During the process, the following searches were done: one that lasted twelve hours, one that lasted three days, and one that lasted two days. During these searches, some soldiers from the Engineers Corps demolished whatever they deemed necessary to obtain a body of evidence, but all these searches were unproductive.

8. As has been made public by the press, not only were the Teruel exiles, who could have testified in his favor, not called, but they were not allowed to make a statement before the tribunal.

9. Finally, not finding a single piece of evidence in all of their investigations, they turned to the Supreme Court prosecutor, asking for whatever evidence he had which could provide grounds for their legal brief. This high official stated that he was echoing the opinion of the people he had spoken to and considered these opinions an expression of public opinion, evidence that, quite simply, is neither reliable nor trustworthy.

Chapter 8

Long before the military tribunal began, the streets surrounding
the Modelo Prison looked strange.

Civil Guard units, Security Guard units, and various other
municipal officers near the building.

At six thirty, soldiers, officers, and other military personnel
involved in the extreme precautionary measures began coming and
going.

This coming and going of the guards contrasted with the few
members of the public who could be seen in the vicinity of the
prison.

In one of the prison's patios, Civil Guards were standing in formation, tasked with guarding the building.

Hours went by like this until it was almost time to begin the
trial, which, as is known, was open to the public.

Nevertheless, at that time, only those carrying a pass from the
regional captain general were allowed to enter the hall where the
case against Francisco Ferrer was to be heard.

At the entrance to the prison, a pass had to be shown and then,
a thorough search before entering the door.

The patio was teeming with guards. Until eight o'clock, the
announced time for the beginning of the trial, they were standing
guard against journalists and some, very few, others who had managed to obtain passes.

The sense of expectation at times like these is enormous.

Promptly at eight o'clock the Military Tribunal was constituted in the case to be heard and judged by the examining magistrate Sr. Valeriano Raso.

The proceedings were presided over by Infantry Colonel Eduardo Aguirre Lacalle from Mallorca, and assisting as members of the panel were captains Pompeyo Martí Montferrer, Sebastián Carreras Porta, Marcelino Díaz Casanueva, Manuel Llanos Torriglia, Aniceto García Rodríguez, and Julio López Marzo. Eduardo Lagunilla Solórzano and José Lojara were alternates.

Acting as prosecutor was Infantry Captain Jesús Marín Rafales from Vergara, while Ensign Second Class Enrique Gesta acted as adviser. Engineer Captain Francisco Galcerán Ferrer was the defense attorney.

Once the Tribunal was constituted, the public entered, mainly journalists.

Colonel Aguirre Lacalle immediately announced that the trial had begun.

There is absolute silence in the room.

The examining magistrate, Sr. Raso, declares that the accused wishes to attend the hearing.

The presiding judge orders him to be brought into the courtroom.

After a few short moments of wait, Ferrer penetrates the room. He looks calm, at peace, somewhat pale. At first, he fixes his attention on the individuals constituting the Tribunal.

He says some short hellos to the Tribunal and asks permission to sit.

Before sitting, he states that he had asked if he could have a dark suit brought to him for the trial, and his request was denied.

Next, they proceed to the reading of the magistrate's report, prepared by Sr. Valeriano Raso.

Ferrer pays close attention to this reading. He leans toward the magistrate and signals that it is not easy to hear.

The report begins with a retelling of the items found by the officers during the search at Mas Germinal. It is precisely the same items, the letters and documents, which we discussed in the previous chapter.

It appears that Ferrer is telling his defense lawyer that everything that is being mentioned in the report is so old that it cannot possibly have anything to do with what occurred in Barcelona. The presiding judge orders the accused to be quiet. The magistrate continues his reading of the report. He reads the statement of the former chief of police, Sr. Díaz Guijarro.

The statement of this ex-prosecutor and ex-chief of police goes over Ferrer's background, as according to the reactionaries, that is, without at all taking into account the Madrid tribunal's ruling which absolved him or the repeated statements of the accused.[1]

Sr. Guijarro's statement ends by asserting that he knows through a police officer that Ferrer had a relationship with *Solidaridad Obrera* and that he was in the offices of *El Progreso*, where he advised proclaiming the Republic.

After these statements of the ex-chief of police, other documents coming from the same source are read. They are Sr. Guijarro's attestations of statements made to him by a few fellows who are not now present.

According to this attestation, these fellows made the declaration to the then chief of police, stating that they told Ferrer what had happened in Barcelona.

"Good, this is going well now."

Ferrer, smiling, says this is all fantasy. He humbly asks the magistrate to read more loudly so he and everyone can hear, since this is about the charges against him and it is exceptionally important. The magistrate promises to appease him.

He reads the declaration of the mayor of Premià de Mar, who said that Sr. Ferrer notified him that Barcelona was in open rebellion and everything pointed to the fact that the Republic would be proclaimed.

The mayor adds that he answered that although everything was quiet in Premià de Mar, if the Republic were to be proclaimed

---

1. A reference to the attack of Mateo Morral on Alfonso XIII in Madrid, which left the King unharmed but killed twenty-four bystanders and soldiers. Ferrer was implicated in this attack as Morral had been employed at the Modern School, and though he was eventually absolved his Modern School was permanently closed.

in Barcelona, the same thing would have to be done everywhere else.

The magistrate then reads a communication from General Brandéis, in which he says that a certain Prene, also not present, told him that the reason Ferrer encouraged these events was because he was after a good stock trade.

Lieutenant Colonel Ponte, in another communication, adds to what Sr. Brandéis relayed from this certain Prene, that another fellow told him that Sr. Ferrer was behind the disturbances in several towns.

Ferrer says he cannot hear well and asks permission to come closer to the magistrate. He is allowed to do so.

At the petition of the accused, the statement he made subsequent to his arrest is read.

In it, he says what he was doing on July 26th. He had gone to several printers to deal with personal matters related to the School and his business. He then went to the Hotel Suizo; the "Maison Dorée," where he ate; the Hotel Internacional; and finally he headed to Montgat on foot.

Later, in Montgat, he found out everything that had happened, and that he was accused of having captained some groups of people. The painful experience of the Morral trial led him to take some precautions.

In response to questions he is then asked, he denies any participation whatsoever in the events, not even having been involved in the political turmoil caused by the war.

He says he was in Masnou, where he did not advise or even discuss the burning of the religious houses, and he did not advocate any violent measures to anyone, something that would not be like him to do, since he is in favor of attaining all social betterment through education, not through violence.

He then states that he should not or could not confess the name of the person who gave him refuge, maintaining that his intention was to turn himself in once passions had subsided a little, thus demonstrating the error and bad faith with which various people accused him of involvement in the events.

In his declaration, Ferrer asserts that he was headed to

Barcelona to turn himself in right when he was arrested, and that that was when he realized that the Supreme Court prosecutor believed he was the perpetrator behind everything that had happened.

The reading of Sr. Ferrer's exhaustive statement makes a great impression on the public. No question is left unanswered, and the answers dispel all suspicions.

Next, statements are read from the workers at the print shops Ferrer says he visited on the 26th, the owner of the Hotel Internacional, and several others that clearly confirm what the accused said.

Following these statements, some editorials are read, such as the documents described previously, which are known since they were published days ago in the reactionary press.

A letter is read from Sr. Estévanez in which he denies knowing the formulas he was asked for, and then a letter from Ferrer to Lerroux offering him leadership of the Republican Party. The context of these documents leads us to believe they were falsified.

A letter from another inquiry of Ferrer is read. He denies authorship of a revolutionary leaflet, and says that the one that was found must be one that was given to him and which he had misplaced among some other leaflets.

He also points out that the Estévanez letter was not written to him, but to Morral, who signed "Roca."

The handwriting experts who have examined the corrections made to the published editorial say that it looks like Ferrer's handwriting, but they do not dare to confirm that explicitly.

After this, a police statement taken by the Guardia Civil of Masnou is read.

Notes from a confrontation with two neighbors who accuse Ferrer are read, along with some other statements: one from the journalist Prene, who associates the movement with *Solidaridad Obrera*; one from neighbors who thought from the beginning that Ferrer was seditious, and they persist in their belief; others from mayors and other authorities who persist in their assertion that Ferrer suggested they rise in rebellion; and one from a neighbor who says that Ferrer supplied dynamite.

Ferrer smiles sadly as he listens to these accusations and watches the magistrate with astonished eyes.

Next, an interview published by *El Liberal* between Carlos Miranda and Soledad Villafranca's mother is read.

Ferrer smiles when he hears that the mother says she had never seen him laugh.

The smile persists as he hears that according to Soledad's mother, Ferrer's fortune had grown to many millions.

In reference to what was said to Carlos Miranda, Ferrer says, "She was only referring to rumors."

He denies ever talking about stock trades or having millions.[2]

Lorenzo Ardid stated that he was at the *Casa del Pueblo* on the 26th, and Ferrer came in and asked his opinion on what had happened. Ardid answered that the republicans didn't care about anything. And Ardid indicates that he left the *Casa del Pueblo*.

A declaration from Emiliano Iglesias is read saying that he has not spoken a word to Ferrer in a long time.

Other editorials and handwritten texts written by Ferrer are read, along with an article signed by Manuel Ruiz Zorrilla.[3]

Another statement by Ferrer is read in which he justifies his visits to Barcelona and Premià in detail.

He also energetically denies the conversations attributed to him, including those that imply he instigated the uprising.

When he was arrested, he was on his way to Barcelona to turn himself in. He reminds everyone of the fact that during Morral's trial, the police rewrote the list of suspects exclusively for the purpose of including him in it. Similarly, the police themselves could have planted compromising documents in his house while he was in prison.

---

2. Ferrer had gained the money needed to establish the Modern School as an endowment from Ernestina Meunier, a wealthy Parisian woman that he had tutored during his exile. Despite his claim in court, Ferrer did have a substantial private wealth, which he used to back anarchist causes and publications from 1900–1909.

3. A revolutionary republican politician, who had served as Prime Minister on two short occasions during 1871 and 1872–73. Ferrer had been involved in a botched Republican uprising led by Zorrilla in 1885, after which he left the country until his return to found the Modern School in 1901.

The editorials were written twenty years ago when Ferrer was a republican and was active in the party.

He has never seen dynamite. He has no idea how it works because he is not an anarchist and believes in evolutionary advancement through education.[4] He denies having been in the *Casa del Pueblo*, as Ardid said.

Next, several statements from neighbors in Premià assert that Ferrer said a Republic had been proclaimed in Madrid, Barcelona, and Valencia.

A confrontation between Ferrer and the mayor is read in which each of them sustain their previous assessments.

More statements from Premià neighbors are read, with Alemán and several others asserting that a man gave them money, and told them it was from Ferrer.

Other statements are then read, including one from General Brandéis saying that Prene's assertions were not based on having seen him, but on what he had heard that he had said, and also two soldiers on horseback, who were in the Plaça d'Antonio López dispersing groups of people, saw a man walking with a blue suit and a Panama hat.

The statement of a correspondent from *El Siglo Futuro* says that he saw Ferrer captaining groups of people, and he recognized him in a line-up.

Once the examining magistrate's long report was finished (naturally it aroused interest), the prosecutor read his report. It says:

PROSECUTOR'S FORMAL REPORT
Sr. Jesús Marín Rafales, captain of the Vergara Regiment, acting as Prosecutor in the case against Francisco Ferrer Guardia in this ordinary military tribunal states:

Being invested, undeservedly so, with representation of the law at this time, he comes before the court with no prejudice whatsoever, ready only to study reality, whatever it may be and

---

4. The conflation of anarchism with terrorism, and in contrast to education, is a deliberately misleading statement. Education was a key revolutionary strategy for many within the anarchist movement, and certainly more widely supported than individual acts of bomb throwing.

without regard to how the proceedings may end. Like all others who make up this military tribunal, he must be encumbered neither by the gloomy vision of these past events nor by pressure from the *vox populi*, even when it is further qualified *vox Dei*. With nothing to guide it except instinct, it lacks a rational basis on which to stand, though it may often be accurate.

The terrifying spectacle of fire and plunder engulfing this capital; the cruelest sectarian spirit pouncing down, mortally wounding the priest standing at the foot of his altar or plucking the flower of purity from the nun in the solitude of her cloister; and the most infamous betrayal destroying the forces of the army who should have been defending our national honor and punishing the murder of our compatriots on African soil—this could warrant vigorous repression, beating back violence in the streets with violence, as harsh as necessary; but since the revolutionary movement has now been subdued, a movement which, were it not the sole work of a few criminals, would have besmirched our entire nation, especially this region, and since peace has been reestablished and the courts are responsible for demanding accountability and redress for any laws that were broken and the order that was disturbed, we must listen only to the voice of the law's august serenity.

And this prosecuting authority, delving headlong into its duties, attempting to fulfill them as concisely and with as much brevity as is compatible with the nature of the case and military procedures, must first make an observation deduced from the origin of these proceedings, that is, this case, stemming from Commander Vicente Llivina's inquiries on the causes of the revolutionary movement and its instigators and perpetrators. This case is not about investigating the arson of a particular religious house, or the demolition of this or that bridge, or the disabling of such and such piece of telegraph line, or the people who raised a barricade and fired at troops from it. No, at its heart, this case is about going after the revolutionary movement in its hidden bowels, investigating the causes that gave birth to it. We are searching for those who created it, prepared it, impelled, or sustained it; we are collecting all the parts that comprise it in a great synthesis, considering it a homogenous, living whole.

The facts! Why go through them? All of you have been eye-witnesses to most of the events, surely the most serious ones, the ones that occurred in the capital city, and spread from there like a trail of gunpowder to the outer towns and Girona. All of you, or almost all, must have taken active part in the repression, some more than others, from June 26th, when the protest began, seemingly peacefully, against the embarkation of the troops to Melilla, until the walls of the churches and friaries were brought down, licked by flame or blasted by dynamite; and the shots fired against you from rooftops and barricades was rampant. Then the lugubrious silence of the defeated rebellion gave way to the victims' sighs, and the savages, in their orgy of blood, blasphemously proceeded to dig up corpses, while repugnant prostitutes came with their obscenities and hyena claws.

And with respect to these events that occurred before our eyes, do we still have to prove they happened? As I said before, all of us are eyewitnesses. The ruins of the buildings attest to what we saw, the shouts of "*Viva la República*" still buzz in our ears, and the facades of numerous country properties are marked with the accusing indifference of their bullet holes.

But what if in this revolutionary movement, it had been mainly women and young boys on the side of these militias who disturbed the peace with their subversive shouts and shot at the military forces, who splashed petroleum on the doors of sacred places and made them burn? What if it had been smaller groups of people who destroyed the railways and disabled the telegraph? What would they be characterized as legally?

Do the events of July constitute rebellion? Is there any reason they could specifically be considered military rebellion?

To answer bluntly, yes. To support our assertion, it would be enough to simply read Article 243 of the Ordinary Penal Code, which defines six cases of general rebellion, and Article 237 of the Military Code, which specifies four circumstances in which rebellion is no longer considered common, but military.

Article 243 of the Common Penal Code says those who rise up publicly and in open hostility against the government for any of the following reasons will be guilty of rebellion:

1. Dethroning the king, deposing the regent or regency of the kingdom, depriving them of their personal freedom, or forcing them to execute an act contrary to their will.

2. Impeding elections for deputies, senators, etc.

3. Dissolving the legislature or impeding its deliberation, etc.

4. Engaging in any of the acts listed in Article 165.

5. Subtracting the kingdom or any part of it, or any corps of land or sea troops, or any other type of armed force loyal to the government.

6. Using and exercising constitutional powers reserved for ministers of the Crown, stripping them of their powers, or impeding or restricting their free exercise.

It seems obvious that the July events fall fully under numbers one, five, and six of the above Article. They fall under number one because the shout of *"Viva la República"* and acts leading to the proclamation of the Republic imply the dethronement of the monarch and the replacement of the monarchy with a republican form of government. It also means attempting to force him to execute an act contrary to his will—to abandon the throne, unless this is the result of his voluntary abdication. They also fall under number five since by attempting to impede the embarkation of troops for Melilla, their aim was to reduce the number of troops loyal to the government. By constituting revolutionary associations that would proclaim the Republic in various towns, they would subtract part of the kingdom from the government, whether in small or large part. Finally, they fall under number six since these revolutionary associations, by creating new centers of government (if they can be called that) that were not tied to the central authorities, abrogated powers belonging to ministers of the Crown. Likewise, those who attempted to impede the embarkation ordered by the government in this city, abrogated constitutional powers belonging to these ministers.

Given that the events under prosecution clearly constitute

rebellion, we will delve deeper to see whether or not they are of a military nature. For this, it would be sufficient to compare the text of the aforementioned article with Article 237 of the Code of Military Justice.

The former tells us that for common rebellion to exist, it is enough to "rise up publicly and in open hostility" to achieve any of the goals listed in the six cases; the latter specifies that for military rebellion to exist, there must be an "armed uprising" against the constitution, the king, the legislative bodies, or the legitimate government, as long as one of four circumstances it lists are "also present."

Therefore, the difference is clear: common rebellion can exist without an armed uprising; for military rebellion, "armed uprising" is the *sine qua non*, and in addition, one of four circumstances it establishes must also be present.

As we have already pointed out, it was not necessary to demonstrate that an armed uprising did exist, since all of you and I have lived through its effects and had to contribute to repressing it within our respective spheres; therefore, all we have left to examine is whether, along with the armed uprising, one of the four circumstances of the abovementioned Article 237 of the Military Code was also present. And of course, not one, but two of these circumstances are present: the third one, since there were militias both in this capital city, in towns across the province, and in Girona; and the fourth one for having attacked the army after the declaration of martial law.

And now having explained the grounds for our assessment of the events, we will do the same for the accusations we have made against the defendant Francisco Ferrer Guardia, who is accused of leading the military rebellion. May the tribunal forgive us, since the copious evidence brought here with praiseworthy zeal by the examining magistrate requires that we have your attention for a short while.

To do this, we must first of all define the concept of "leader." A leader is a boss, a superior, or head when they find people, motivate, and direct them; when they become their voice; when they communicate the goals of the revolution; and when they provide and distribute the means to its attainment. If this is the nature of a leader of a rebellion, is it applicable to Francisco Ferrer Guardia during the events of July, according to the evidence in the case file? Absolutely, and we will demonstrate such.

We begin our prosecution in this sense with the declaration of Civil Guard Lieutenant Colonel Leoncio Ponte, page 26 reverse, who points to Ferrer taking active part in the movements in Masnou and Premià and telling his supporters to go to Barcelona to defend their brothers and sisters there. This military chief thought the Republican Fraternity of Premià appeared to be a headquarters for the arsonists and seditionists. Next, the journalist Sr. Manuel Giménez Moya—not at all a suspect witness since he was exiled to Mallorca for his "overexcited" ideas—further clarifies the charge, page 31 reverse, saying that in his opinion, the rebellion started at *Solidaridad Obrera*, where a clandestine meeting was held, and "where [delegates] left from" to go to various towns. He points to Ferrer and his associates from the Antimilitarist League as directors. Councilor Narciso Verdaguer Callís continues in this same vein, page 31, asserting that according to information he is unable to verify, "but which he believes is accurate," the events began through the initiative and direction of more or less anarchist elements, "motivated and guided by Ferrer Guardia" and a young language teacher named Fabré. Sr. Juan Alsina Estival, councilor from Premià, further elucidates the charge. In his first declaration, page 77, he confirms "the serious turn of events that occurred in that town after Ferrer came and had his conference with the mayor." The neighbors of Sr. Jaime Comas Alsina affirm on page 161 that "one hour after Ferrer left, the violence began." Sr. Valentín Alfonso, a carabinero lieutenant, page 162 reverse, indicates that after the defendant arrived, the events took on a different character than before. Sr. Adolfo Cisa Moragas and Sr. Pablo Roig Cisa sustain, pages 214 and 216 reverse, that ever since the "conference with Ferrer, the attitude of the revolutionaries changed." The councilor from Barcelona Emiliano Iglesias likewise points to *Solidaridad Obrera*, albeit in very vague terms—he says only that he thinks it spent more money than it had. On the other hand, a crucial witness like Baldomero Bonet, who is charged with serious crimes in connection with the arson at the convent of the Conceptionists, confirms this during the investigation of the aforementioned case, attached on page 370 of these proceedings. He said he believes that "the original source of what happened is in *Solidaridad Obrera*, and 'since they do not abound' in resources, he concurs with public opinion that 'the known anarchist Ferrer helped them.' This witness testimony is certified on page 371 of this case file with the addition that 'he confirms his belief.'" It is understood that "nothing else could have caused the events." The declaration of Civil Guard First Lieutenant Modesto Lara, page 210, follows suit regarding *Solidaridad Obrera* and Ferrer as its director, as does retired First Lieutenant Alfredo García Magallón, Artillery, who, in reference to a meeting at *El Progreso*, says, page 480, that the journalist Pierre expressed what he in turn had heard, that the July events were of an anarchist nature and were promoted by *Solidaridad Obrera* "under the direction of Ferrer as his project. As if that were not enough, Juan Puig Ventura, alias Llarch, tells us regarding this in particular (later, we will examine other details of great interest from his two declarations), page 24 and 76 reverse, that he believes Ferrer was behind everything, and that the excesses that were committed coincide with that individual's destructive ideas and his markedly anarchist goals, which are active in *Solidaridad Obrera*. Mayor Domingo Casas Llivre, who met with Ferrer, as we shall see later, was prosecuted for the events that occurred in his town. He indicates in his declarations, pages 138 and 305, that he formed the opinion that Francisco Ferrer Guardia was "the directing element" of all the violence that occurred in that region. Sr. José Álvarez Espinosa, assistant secretary of the Premià town council who also met with Ferrer, and like the previous defendant, was prosecuted for the events there, profusely concurs in this opinion and affirms his belief, pages 139 and 313, that Ferrer was the "true instigator and inspiration for the events of July."

Fortunately, we already have testimony evidence from fifteen individuals pointing to Ferrer as directing the events. Some of these individuals also added to the charges his relationship to *Solidaridad Obrera,* its participation in the events, and their mutual affinity, while others also discussed the monetary aid. Some point to the defendant's personal participation, using the events in Premià and the acts of violence committed there as their basis. These events did not take place until his arrival in town and his meeting with Mayor Casas, Deputy Mayor Mustarós, and Assistant Secretary Álvarez Espinosa of the town council. According to the aforementioned Sr. Jaime Casas Alsina, the acts of violence began precisely after Ferrer left, something like one hour later.

But there is still more significant evidence. The honorable Supreme Court Prosecutor says that the events in Barcelona and the surrounding region began with a seemingly peaceful protest against the war and the embarkation of troops. That is true, but it would be a good idea to go over these facts in detail. Yes, a protest began on the morning of July 26th and it intensified by the afternoon. However, we should note that this protest was never a spontaneous occurrence, not on the part of the general population nor on the part of the workers in particular. The evidence of this is clear inasmuch as the workers did not walk off their jobs; they were forced to stop work by the attitude of groups circulating around workshops and factories. The streetcar personnel, who you will remember have endorsed strikes on other occasions, did not abandon their posts for a single instant, and kept service running as long as possible. They defended the streetcars with true zeal, in some cases putting themselves in danger, only leaving when they no longer had the means to control the crowds of people who tried to stop them.

That same afternoon, as we said already, the events took on a life of their own, and just as the witnesses from Premià pointed out the change that occurred after Ferrer showed up, we can observe the same phenomenon here if we follow him step by step, starting with the afternoon of July 26th when he returned from the railroad station (since trains were not running) and headed to the Plaça d'Antonio López in this capital city, until the 29th when he reappears, having taken refuge in an unknown location, where he says he was secluded until the day of his apprehension.

In fact, the officer charged with tailing Ferrer, Sr. Ángel Fernández Bermejo, tells us in his declaration, page 481, that at six o'clock in the evening on Wednesday, July 28th, he saw Ferrer approach seditious crowds in the Plaça d'Antonio López, in this capital. At one point, a couple of cavalry soldiers there dispersed the crowds, and after this, Ferrer was found in a group walking toward the Portal de la Pau, finally ending up in front of Atarazanas, where he spoke to a group. He later continued along La Rambla. During a charge of the security forces, the officer lost sight of him, but then saw him again on La Rambla again heading to the Hotel Internacional. The clerk there stated that Ferrer had dinner, but he was not sure whether he would return to spend the night.

The declaration of a witness from Masnou, Francisco Doménech, a barber, fits together nicely with the previous one, saying, on pages 21 and 23, that at nine thirty at night on the same day, July 26th, he saw Ferrer at a café located below the Hotel Internacional. Ferrer invited him to something, and he accepted. From there, they went to the offices of *El Progreso* to see, as Ferrer put it, "what the fellows were up to." Later, they went to Café Aribau, although in his second declaration, he corrects that, saying it wasn't at that café, but at a different one on Carrer d'Aribau and Ronda de la Universitat, where they saw Calderón Fonte, Tubau, and Sr. Litrán and his wife. Ferrer spoke with them, but the witness was unable to hear what it was about. Ferrer later suggested that he go to Carrer Nou de Sant Francisco, to *Solidaridad*, to see if some of his supporters were there. He declined but Litrán went instead. Ferrer and Doménech later returned to the offices of *El Progreso*, and as they were leaving, Ferrer said he did not find what he was looking for, adding that Iglesias and others did not want to sign a document he had which was to be sent to the government. The document called for a halt to the embarkation to Melilla and "if that did not happen, they would make revolution, and the signers would stand at the head of the people." Iglesias had told him it would be better to go back to work. He also asked what forces he had to do what he was proposing. From there, they decided to go home, but on Carrer Princesa, they were stopped by two gentlemen, one named Moreno. Ferrer told him that representatives of *Solidaridad* were at *El Progreso* to see if they could come to an understanding with the radicals (previously they had declined). He asked Moreno to return there to see if they had reached an understanding, and Moreno said, "they were already compromised," and according to Doménech, Moreno added, "Anyone who is not with us can go to hell because we'll treat them like they treat traitors in Russia!"

These declarations attest to Ferrer's directing the events on July 26th, highlighting his leadership and his impulsion of the movement, but his significance in this movement, already enormous, is magnified by the declarations of Lorenzo Ardid and those of the soldiers of the dragoon regiment of Santiago, Claudio Sancho Yugo and Miguel Calvo. In a statement given during the proceedings against him, Ardid tells us, page 368, and again, certified copy page 396, that on Monday, July 26th, he was having a coffee in the *Casa del Pueblo*. When Ferrer came in and greeted him, saying he needed to speak with him alone, he answered, "any time, sir." Ferrer asked him, "What do you think about everything that is happening now," and the witness answered, "It's over. It's the kind of protest that can't go any further." Then Ferrer asked him again, "Do you believe that this cannot go any further?" When the witness answered more vehemently, Ferrer became quiet. Ardid then turned his back to him, went to one of his associates, and said, "Tell that gentleman," (pointing to Ferrer), "to leave by the side door right away," and he did so. The witness also adds that Litrán was at the table with him and that he suspected Ferrer was one of the organizers of the events. This declaration is of utmost importance, not only in and of itself, but because during a confrontation with the accused, entered on page 414, Ardid stated his account with extraordinary energy, while Ferrer, who, during his investigation, denied having been at the *Casa del Pueblo*, had to concede, saying that he did not completely deny having been at that location and that it was only natural for him to look for Sr. Litrán there if he wanted to see him. He also had to admit he remembered seeing Sr. Ardid on July 26th.

Meanwhile, with respect to the occurrences in Plaça d'Antonio López, the soldiers Claudio Sánchez and Miguel Calvo corroborate what was said by the officer who kept watch on Ferrer, Sr. Ángel Fernández López, pages 485 and 484 reverse. They say that at approximately five thirty on the same day, the 26th, they began patrolling the plaza together. There were struck by the presence of an individual who looked different than the rest of the group of workers. He was wearing a blue suit and a straw hat with the brim turned down in the front and up at the back. When they dispersed the group, this individual confronted Claudio Sánchez, and, pointing to the decree that was pasted to the wall, he said, "Aren't we allowed to read this?" The two soldiers' statements are incredibly important, not only for their intrinsic value, but because during three different line-ups, they both identified Francisco Ferrer Guardia as the individual they were referring to in their statement, pages 488 and 489.

In regards to the next day, July 27th, Ferrer had breakfast with the previously mentioned witness Francisco Doménech at a café in Badalona, and they returned to his Mas Germinal estate by early morning. However, it is known that he cannot remain idle, and he must have thought his leadership and presence in Barcelona was necessary in case his followers' enthusiasm were to wane. This is evidenced by the declaration of Sr. Francisco de Paula Colldeforns, page 492. He affirms that on Tuesday, the 27th, between seven thirty and eight thirty at night, he saw a group of people across from the Liceu Theater on Las Ramblas "captained," (pay close attention here), "captained" by a gentleman who looked like Francisco Ferrer Guardia. Although he only knew him from photographs, he became convinced that it must have been him because he heard people walking through that place saying it was. This group was walking along Carrer de l'Hospital. And the examining magistrate then carried out the appropriate procedures, page 483, and the witness identified Ferrer three times during line-ups as the person he had seen on that day in that situation.

The 28th is a day of extraordinary activity for Ferrer. He was everywhere, and where he was not able to be directly, his agents came and brazenly spoke to the crowds in his name, pushing them to commit the excesses that all of us regret. This is the very reason, however, that this day provides the most clues as to his movements and the greatest number of witnesses pointing to him. Perhaps this was why he began his day's work by having a shave in Masnou—so that he would not be recognized and could evade justice.

Francisco Doménech, who has been mentioned several times already, tells us on the same pages previously referenced, that on the 28th, Ferrer came to the barber shop where he worked in Masnou to have a shave. He asked him to find the president of the Republican Committee, Juan Puig Ventura, alias Llarch, to "see what he was up to." When Llarch came, Ferrer proposed that they go to Town Hall to proclaim the Republic, but like the others, he declined, thinking that Ferrer would put them at risk. Late in the evening that day, there were numerous unruly crowds of people from the towns immediately surrounding Barcelona who said that they "were waiting for Ferrer to come, but he did not show up." They added that Ferrer disappeared from his house on the 29th, and he was not seen again.

The above statement is expanded upon and corroborated by Juan Puig Ventura, alias Llarch, who, as we have seen, Doménech previously alluded to as a man of integrity who, despite his ideas, effectively assisted the mayor of Masnou in maintaining order against the interference of outside elements. In his four declarations (pages 24, 76 reverse, 136, and 457), this same man said the same thing without hesitation or retraction, and in his confrontation with the accused, entered on page 498, he was steadfast in his account.

So Llarch, after confirming that Doménech did call him on behalf of Ferrer, says in his declarations that the two of them went to a site that was unoccupied on Carrer Puerto Rico, and there, the accused expressed that it was necessary for that town to endorse the movement in Barcelona, to which Llarch answered that he did not think it was a good idea in any way. Ferrer insisted, saying he should "begin by exciting the people so that some of them would go out and burn the churches and friaries." The witness answered by saying he did not understand how that would bring about the Republic, and Ferrer replied that "he didn't care about the Republic; the issue was revolution." Ferrer then proposed that they go to Premià de Mar together, since he wanted to see Mayor Casas, and Llarch did not have a problem with that. Once there, Ferrer made the same proposition to him. When they returned to Masnou, they found a group of young people who had come from Barcelona, and they related what was happening there. Once Ferrer heard this, he said, "Don't worry, stay strong—we must destroy everything." When they arrived in Masnou, Ferrer once again began insisting on his propositions, and Llarch once again said no, as he had done all throughout their walk. Llarch also stated that he believes that if it were not for Ferrer, the strike which began on the 26th would not have had such sad consequences.

The meeting alluded to by the previous witness between Ferrer; himself; the mayor of Premià de Mar, Sr. Domingo Casas Llibre; the deputy mayor, Sr. Antonio Mustarós; and the assistant secretary of the town council, Sr. José Álvarez, was held on the premises of the Republican Fraternity in that town. To begin with, there were five eyewitnesses, that is: the four individuals who took part in the meeting with Ferrer, plus Calvet, the waiter who served them. Another two witnesses, Lorenzo Arnau and Jaime Calvet, accompanied Llarch and Ferrer to the meeting site. Another two witnesses were in the Baldomero Café and saw them enter. Their names are Sr. Jaime Casas and Sr. Pedro Cisa y Cisa. Witnesses Sr. Francisco Cahué, Sr. Juan Alsina, Sr. Vicente Puig Pons, Sr. Valentín Alonso Poblet, Sr. Pablo Roig Cisa, Sr. Adolfo Cisa, Sr. Jaime Font, and Sr. José

Canes, who heard the mayor's name mentioned during the meeting of that town's major taxpayers held last July 30th. Another witness, Antonio Costa Pagés knows about it from Lorenzo Arnau, who accompanied Ferrer. A total of nineteen witnesses confirm the fact. We will relate the story of Francisco Calvet in his declaration on pages 412 reverse and 477, whose account, except for a few incidental details, is consistent with all the others. He says that on Wednesday, the 28th, at around twelve thirty, he was in a room used by the Republican Fraternity on the building's mezzanine when two gentlemen came in. One of them was Llarch, and he did not know the other one, but he was wearing a light suit and a straw hat. This second gentleman asked if they could take a seat and ordered a soda and a beer, to which he assented. A short while later, Casas, Mustarós, and Álvarez Espinoza arrived and this unknown individual said, "I am Ferrer Guardia." The witness adds on his own that this created a sort of fascination among those who heard him, and especially for him, since he had heard such terrible things about him. Later, Ferrer added, "I have come to tell you," (speaking to the mayor) "that the Republic must be proclaimed in Premià." To this, the mayor responded, "Sr. Ferrer, I do not accept these words." Ferrer replied, "How do you not accept it, when the Republic has been proclaimed in Madrid, Barcelona, Valencia, and other capitals?"

But the importance of what Ferrer did in Premià is not only this. We have already listed the names of the witnesses who point out how the events there became violent barely an hour after Ferrer left the town, and now we should add that the same waiter, Calvet, indicates that another individual nicknamed "Casola" frequently entered and exited certain rooms of the Republican Fraternity during these events. Juan Alsina declares with moral certainty that this "Casola," whose real last name is Solá, received instructions for the revolution "directly" from Ferrer. He also maintains (and the witnesses Puig, Pons, Comas Alsina, Roig Pisa, Cisa Moraga, and Font Alsina agree) that during the July 30th meeting of major taxpayers, the municipal judge asked the mayor if he knew whether any of the attackers of the monastery of the Brethren of Christian Doctrine carried dynamite. When the mayor said no, the judge said he would investigate to find out who the municipal employee was who was carrying the dynamite cartridges, and if the investigation did not produce results, he himself would say who it was. The town's night watchman, Jerónimo Cardona, verifies the use of dynamite at the aforementioned monastery, declaring on page 476 that when the attack occurred, two very loud charges were heard, which sounded like dynamite or some other explosive, along with gunshots. And in another declaration on page 406, he states that his partner, Jaime Cisa, had told him that Ferrer was in Premià to take leadership of the revolutionary movement.

Meanwhile, witness Sr. Salvador Millet, page 364, says that he heard that groups of rebels had gone to Masnou and attacked the town hall on either the 27th or 28th of July. They also gave speeches from their balconies to encourage the crowds to join the movement. One of the orators said he was speaking on behalf of Ferrer, "who could not be there because he had to deal with the revolution in Barcelona." Aside from what was said by Llarch and Doménech, which we have already dealt with, the declaration of "eyewitness" Esteban Puigdemón confirms these facts. On page 473, he maintains that from the door of his house, which was next to the Town Hall, he witnessed a group of rebels, who were outsiders, arrive in Masnou on the 28th, and one of them gave a speech in front of a crowd saying that he had come on behalf of Ferrer, who was unable to be there.

Surely everything that has been set forth here would be enough to characterize Francisco Ferrer Guardia as head of the rebellion. At times, we see him leading it personally, as we pointed out when he was at La Rambla in Barcelona on the night of the 27th, while at other times, we see him setting the goals of the rebellion and recruiting individuals to accomplish them, as we can see from the presentation of his manifesto to the Committee of radicals meeting at the offices of *El Progreso* on the night of the 26th, his work with the *Solidaridad*

Committee drawing in others that same night, his insistent arguments with Llarch, and his meeting with the mayor of Premià de Mar. But I believe there is still more which should not be ignored.

I will remind you of the soldiers Claudio Sancho and Miguel Calvo—as they were dispersing the crowds at Plaça d'Antonio López, an individual in a blue suit and a straw hat drew their attention. Do you remember that they pointed out Ferrer during a line-up? Well, fine. Both the Colonel and Captian Ramón Puig of the dragoon regiment of Santiago state in their declarations, pages 486 and 487, that on July 28th, they were with their regiment in the streetcar yards at Carrer del Comte Borrell and Ronda Sant Pau. They detained and searched several individuals who had new Smith revolvers. When they asked these individuals where they had obtained them, they said they were from a man they did not know, but that he was wearing a blue suit and a straw hat. Doesn't this peculiar coincidence mean something to you?

Even more, the witness José Canes points out an individual nicknamed "Mamadits," who, during the events, frequently came and went from the Republican Fraternity. He would arrive by bicycle from Masnou, and would go back in the same direction when he left the Fraternity. Sr. Vicente Puig Pons tells of a gang of thirty men appearing in Premià, whom he believes Ferrer recruited. We will note that although he does not personally have knowledge of the recruitment, this must be the case, given that when people were asked where this gang came from, it was heard said that "They are the stonecutters Ferrer had sent." Sr. Jaime Comas declares that on the afternoons of July 26th and 27th, he saw several cyclists that people said were passing messages for the rebels, and they didn't know where they ended up going in town. Sr. Pedro Pagés references an article he read in *La Almudaina* of Palma de Mallorca, in which a contractor from San Andrés de Palomar, coming on Tuesday the 27th by coast road, was detained by a group. He recognized some of his workers among them and thought they were behaving strangely. They told him they would do him no harm, but they had to follow Sr. Ferrer's orders, as he had been there that morning and given them money. Sr. Bruno Humbert, First Deputy Mayor of Montgat-Tiana, the municipality where the defendant's estate (known as Mas Germinal) is located, says that from July 27th through the 29th, from the road in front of his house, he saw from afar groups of five or six individuals who seemed to be watching something, and they forced carriages and bicycles to stop. Finally, the worker Rosendo Gudás relates that he was fixing a door in Ferrer's house, although he doesn't remember if it was on the 27th or the 29th, and Ferrer approached him and said, "Rosendo, what do they think in Tiana? Now is the time to burn everything down."

This examination of the witness evidence must surely have seemed to you to be dull and bothersome due to the great number of declarations that it was necessary to analyze and the inevitable repetitions that exhaust the public's attention in cases like these; however, now that we have completed this examination which has confirmed the defendant's role as leader of the rebellion, I will briefly turn to studying the confrontations. Before we get to that, though, I will note a detail that stands out to me, which I believe will have the same effect for you: in this case, the number of witnesses who made statements during the *sumario*[5] came close to, or perhaps, exceeded seventy, and while there are some (though not as many as one might expect) who maintained that they do not know anything or have not seen anything, not one witness said a word or gave any indication of something that could have served to exonerate the defendant.

And turning to the confrontations, suffice it to say that the four that took place have had astonishing results—the witnesses have sustained their assertions with absolute firmness, in a way that rarely occurs.

---

5. The military tribunal is divided into three parts. During the *sumario*, the examining magistrate presents evidence, and a decision is made whether to move forward with a trial. During the *plenario*, both sides go over the evidence, and witnesses may be reexamined. These first two hearings are behind closed doors. Finally is the *vista pública*, which is described in this chapter.

The first one between Lorenzo Ardid and the defendant, page 414, completely discredits Ferrer's assertion from his second examination, entered on pages 195 to 201 of this case file, in which he flatly denied having been at *Casa del Pueblo* at any point since June. In a self-possessed manner, Ardid maintained that he was there on July 26th and they discussed the matters specified in his declaration. Ferrer had to admit he did not completely deny this; he remembered seeing him on that day, adding that he needed to see Sr. Litrán and it would not be out of the ordinary for him to go there to look for him. With respect to his opponent's other assertions, he doesn't deny them, either. He says he does not remember, which is not the same thing, and adds that it doesn't matter what was discussed at a café table.

In the second confrontation, between Juan Puig, alias Llarch, and Ferrer, page 458, when the former saw the attitude of the latter, blatantly denying everything, he said to the defendant, "neither your diplomacy nor any personal interest will stop me from speaking the truth." To subsequent denials, he responded emphatically, "I don't retract anything. . . ."

The third, page 400, was between the mayor of Premià, Casas Llibre, and Ferrer. Faced with Ferrer's denial of what he said during his interview at the Republican Fraternity, the mayor, in an outburst, says this sentence: "A person who denies the truth like you do is capable of denying the sunlight." In addition to what he had already stated in his declaration, he added that Ferrer said "that he could also captain a group, but his contribution was being reserved for more important things."

Finally, in the fourth confrontation, page 461, with Álvarez Espinosa, Ferrer tries to minimize the importance of the Premià interview, saying that the two of them left the conversation on good terms and shook hands. His opponent replies that they did not leave on good terms since there was a protest, but that that did not stop them from saying goodbye in a cordial manner.

And if thus the witness evidence points to Francisco Ferrer Guardia as the leader of the rebellion, the documentary evidence confirms it.

In an autobiographical article written in French for Monsieur Fournemont, page 191, Ferrer describes himself to us as a perpetual agitator and rebel. In another such article published by *España Nueva*, issue 16, dated June 16th, 1900, pages 372 and 373, he boasts of his participation in every movement that has occurred in Spain since 1885. Last and most importantly, he paints us a complete picture with these words: "I cannot conceive of life without propaganda. Anywhere I may be, in the street, in some establishment, taking a streetcar or a train, no matter who is before me, I must pass out propaganda."

These sentences might seem somewhat vague since they do not specify what kind of propaganda Ferrer is talking about, but in the documents on pages 374 to 383, it becomes completely clear—they demonstrate that his propaganda is unambiguously anarchist. If you doubt that, look at his handwritten announcement from 1892 to the Congress of Freethinkers. In it, he oayo that thooc who subscribe to these ideas should send their names and addresses to Monsieur Ferrer, poste restante, rue de Lafayette, who will give them the address of the executive board. He then adds that they should write three times per month, on the 10th, 20th, and 30th, beginning with the 30th of that month, and say one or more of the following things: "'I have one, two, or three, etc., more friends,' (with names and addresses) 'with protection' (arms) 'or without,' 'who are able to travel,' (meaning they can pay for their trip to Madrid) 'who want to travel,' (meaning they want to go, but do not have the money) 'with supplies for one,' (meaning dynamite)." If by 1892, he is already telling his supporters to address themselves to him and let him know what weapons they have at their disposal, does this not reveal him to be an organizer, a leader, a boss? In this document, as well as in the following ones included in the aforementioned pages, he talks of the creation of a group of three hundred individuals who will follow him and be the first to go to combat on the appointed day. He says, "We will find an opportune moment, for example during a strike or on the eve of May 1st."

Don't you see how this is perfectly consistent with what has happened here?

Is it any wonder to you that *Solidaridad Obrera* was described as supporting Ferrer, as you have seen in several previous witness declarations? He himself writes in this document, "We have relationships in the workers party and with other revolutionary forces."

In other words, this did not just happen in one day or one year, but it was over the course of many years that Ferrer has been laying the groundwork, distributing propaganda, recruiting people, and waiting for an opportune moment such as this one to put his plans into action.

The fact that he saw the right occasion approaching and "went all in," as they say colloquially, is evidenced by the two typewritten circulars on pages 177 and 179, the program on page 178, and the printed copy of the first circular with the program attached on pages 180 to 183. In the first circular, referring to bourgeois politicians and traders, he says that the clergy and the Army enable their thievery and fraud. Then this: "they exploit us, they sacrifice us, they kill us, and they dishonor us, because either we are not men, or we do not act like men. They think we are a vile flock of mangy sheep, and they are almost right because we have consented. Fortunately, the time has come to demonstrate before the world that we will no longer be exploited. The moment for rebellion is approaching; rise above the shameful bourgeoisie and their ridiculous programs. Before building, we need to tear down the ruins. If there are any men among the politicians who are worthy of respect, a citizen who is popular, whether justly or unjustly, you will see how they will try to contain you in a critical moment, how, under the pretext of humanity and kind sentiments, they will put out the lit fuse. Well, don't pay attention to them. Kill them if necessary. Let revolution come because it is as inevitable as bankruptcy; but do not leave it in the hands of a bourgeoisie that is as hateful as it is reactionary. And do not rest until you have taken the revolution as far as it will go. Without you, it would be as shameful as it would be sterile."

The second circular says, "We need and want to destroy everything, and we say this with true candor," then adds, "Let us fight for their redemption and for our own until they are convinced that militarism and clericalism are the two arms of capitalism, the executioners of men. Let us finish off the arms so that later it will be easy to cut the head off the beast. Be ready, workers, for the hour is near." And this peculiar document ends with the following: "attached is the recipe for making panclastite."

Regarding the program on page 178, true program representing the rebels' work this past July, we will only say that it includes, among other things: the abolition of all existing laws, the expulsion or extermination of the religious communities, demolition of the churches, expropriation of the Bank, and expropriation of the railroads.

It is quite noteworthy that in the second of these circulars, which was typewritten throughout, there were two corrections: the "*t*" in the word "*actos*" and the syllable "*ba*" in the word "*trabajando*." Having done a timely analysis, the expert witnesses affirm that the similarity of handwriting between the accused and the writing on the documents shows that these corrections must have been made by Ferrer. During his examinations, the defendant denied that the documents belonged to him and that he made the corrections. But isn't it odd that although he had the opportunity during the *plenario* to propose a new examination by different experts designated by him, he didn't do it? Despite his denial, wouldn't this appear to indicate an implicit acknowledgment of the authenticity of these corrections?

As prosecutor, I found it very strange that a man like the defendant, who gives the impression of having such foresight, would write a letter to Odón de Buen (page 100), saying, "It has been a while since I promised I would not go back to being a member of any parties. I ask you, therefore, not to use my name, since *it has to stay in obscurity*. Nevertheless, and I'll discuss this with you the first chance I get, I am always ready to help bring about the Republic." I repeat—how odd that while desiring to stay in obscurity, he would allow himself to be seen so much during the events of July, as we have previously demonstrated, thus allowing these charges to be brought against him. What could have moved him to change his behavior? Could it be self-interest? It's a mere suspicion, just a suspicion of mine, which came to me upon examining the declarations of Sr. Pablo Roig Cisa, Sr. Adolfo Cisa Moraga, and Sr. Jaime Font Alsina, especially the first two, who affirm that days before the events occurred, Lorenzo Arnau, who accompanied Ferrer to the meeting in Premià, told them they should play the market because the exchanges would go down three or four points. Of course, Arnau says that if he did say this, it was because he had heard it in Barcelona. But there is another declaration from Sr. Alfredo García Magallanes, who says that Piérre told him on August 10th that he had heard that Ferrer had played the market, and since in fact, the official share price bulletins attached to the case-file show a decrease during the events with respect to the previous days—well if you put two and two together, we would be hard-pressed to deny this idea.

Thus having shown the liability of Francisco Ferrer Guardia as perpetrator of the crime of rebellion, having the character of leader, let us turn to the attendant circumstances. We reaffirm our assertions from our provisional statement, in which we showed that all of the circumstances listed in Article 173 of the Code of Military Justice are present in this case. That is, the perversity of the criminal could not be greater. Consider the goals he set for the rebellion, which can clearly be deduced from the aforementioned documents on pages 177, 178, and 179—he did not just advocate ordinary political change, however profound it might have been, but true social revolution of an anarchist nature. Or consider the constant, early propaganda, evidenced by the documents from 1892 found on pages 374 to 383. Or the hypocrisy and depravity of spirit found in his letter to Sr. Odón de Buen, page 190, where he "wants to remain in the shadows," as he says, not so much due to a lack of ambition to serve or achieve recognition, as the defendant asserts during his examinations, but rather, it seems, to obey a desire to find a safe way to avoid liability for his conduct. Instead, encouraging others to action while he remains hidden in the shadows, as we have seen, is so pleasing to him.

The magnitude of this crime is immense. Just thinking about how the rebellion isolated this land from the rest of Spain and the world, and how the capital was almost left without electricity and supplies during Tragic Week—it would be enough to make us realize the extent to which these events have pervaded every sector of our nation, from industry and commerce to our private family lives.

The harm, not the hypothetical harm, but the real harm that was in fact done to public utilities, to the interests of the state, and to individuals has been so enormous, that we can truthfully, decisively say it was immeasurable. The public utilities were paralyzed by the damage done to railways and telegraph lines, and the chaos created by the rebellion made it impossible to remedy the situation in a timely manner. The interests of the state have been doubly harmed: first since troops headed for the Rif to avenge our nation's honor had to be detoured to subdue the rebels, and secondly due to the great monetary sacrifice that resulted from mobilizing the troops to be sent to this region. We don't need to even say how much our civilians have suffered. Statistics on the number of dead and injured as a consequence of the street fights speak for themselves, as do the murders committed in their name, the buildings that were destroyed, and the elderly, the infirm, and the children thrown out of their asylums who are now on the street, homeless.

And as we say this, we cannot help but also remind you that in this rebellion, along with the armed fighting, there were fires set, there was looting, and damage was also done to railways and telegraph lines. The Supreme Council of War and Navy has ruled in multiple similar cases, especially the one from March 30th, 1897, that while these are all common crimes, they are also intrinsic to the rebellion and share the same goals. It is true that each of these crimes had their own perpetrators, but they are unknown to us as of yet, given that the numerous cases that have been initiated against these individuals have not yet been adjudged. We therefore have no other choice but to confine ourselves to what is stipulated in Article 242, paragraph 2 of the Code of Military Justice and declare the defendant Ferrer

Guardia as having subsidiary personal liability, both criminally and civilly. As principal leader of the rebellion, his civil liability should be paid from his assets, even if at this moment an exact appraisal of the amount of damage caused by the fires, the looting, and the destruction of communication lines would be impossible to ascertain.

Therefore, having characterized the consummated crime as military rebellion under Article 237, paragraphs three and four of the Code of Military Justice; having demonstrated that the defendant is the perpetrator of that crime in his capacity as leader; and in consideration of all the aggravating circumstances listed in Article 173:

I do hereby, in the name of the King (God save him), and in accordance with Article 238, clause 1 of the Code of Military Justice, ask for infliction of the death penalty against Francisco Ferrer Guardia, with the accessory penalty, in case of pardon, of perpetual absolute disqualification. Furthermore, half the time served in preventive imprisonment should be credited to him in accordance with the Law of January 17th, 1901. He should likewise be liable for damages occasioned by the fires, looting, and the destruction of railways and telegraph lines which occurred during the rebellion. All assets of Francisco Ferrer Guardia's should be used to discharge this civil liability, insofar as the amount can be determined.

This is in accordance with Articles 172, 188, 219, 237 (paragraphs 3 and 4), 238 (clause 1), and 242 of the Code of Military Justice; Articles 11, 13, 18, 53, and 121 through 126 of the Ordinary Penal Code; and the aforementioned Law of January 17th, 1901.

Nonetheless, the Tribunal, with its superior reason, will resolve the matter justly.

The Defense

Next, Francisco Galcerán, captain of the Fourth Mixed Engineer Regiment, read his report, which says:

First of all, I should remind you of the circumstances in which the proceedings against Francisco Ferrer have unfolded. During the *sumario*, all his enemies made declarations. Any anonymous accusations that might hurt his case were received and added to the record. Opinions from authorities piled up, some having more, some having less knowledge of the affair. Anyone who could have illustrated for us details on his life, customs, and work has been exiled. Also, after the reading of the charges, I was denied the right to present any evidence as requested. I was not able to have witnesses heard because the legal time limit had elapsed, and now I find myself with a finished process, in which the constant zeal exhibited in search of charges against him was at no point employed in search of clarity. Instead, the opposing side, using many different means, has managed to tarnish my client's name.

But with this commentary that I am offering as calmly as possible, but in protest, I do not wish to indicate in any way that I am discouraged or at a loss for words as I stand here before you. These obstacles have redoubled my energies, and this energy has sustained me in this forced march forward that unknown interests have imposed upon me. Supported as I am by reason, as long as my faculties remain as strong as my will, I do not fear what may happen. The accusations will falter on their own, and as I do, you will reject this undignified pressure that has been placed upon us for some time to separate this case from the truth and reason.

All the reactionaries and the conservative elements—that group that pompously refers to itself as the forces of order, but perhaps which egoistically prompted the events of July—have tried to hide their cowardice during those days by vigorously punishing their opponents, desiring society's vengeance to be vicious and long lasting. Constantly, they bring up the events of Tragic Week in their press organs, focusing their attention on a mutilated priest and a septuagenarian nun whose modesty was offended by the rebels. They aim to transform their hatred into a noble desire, but they do not realize that as much as it may rise, such a repugnant passion can never be elevated.

This campaign is directed mainly against Ferrer out of hatred and the fear of educating the working class, whether through the Modern School, which they managed to close down a while ago, or through the series of books issued by the publishing house he founded. I repeat: it is out of fear of the enlightenment of the needy, the fear that they will find dignity and shake off their yoke, which is unworthy of the human race. To that end, they have mangled and then published certain paragraphs from books to make gullible individuals believe that they are only about anarchism, based on the sole fact that their teachings do not include religion (and religion should purge itself of anyone who cannot forgive and whose usual behavior is vengeance).

This campaign, directed skillfully in some cases and clumsily in others, has yielded fruit—it has created an enormously negative portrayal of my client, who finds himself in a noxious atmosphere that would be enough, by itself, to finish off an individual whose character was less accustomed to human injustice. There have been disgraceful accusations, which have been serious from the point of view of the police. Certain people must have had time ample time to ponder them while they bravely and voluntarily confined themselves to their houses during that week.

By the way, I must observe it is quite noticeable that a copy of the ruling from Madrid was not brought to the *sumario*— that tribunal was aware of this series of documents and Ferrer's activities before the attempt on His Majesty's life. If that had been brought, there would have been no need to complicate this case with a series of pages that might disrupt the dispassionate march of justice, pages whose purpose, it seems, was to contribute to increasing that sentiment which accuses Ferrer of being so terrible because of his ideas and his accomplishments.

That judgment of acquittal would have removed all importance from announcements and letters written twenty years ago, all prior to the assassination attempt, or it would have completely stopped any discussion of them, since they cannot be judged again without reviewing those proceedings. It is not possible, and it would be an enormous injustice if the same thing that was deserving of acquittal in another case was used to deliver a guilty verdict in a case that proceeded so quickly. It is not possible for something cleared by legal science after slow, thoughtful deliberation to be destroyed by another jurisdiction.

Add to this the small loan of a few pesetas made to *Solidaridad Obrera* when several of its associates were struggling against the abuses of the *El Progreso* organization, which, after maintaining in every possible way that the struggle of the working class would regenerate Spain, behaved towards its employees in a way that those it labeled exploiters of humanity could learn much from.[6] Ferrer had always been so respected and was responsible for organizing the Radical Party's schools, the only source of income for the *Casa del Pueblo*, something that is recognized by his own enemies. But this loan was enough for Ferrer to be declared an enemy of the Radical Party, which has paid him back with the most appalling ingratitude known to humanity, contributing to his enemies' work with their false informing and stealthy declarations. It will not take long to see whether justice has disappeared from this world.

In short, these are the elements of this anti-Ferrer coalition. United by stubbornness, egoism, hatred, and ingratitude, they began by having my client imprisoned, and are continuing, at this moment, their hateful campaign to make sure his innocence is doubted. They want to make sure he can no longer upset their plans through his peaceful, educational activity, that he can no longer loosen their grip on those they try to use for their bastard ends, each in their own spheres.

Has this environment been at all able to influence the honorable examining magistrate in this case? In my view, yes, it has aroused his zeal to the point of obfuscation. And in attempting to clarify the how and the why of these events, which the prosecutor has so masterfully painted for us, his aim (with the noble eagerness to put an end once and for all to the repugnant

---

6. Lerroux's *El Progreso* and the syndicalist *Solidaridad Obrera* had been in conflict since early 1909, with the latter calling for a boycott of the former. See Smith, *Anarchism, Revolution and Reaction*, 167–78.

scenes that have shamed Barcelona and have had such serious, frightening consequences for the city) his aim was to discover the head of the movement and disable it, bury it for good. To do that, he had to start from the unfounded premise that this movement had a perfectly organized origin; that it was led by people with advanced ideas, who by sheer talent have been able to spread and gain respect among the working classes and the dispossessed; and that they were capable of pushing these masses to carry out the most outrageous acts, the most unimaginable folly.

The magistrate and the prosecutor and the majority of those dealing with the events that have brought us here have not wanted to understand that the way this inaptly-named revolution unfolded. The damage done to inoffensive entities, and the incidents at the centers for needy children indicate precisely that there was no leader to direct the mobs. If there had been, they would have prevented all manner of excesses. If there were revolutionaries at the helm, they were not honored, and without honor, without prestige, without the moral force to be able to assume control, the leaders would have even found themselves aided by the powers that be, but as some deluded individuals and many cowards watched them falter, only to fall into the grimy, bloodstained hands of a few arsonists, killers, and thieves.

The magistrates have directed their enthusiastic and muddled gaze at those who, having ideas contrary to the current state of things, delude themselves with changes to our society's constitution, mainly against those who, having these ideas and these illusions, also have intelligence, education, and knowledge. Thus, council members and deputies from the Radical Party have fallen under suspicion; thus, my client is here before this Tribunal.

So do not be offended, dear members of the panel, that before going into concrete facts, I have drawn your attention to the power of this mania composed of such varied elements. If you'll allow me to say it, resist its pull. I have suffered so much disappointment these past eight days! I have been through so much disillusionment since Ferrer honored me with his trust! Either I must be completely deranged or there is in our society such immorality, degeneracy, such a dearth of noble ideas and an abundance of vile passions. But I have not lost hope in your rectitude, in your nobility of sentiment, and your benevolence, and despite everything, I still trust that you will pay close attention to the little that after twenty-four hours of study I have been able to glean from the 600-page case-file to refute the terrible accusation we have just heard. I hope that you will not rule according to the *vox populi*, as the prosecutor has advised (though to my mind, only that could have guided his report).

Next, the defense lawyer analyzes the witnesses referred to in the accusation. He deduces that the Premià witnesses lack validity, and here is what he says about the Barcelona witnesses:

Manuel Giménez Moya, an important witness according to the prosecutor "since he was exiled" explains perfectly well how Ferrer was a leader but "without the basis of evidence and only through a personal opinion" that the Antimilitarist League and Ferrer were the source of the rebellion. But he ends up admitting in his declaration that "he doesn't know anything since he was not in Barcelona after July 15th." And Sr. Narciso Verdaguer y Callís says, "according to information he has no way of verifying," that his political enemy Ferrer organized the movement.

Sr. Emiliano Iglesias says he does not know about Ferrer's relationship with *Solidaridad Obrera*, and Baldomero Bonet, who the prosecutor considers a crucial witness, does not give any specific details despite what was laid out in the accusation. He affirms that he has no knowledge whatsoever of Ferrer's participation in the events.

Juan Puig y Ventura, alias Llarch, believes that Ferrer was behind everything because of the sole fact—a baseless claim— that his ideas coincide with the excesses that occurred. Well, the court can see that this first lovely bit of witness evidence has now been reduced to two suppositions based on rumors.

Next, the defense analyzes the declaration of the barber from Masnou, Francisco Doménech, whose memory is so original that "while he remembers word for word what Ferrer said that night," he cannot remember what café they were in, and after taking advantage of what was said to falsely smooth over the differences between *Solidaridad Obrera* and *El Progreso*, he finds it easy, at the age of twenty-two, to leave the country of his home in a difficult moment when there is excessive scrutiny, perhaps so he can taste the fruit of his slippery tongue in a faraway land.

Let's take a step back from the prosecutor for a moment so he has some time to think carefully and tell us something that occurred on the 27th. In a space of 24 hours without noting the presence of the supposed leader of the rebellion or pressure from him to act, one might think that the rebels knew what they had to do, and they didn't at all need instructions from someone who was quietly waiting for things to calm down so he could continue his work at his publishing house.

Since the Modern School was now closed because of the pressures mentioned previously, considered an extremely harmful point of contagion, he is moved by his desire to educate through publishing. He founds a publishing house, and with that ceaseless energy that is so characteristic of him, he undertakes the publication of any books from abroad that defend the rule of reason against stale traditions. This brings him into contact with writers and philosophers from Paris, Brussels, London . . . and thus we see his sway over thousands of volumes. We see his publishing house grow in importance, and his misfortune is that it once again shines attention on him. Because of these advanced but rational ideas, his enemies return, and if previously they closed his school, now they aim to destroy him in order to put an end to these ideas. But they forget these ideas belong to a human being, and sooner or later, these ideas, this raging current will overwhelm those old, inquisitorial dams that will only be in their way for a short time.

The defense lawyer then explains that his return from London was due to the illness and death of a relative, describing the constant campaign against him, the purpose of which was to negate his efforts in favor of the publishing house, explaining, in passing, his short stay in Barcelona during the month of July, peripheral to the events. This was according to the declarations of several witnesses who saw him at paper factories, printing presses, etc.

He denies the validity of an affirmation by a Catholic daily with respect to Ferrer's return to Mas Germinal and the declaration of that newspaper's correspondent.

In reference to Llarch and the mayor of Premià, indisputable leaders of the Republican Fraternity there and in Masnou, he says that nothing illegal happened during the first few days of Tragic Week.

All of you must have read articles in the press stating that neither of these authorities, the one being a moral authority and the other an elected official, had opposed Monday's endorsement of the movement in Barcelona, and therefore, we should assume they were supporters of a very different legality than what we have heard. Of course, the courts had the same understanding—they were incarcerated and proceedings were initiated against them. Then as a result of actions and statements made in these and other cases, as well as the protection and influence of a certain character, they were granted a conditional release, throwing death to another individual like Ferrer, who is less favored, hated rather, by those with influence today, who were satisfied to see their favors paid back by neutralizing one of their longstanding enemies. Throwing enormous weight to his shoulders, he finds he must carry that burden alone.

He relates a detailed story about what happened in Masnou and Premià on the 28th, also presenting Ferrer's ideas with respect to politicians and his alienation from all political parties. Next, he skillfully contradicts the depositions of 19 witnesses from Masnou and Premià. He says:

One point has not yet been sorted out during the *sumario* which could illustrate whether the discussion between Ferrer and the mayor of Premià was a planned meeting or just a casual encounter—that is, whose initiative was it to meet? Why did the mayor voluntarily go to the Republican Fraternity? Was he notified by someone? Who was the messenger? I have not been able to find any diligence whatsoever in this regard, and this would have been much more useful than taking three or four declarations from Cisa, Espinosa, Comas, and Moragas on the same point, which may have led you to believe (as I was led to believe during the reading of the charges) that there were 200 different declarations, when in reality there were fewer than 50 interrogations in Premià. We cannot now confirm that this casual encounter was a planned meeting.

He highlights a few contradictions and ambiguities which cast doubt upon the declarations of the Premià witnesses, deducing, logically, that based on these witness statements alone, Ferrer cannot in any way be considered a leader of the rebellion—many of them were based on hearsay, while others were obviously biased.

Analyzing the events in Masnou, he argues that what occurred there does not have the importance it is claimed to have. Moving on to the documentary evidence, he repeats arguments from his opening. On the two leaflets, he says that although they were not dated, they have been brought over and over again as this overwhelming charge against Francisco Ferrer, and he remarks that maybe if the thick veil shrouding these strange circumstances were to fall away, we would discover other, more damaging things than these leaflets, since his theories are so anarchistic.

These leaflets were found during a police search, the only one at Mas Germinal where no expert was present, and the only one that had a favorable result. But these leaflets, which my client does not recognize as belonging to him, have such monumental errors that they show, regardless of what anyone tries to say about them, that they were written long before the events. On July 1st, there were no suspicions about them, and there can be no doubt that they were written for another day or another purpose.

These supposed leaflets, old and unpublished until recently, have appeared in almost all the newspapers in Spain. Writing these leaflets and locking them away in a file is no crime, but publishing them is. Therefore, the true guilty party, the one who should have been held accountable by the Code, was the person who scattered these destructive and incendiary leaflets to the four winds. They have been published despite the secrecy of the *sumario*, and I swear by my honor that there was no way they could have left the *sumario*, which means we must admit something extraordinary occurred before they were passed along to us.

Although I do think it is appropriate to draw your attention to this repugnant slippery slope, I would rather not go into it further, and in order to avoid too great a dust up, I will only touch upon two tangential points arising from the *sumario*.

First: some corrections found on page 29 (which was typewritten) have been subject to expert evaluation, and two young men are of the opinion that the added syllable "ba" and also a corrected letter "t" appeared to have been written by the same hand as some of Ferrer's letters, which they showed the court. However, they cannot confirm this categorically. This is very different from what the prosecutor claims when he says these corrections must have been made by Ferrer. I should also add, and you can verify this yourselves, that the "t" looks nothing like my client's "t."

The second point is a different kind of idea. That is that we should consider these leaflets as having never been published or, at minimum, that they have nothing to do with this rebellion. The examining magistrate has looked at several other cases to see if anything could be related to Ferrer's case, and yet there has been no testimony whatsoever showing that a copy or reproduction of these leaflets has appeared during any one of the thousand searches of rebels' houses or in the possession of any of the prisoners. This proves that either the circular was never distributed or that its effects have been nil.

In summary, Your Honors, Francisco Ferrer Guardia, persecuted for his rationalist ideas, pressured and harassed to the extreme, surrounded one day by accusations of abominable crimes, his schools closed, constantly insulted by stubborn groups of people—he does not give up or ask for a truce. Instead of presiding over the masses, he educates them. He encourages and directs others toward splendorous reason. He points out humanity's true goal. He learns the science of the wise and shares it with others—these are the true weapons of his rebellions.

And if we have seen in detail that he has not taken part in military rebellion, not as a leader nor as a participant, what would be the drawback to recognizing his innocence, giving him back his freedom, unfreezing his assets, and allowing him to embrace his family where they are exiled and tell them how justice is administered in the army?

I don't have to hide from you that if you were to grant my petition, our courage might be called into question, since those who are blinded by hate cannot conceive of justice without punishment, but it will not be long before we come to our senses, and those who are blind today will applaud your strength.

If, to their misfortune, the light of justice has forever ceased to shine upon them, keep in mind that the cheers of public opinion will cause sadness and inner regret, but the approval of your conscience will amply compensate for the public's scorn.

I ask that you rule on the basis of your conscience, nothing more.

Ferrer's Declaration

Asked by the presiding judge of the military tribunal if he had anything to add after his defense lawyer's report, the defendant made the following statement:

If it please you, your Honor, I will allow myself to ask the tribunal if you would be so kind as to judge me only on the events of the final week of July, or the days before, during which time someone or *several people* could have taken the initiative to plan the general strike on the 29th. I am completely sure that if you do this, I will be absolved, since I have taken no part in these events, as the case file shows.

I must also allow myself to observe that it would be unfair, in my opinion, if I were to be reproached today for my political activity from the last twenty years of the last century, although you don't believe any of it was sinful. And it would be unfair to reproach me for the educational work of the Modern School or its publications, which began in this century. And in saying this, it is not that I am refusing to deal with it. On the contrary, I would be more than happy to go before any tribunal that is charged with judging the Modern School's books. I am sure that I do not deserve punishment for having published them since all of the writings are signed by classical authors whose names are considered glorious or by modern authors whose wisdom or highly humanitarian sentiments are recognized. I conclude by saying that the people who criticize the publications of the Modern School either have not read them or they are not in a position to judge them because of their out-of-date prejudices, which unfortunately all of us have. I didn't have anything else to say.

SENTENCE

Having met in Barcelona, October 9th, 1909, to hear and pass judgment in this case, having heard the examining magistrate's summary of the case file, the accused being present, having heard the prosecutor's accusation and the defense, and in accordance with the adviser's report, this Ordinary Military Tribunal unanimously declares:

that the events prosecuted in this case constitute the consummated crime of military rebellion, as defined in Article 237 of the Code of Military Justice, with the presence of the third and fourth circumstances therein:

The accused Francisco Ferrer Guardia is considered liable as perpetrator and leader of the rebellion, with the aggravating circumstances listed in Article 173 of the same Code.

By virtue of the Code, and pursuant to Article 238, clause 1, the death penalty will be imposed, with the accessory penalty of perpetual absolute disqualification in case of pardon; and he is furthermore sentenced to indemnify all damages occasioned by fires, looting, and damage to telegraph lines and railways that occurred during the rebellion, with all the assets of Ferrer Guardia subject to forfeiture; and in the aforementioned case of pardon, he will be credited with half the time spent in preventive prison as a result of this case.

The above is pursuant to Articles 173, 188, 219, 237 (3) and (4), 238 (1), and 242 of the Code of Military Justice; 11, 13, 18 to 21, 53, and 121 to 128 of the Ordinary Penal Code; the concordant provisions of both Codes; and the Law of January 17th, 1901.

Eduardo Aguirre, Pompeyo Martí, Sebastián Carreras, Marcelino Díaz, Manuel de Llanos, Aniceto García, and Julio López.

DECREE

From His Excellency, the Captain General of Catalonia, approving the ruling of the Military Tribunal.

Barcelona, October 10th, 1909.

In accordance with the previous report and due to the reasons cited therein, I hereby approve the sentence of the Military Tribunal that has heard and passed judgment in this case against the defendant Francisco Ferrer Guardia, liable as perpetrator of the crime of military rebellion and leader of it, with the aggravating circumstances in Article 173 of the Code of Military Justice. He is to be given the death penalty, with the accessory penalty in case of pardon, of perpetual absolute disqualification, and he is also sentenced to forfeiture of all assets in payment of his subsidiary liability for the damages occasioned by fires, looting, and damage to telegraph lines and railways during the rebellion, pending establishment of the exact amount. In case of pardon, half the time served in preventive prison will be credited to the defendant.

Pursuant to Article 633, paragraph 3 of our Code, the Government will be notified of this resolution through His Excellency, the Minister of War. To that effect, the examining magistrate will gather the written prosecutor's accusation, defense, adviser's opinion, sentence, previous report, and this decree, and this document will be immediately forwarded by this General Staff to the proper authority. Execution of this judgment will be postponed until such time that a response is received.

✯✯✯

Regarding everything that happened, the universal consciousness affirms:

1. Ferrer did not intervene in the movement.

2. He did not provide money, given that the funds for delegates who went to various locations around Catalonia were collected from dues paid by workers at their meetings.

3. Ferrer did not supply anyone with arms. Some of the weapons acquired by the people came from attacks on armories and several loan institutions, requisitioned from neighborhood watchmen and infantry troops, from the veteran's barracks, and from those guarding supplies—all these weapons were seized through violent means. Others, the majority, came from night watchmen, vigilantes, and various police officers.

And finally, as one Barcelonan newspaper so aptly observed, if you reflect on it calmly, the only substantive evidence shown to the court was:

A bulky packet of books and documents, a Masonic apron and sash, several medals, leaflets, and letters.

Estévanez reminds us that Schiller, talking about Wallenstein, said, "No one since the days of Samuel, the prophet, has yet come to a fortunate end who had quarreled with the Church."

Chapter 9

The world has never seen such a magnificent dawning of something, which is how we should describe this towering, unanimous voice that announced the moment for solidarity with such apocalyptic ring.

This solidarity has been offered not only by the Latin peoples, but all nations of the world have been shaken, thus shrouding the victims of Spanish barbarity with a glorious halo.

Paris, Rome, London, Berlin, Vienna, the Hague, Lisbon, and many other European capitals, and all over the Americas, from East to West, they have raised their protest, which the passage of time will never erase, as if these protests were sculpted in bronze.

Some around the world have been paying attention to the popular movements in Spain ever since the war began in the Rif. After the events of July, when they saw the government's cruel repression and injustice, a government they considered responsible, so many exceptionally honorable individuals from all around the world launched a campaign of political agitation against it. This government did nothing to avoid the protests; very much to the contrary, it officially or unofficially began another campaign of insults and defamation in the pages of *La Época*, *ABC*, *El Universo*, and others, against those who had inspired the universal movement.

Even before Ramón Clemente García was executed, appeals had come from France and England to warn Sr. Maura's government that there would be further conflict if he did not contain his despotism. The Defense Committee for the victims of Spanish reaction, constituted in Paris, published a manifesto to this end.

When they learned of the Ferrer trial, the movement intensified, but, far from the streams of solidarity that unite modern peoples—who understand that when liberty dies in one nation, it threatens all the rest—Maura and his ministers' arrogance grew to the extreme, rejecting the intervention of those who abhorred his ruinous work from beyond borders and seas.

Parroting his Spanish colleagues, one reactionary aristocrat, the Marquis de Castellane, a deputy in the French Parliament, admonished this intervention, considering it an attack on international social conventions. But Alfred Naquet, a writer and elder, interrupted him with these words of a true man[1]:

> When it is about saving the lives of our brothers and sisters, we must not be held back by questions of form and protocols.
>
> The Spaniards who are living through the oppression of the current regime have placed their hope in us because they know we can speak.
>
> A letter from a citizen in Madrid says that our call to a conscious Europe has created deep vexation in ministerial circles, and that La Cierva, minister of the Interior, told reporters from the legislature's newspapers on the subject of our call, that if we resided in Spain instead of living on the other side of the Pyrenees, (quote) "if we were within his reach" he would show us what should be done with our people.

And the same letter ends with these paragraphs:

> The Paris Committee can exercise a profound influence on our government to save Ferrer and the other arrestees. Maybe the dishonorable individuals who rule us will back down in the face of the civilized world's verdict.
>
> Our words dictate our conduct, and we are prepared to

---

1. A French politician of the far left, who famously campaigned against misogynistic marriage laws.

violate international decorum for Solidarity, a sentiment that unites all those who are oppressed in a single desire.

The thinking and working world is as one, and dignity disappears where there is degradation and crime; therefore, we are obligated to cleanse these criminals' affront to civilization.

This call which was so imprudently received by the Spanish government began having results very quickly.

Delegates from all member unions of the Labor Council of Bouches-du-Rhône, meeting in General Assembly at the Labor Council of Marseille made the following resolution, among others:

To enthusiastically interest all conscious individuals belonging to all social classes around the world to carry out the practical action of boycotting Spanish industry and trade in order to use all possible means to compel the government of Alfonso XIII to cease its bloody and iniquitous repression and force him to release all imprisoned workers, since this is an attack on their most basic rights.

The Parisian Typographic Syndical Chamber, meeting in General Assembly resolved to publicize the following resolution:

Strongly moved by the danger threatening militant Spanish syndicalists, whom the government wants to do away with by means of imprisonment, torture, and execution, we protest against this barbarity and resolve to use any necessary means to put an end to this odious repression.

The General Confederation of Labor proposed intensifying the movement, and to that effect, it issued the following circular to its members titled "For our Brothers and Sisters in Spain"[2]:

2. The French Confédération Générale du Travail (CGT) was established in 1895, and adopted revolutionary syndicalism in 1906. Syndicalists in Spain were greatly influenced by this organisation, to the extent that the original name for the CNT was a direct Spanish translation: the Confederación General del Trabajo. After around six months from its foundation the name changed to Confederación Nacional del Trabajo.

Fulfilling the second set of resolutions taken by the Confederate Committee with respect to the events in Spain, it is necessary to organize regional demonstrations in all the main provincial centers.

To give greater visibility to these rallies, we encourage all Labor Councils to delegate as many fellow workers to them as possible.

The situation of our Spanish brothers and sisters is critical; therefore, it is essential to act quickly and with force.

We trust that all worker organizations will take stock of the importance of this political agitation work and will use every effort to ensure its complete success.

Regarding the organizing of these demonstrations, we have no intention whatsoever of standing in the way of the multiple and varied rallies that may arise. What we want is to demonstrate, by rallying in unison, that the French proletariat cannot be indifferent to the events in Spain.

Through a unified protest movement, we wish to force the Spanish Government to desist in its work of hate and repression.

It is up to all the workers to define the character of these demonstrations.

The following Labor Councils organized public protests and meetings with the help of distinguished personalities: Clermont-Ferrand, Montpelier, Lyon, Tunis, Narbonne, Avignon, Cette, Boury, Bordeaux, Toulon, Béziers, Nice, Limoges, Nancy, Belfort, Nantes, and other towns.

There were rallies in Paris every day. Innumerable respectable individuals supported them. Reporting on all of them would be too lengthy of a job for us.

A considerable number of people protested in the Learned Societies, including Albert, Naquet, Malato, Moreno, Fauré, Bonzon, Tarbouriech, Marmande, Yvetot, and Sicart de Plauzolles.[3]

---

3. Charles Malato was a prominent French anarchist theorist and publisher, accused of planning an assassination attempt on the Spanish King Alfonso XIII when he visited Paris in 1905.

Letters of support were also sent from notable writers Anatole France and Gabriel Séailles.

Over 6,000 people gathered at the Tivoli-Vauxhall Theater to brutally denounce the Spanish Government.

Orators from different countries took part in the demonstration held at L'Egalitaire:

R. Kocker, German; Tumarinson, Russian; Artur Gas, Spanish; Molnar, Hungarian; Em. Cipriani, Italian; Cornelissen, Dutch; Vas. Heyno, Bohemian; Ch. Roth, English; de Marmande, Social Defense Committee; Thuillier, Association of Trade Unions of the Seine; Violette, Jewelers Union.

The agitation continued ceaselessly. Francisco Ferrer Guardia was soon to appear before the military tribunal, but the Spanish political world was inexplicably silent. Meanwhile, the most notable event in Paris at this time was arranged by the young revolutionaries of the Defense Committee, who organized three demonstrations composed of a procession of sixty automobiles that departed simultaneously from the Luxembourg Palace, the Bastille, and Place de la Concorde, drove along the principal arteries of the French capital, and ended up at the Spanish embassy.

The procession was quite compelling and every automobile had a sign with thick letters saying: "There are still firing squads at Montjuïc! The monks want Ferrer's head! The Spanish press is stifled!"

When the police saw a group of these cars, they tried to intervene under the pretext of ensuring that carriages coming and going from Avenue de l'Opera could circulate freely, but the result was that traffic was blocked along adjacent streets due to the accumulation of automobiles, carriages, and the enormous crowds surrounding them.

Then the demonstrators began distributing hundreds of pamphlets with the first lines: "The Crimes of Spain. To anyone with a heart in any party and all classes!"

The police intervention helped set the stage for more propaganda distribution. The organizers were not expecting that. They were parked in front of Avenue de l'Opera, number 39 for half an hour, and the crowd swelled at times. Finally the police gave the order to move on, and the cars headed very slowly toward the

Place de la République, continuing the pamphlet distribution. At that point, they met another group of twenty automobiles, and the forty stretched along the great boulevards at the same time. Meanwhile, the twenty remaining cars took the Boulevard de Magenta to the Spanish embassy.

Some 800 police officers stepped in front of the forty automobiles, blocking their path. This created serious disturbances, and the people were shouting insults at Maura and La Cierva. The procession was led to the police station, and after the demonstrators were interrogated, they were released. After this maneuver, the authorities could see that the crowd which had gathered along the major boulevards dispersed, moving to the Boulevard de Courcelles, where the Spanish embassy is located at number 34.

Early in the evening, when the demonstration was much larger, a yellow automobile appeared at full speed and stopped in front of the embassy. It was showing off the sign that we described earlier. Occupying the car were Malato and Lefebvre from the Committee, who the police captains ordered to leave. There were some collisions, and the worst part of the police were carried away. Around one hundred were arrested and later released.

In all the other European capitals, the protest movement was extraordinary.

In England, the National Council of the Independent Labour Party approved the following resolution:

> The National Council of the ILP manifests all of its horror and indignation at the policies of the Spanish Government, which has shut down the democratic press, prohibited demonstrations in favor of peace, mass incarcerated workers, including women and children without taking into consideration their non-participation in the events of July. It dictates the decisions of the courts, arbitrarily tries militants in military tribunals and locks them away in prisons where they are subject to ill-treatment.
>
> The National Council of the ILP trusts that all civilized governments will launch an immediate diplomatic intervention in favor of all of humankind.

It also published a call to all workers in Great Britain encouraging them to hold meetings in industrial cities and agricultural centers. In Sheffield and Liverpool, these meetings were very large.

The Morning Leader, a Ministerial daily; Reynold's, a radical paper; and John Bull, an independent paper, began an active campaign against the conduct of the Spanish Government.

In London's Mile End district, a gigantic demonstration was organized by the Federation of Freethinkers and the Nationalist Association.

Thirty-three Labour Party deputies protested in Parliament.

A conservative newspaper, The Sheffield Daily Telegraph, protested against El Mundo, La Correspondencia de España, La Época, and ABC for helping justify the atrocities of the Spanish reaction and fueling exaggerations of atrocities which the revolutionaries never carried out. The following French publications also joined the abovementioned newspapers in their extremely noble work, which continued every day as soon as the Spanish reaction began: Le Radical, Le Rappel, La Petite République, L'Action, L'Intransigente, L'Humanité, La Guerre Sociale, La Libertaire, Les Temps Nouveaux, L'Anarchie, all of the Parisian newspapers, and La Depêche from Toulouse.

In Italy, the demonstrations took on a solemn character, especially in Rome, where most of the authorities did not object to contributing to such a just cause. They established a General Solidarity Committee supported by numerous subcommittees which carried on the agitation work in the Italian provinces. The League for Rationalist Childhood Education published a stern manifesto inviting all free individuals to join them, along with all the associations created to defend and spread liberty in thinking and action.

In Belgium, besides the demonstrations in Brussels that were attended by university professors and deputies, several committees were constituted, including in the capital, in Anvers, Charleroi, and Ruan.

In Germany, the Socialist Party unanimously declared their indignation during their General Assemblies.

Amsterdam, The Hague, and Rotterdam (Holland) contributed to this movement with numerous demonstrations, also issuing 20,000 copies of a leaflet outlining the Spanish Government's conduct, which it distributed in other Dutch towns.

The Swiss were not indifferent, either. A Committee was formed in Geneva that began its work with a call to all social classes. It said: "All those who have been moved by the martyrs of the Spanish proletariat, all those who feel the ignominies of reaction in their heart, join us in protesting just as our brothers and sisters in France, Belgium, Germany, and Italy have done and continue doing."

Large public events were held there.

The republicans of Lisbon, Portugal issued the following protest message signed by 8,136 individuals:

Profoundly and painfully moved by recent events in Catalonia, we who dream of attaining a society in which liberty is not just an illusion and justice is more than disguised iniquity, we who are outraged by every injustice and all oppression, we who show solidarity alongside others who share our outrage—we cannot remain silent in the face of the brutal and iniquitous repression of the Spanish rulers; if we did, we would consider ourselves in a way complicit in the iniquities against government justice.

We would like to protest, loudly, against the violence of the repression, against the mass prisons, and against the unenlightened school closures and the persecution of teachers.

We would like to protest against the imprisonment of Francisco Ferrer, who, because of the social education work he has done with such intelligence and tenacity, is the principal target for the hatred of those who feel their privileges threatened by his emancipation work.

And we who would like our protest to be used in the best way possible, have resolved that you who are one of the most glorious representatives of educated Spain, you who have translated, with such beauty and intensity, the suffering caused by a most imperfect society as well as the most generous, elevated human sentiments—we have resolved that you should use our names as you see fit and we are certain there is no one better to use them in the defense of liberty and justice.[4]

In addition to the above message, the workers associations of the Kingdom of Portugal also carried out political agitation to likewise protest against the atrocities.

This beautiful solidarity also became extremely important in Buenos Aires and other towns in Argentina, and they also made their outrage at the Jesuitical Spanish government known in Montevideo, Cuba, Brazil, Concepción (Paraguay), Chile, and Peru.

A shudder of horror came over these demonstrations.

The Times, an accredited newspaper published in London, published the following note:

> Madrid, October 13th, 12:30 a.m. The Council of Ministers has examined the sentence against Francisco Ferrer.
>
> No reason was found to advise a royal pardon.

It is believed the sentence will be carried out within a few hours.

Immediately, various points in Spain were sent telegraphs from many capitals asking for concrete news. The only response that was obtained was this laconic telegram:

> Due to censorship, the solicited information cannot be provided.

The impression this created was indescribable. Hundreds of petitions asking for clemency were sent to the Spanish press and the King's government. Telegraph and telephone offices buzzed across many nations as people learned the news that the execution was close at hand.

Fearing sadly that such a thing was close, the news produced loud demonstration before the Spanish embassies in Paris, Rome,

---

4.   [Author's note] This was sent to the director of *El País*, Madrid.

London, Turin, Livorno, Vienna, Berlin, Brussels, Ghent, and other points, which we will succinctly recount elsewhere.

Chapter 10

From Prison to the Castle • Ferrer in the Chapel •
Ferrer's Testament • To the Moat • Execution •
Long Live the Modern School!

At three o'clock in the morning on the 11th, the prisoner Francisco
Ferrer Guardia was transferred from the Modelo Prison to
Montjuïc Castle.

The transfer was carried out with Sr. Ferrer locked in a prison
carriage guarded by a unit of twenty Civil Guards.

The news did not become known until very late in the evening,
and even so, officials would not confirm it. Censorship interrupted
telephone and telegraph communication by the press, which
increased the sense of alarm—exactly what the authorities wanted
to avoid.

When he arrived at the castle, he was housed in a well-furnished
wing of the building. It was clean and well ventilated.

At seven o'clock in the evening, the examining magistrate came
in to read him the sentence. Ferrer was imperturbable, so extraor-
dinarily serene that it made an impression on the military judge.

He refused to sign the sentence.

At eight o'clock in the evening, the Montjuïc Castle chaplain,
Sr. Eloy Hernández, went to the chapel.

A captain, assistant to the general, the castle's governor, let
Francisco Ferrer know just before he entered the chapel that he
would accompany him until it was time to carry out the sentence.

The reverend, Eloy Hernández, said to Francisco Ferrer as he
entered the chapel that he supposed he already knew the sad mission that was his duty. Francisco Ferrer asked the reverend, Eloy

Hernández, to leave, very politely, since he was in the mood to write and was accustomed to writing in solitude. "Your presence— which pleases me very much—would distract me. So I am asking you to take your leave and please forgive any irritation that my apparent discourtesy might cause you." The reverend Eloy Hernández answered Francisco Ferrer that the castle's regulations obliged him to be by his side. "I will make sure not to bother or distract you," the reverend Hernández said to him. "I'll go to the other side of the chapel, and you'll have peace and quiet to write."

Francisco Ferrer insisted very politely that he wanted the chaplain to leave the chapel entirely.

Since Ferrer insisted, the chaplain told him that to fulfill his duty, he would leave the chapel and come in every half hour and freely supply him with any corporeal support that might be necessary.

Shortly after the chaplain left, Ferrer was visited by the captain assistant to the military governor, Sr. Parga, and several officers from the Constitution Regiment, which was then stationed at the castle.

Ferrer appeared satisfied at the presence of the supervisor and the officers and conversed with them for a long while, explaining the structure of the Modern School in detail.

After Ferrer wrote some letters on fifteen or twenty sheets of paper (which was given to him by the secretary, Commander Dionisio Terol Orozco, and authorized by the governor, General Fernando Parga) he asked for the senior member of the Notaries' Association so he could write his will.

The notary, Sr. Permanyer, arrived at Montjuïc at ten thirty and spent six and a half hours performing his duty.

At close to two in the morning, the notary and the prisoner took a break from their work to rest for a few minutes, and after Francisco Ferrer finished a cigarette, he told Sr. Permanyer they could continue. The member of the Notaries' Association left the fort shortly at five o'clock in the morning.

The prisoner then continued writing his letters, saying goodbye to his friends and intimate associates.

The main clauses of the will were as follows:

I am protesting as vigorously as possible, first and foremost, against the inexplicable situation I have been placed in and the penalty that will be applied to me. I am completely innocent and firmly convinced that in a very short while, my innocence will be publicly recognized.

I hope that on no occasion, not in the near future or later, will demonstrations of a political or religious nature be organized at the site of my remains. I believe the time spent worrying about the dead could be put to better use improving the conditions of the living, who find themselves in such need.

With respect to my remains, I find it deplorable that there are no crematories in this city like in Milan, Paris, and so many other centers; I would have asked for my body to be cremated. For hygienic reasons, let us pledge to make sure that cemeteries soon disappear and are replaced by crematories or any other facility that allows for the fast elimination of corpses.

I also hope my friends will not talk about me too little or too much, since that is how we come to create idols, which later becomes an obstacle to progress. One's ideas are taken to be intangible precepts, and this is unfortunate for the future. A man's ideas should be debated, and before applying them, they must be studied to see whether they are good or bad.

Later, Ferrer stipulated the following:

He designates his brother José as sole heir of his assets, with Mr. William Heaford, secretary of the Association of Freethinkers, from London, and Cristóbal Litrán, his secretary and director of his publishing house, from Barcelona, as executors of his estate.

Ferrer Guardia states he will leave six thousand francs to each of his three daughters, Trinidad, Paz, and Sol, since that is the smallest amount the law obliges him to provide to them. At the same time, he asks his three daughters not to touch this money and to deposit it in a fund for the continuation of his work, since he owes his inheritance to mademoiselle Meunier, who had left him the money so he could promote his ideas.

In this regard, Ferrer Guardia protests against what had been said accusing him of having abused Mlle. Meunier's trust so she would make him her heir. He then explains that this money was used to open lay schools, as per his agreement with the deceased. He leaves Soledad Villafranca a modest sum that would allow her to support herself.

He leaves his publishing houses in Barcelona and Paris, as well as some cash, and property, etc. to Monsieur Lorenzo Portet, with the condition that this should be used to continue his educational work.

If his daughters; his son, Leopoldo Ronald, better known as Riego; or Soledad Villafranca find themselves living in poverty, Ferrer Guardia asks M. Portet to assist them.

He asks him to especially look after Trinidad, since he says the others have a lifestyle that is not compatible with his way of thinking.

Finally, Ferrer Guardia instructs Lorenzo Portet in his will on what works he should have translated immediately and what other works should be published.

Among the publications that should be printed first are the first three volumes of the *Encyclopedia of Higher Popular Education* (*The Evolution of the Worlds*, *The Story of the Earth*, and *The Origin of Life*); *The Great French Revolution, 1789-1793*, by Kropotkin; *How the Mind is Shaped* by Doctor Toulouse; and five other volumes that were brought from England and notated in his own handwriting.

He says a weekly newspaper dedicated exclusively to rational education and syndicalism in education should be published as soon as possible. The Modern School's work will be announced in this publication.

Ferrer Guardia advises his friend to go Germany and Italy as soon as he can to obtain good textbooks there, something he himself was intending to do given the results of his investigations in England.

Once the will was finished, the notary and the prisoner started a conversation on religious matters. Sr. Permanyer asked Ferrer:

"Don't you believe that something else exists beyond this life?"

"No, señor. I believe everything ends here. Everything is finished when a person's life ends. As soon as I became convinced of that, everything I did was shaped by that.

The friendly conversation between the prisoner and the notary continued, and Sr. Permanyer brought up Ferrer's childhood. In reminiscing, he tried to awaken some religious sentiments, also evoking the good memory of the prisoner's mother.

Ferrer cut him off, saying:

"Yes, indeed, my good mother educated me in the Catholic religion. But my mind belonged to me, and by meditating on life and studying books, I became convinced that this was a mistake, and I hurried to correct that."

Next, using very short sentences, Ferrer firmly professed rationalist principles and offered sober praise of the Modern School that he founded.

At around five o'clock in the morning, a company from the Vergara Regiment began its march to the fort. A short while later, two squadrons of the Montesa Cavalry Regiment followed these forces. At six o'clock, General Escriu of the Engineers penetrated into the castle with his aide.

Almost at the same time, Captain Galcerán of the Engineers, Ferrer's defense lawyer, went up to the castle.

Ferrer was visibly delighted to see him, greeting him effusively. Sr. Galcerán could not suppress his emotion, which was only natural in such a painful scene.

Sr. Ferrer asked him to sit, and they spent a long time talking. Minutes before the scheduled execution time, Sr. Galcerán left the chapel.

This goodbye was extremely emotional. Sr. Galcerán did not leave the castle until the sentence was consummated.

Sr. Ferrer was left alone in the chapel smoking his last cigarettes. Someone told him that a priest wanted to see him, and he answered that it was his ideas that put him at the point of death, and not any crime, so it was extremely impious to want to disturb him like that.

At eight o'clock in the morning, news of Sr. Francisco Ferrer's execution had spread throughout Barcelona. A few groups headed to the castle. The sentinels forced them to disperse and leave. A few stubborn curious onlookers insisted on approaching the castle. A handful of soldiers and a corporal came, and that was enough to make them leave.

A short while later, by order of their superiors, the cavalry members took a position at the top of the mountain. Only a very small number of people including the Brothers of Peace and Charity were allowed entry into the castle.

At a quarter to nine, Ferrer made out the castle's chaplain walking to him. He stood up quickly and asked very calmly, "Is it time?" The chaplain nodded, and so Ferrer left the chapel. The firing squad, at the command of an officer, had already taken its position. Ferrer walked hastily to the site of the execution. On his way from the chapel to the moat at Santa Amalia, Ferrer waved politely, without affectation, to everyone he saw along the way.

On the way, a priest approached him and tried to persuade him. Ferrer begged him, very courteously, to be quiet and let him go by himself. Nevertheless, the priest continued walking next to him, but without saying anything.

He thus arrived at the moat of the Santa Amalia bastion, where the castle governor was already present. When he found out where he was to be executed, he saw that they were going to blindfold him, but he asked them not to blindfold him and also not to force him to go down on his knees.

The officers consulted with the governor, and they permitted him to stand for his execution, but said he would be blindfolded.

With his head held high, facing the firing squad, he fell to his death, pronouncing these last words: "My children, aim well! You are not to blame! I am innocent! Long live the Modern School!"

He was shot in the head three times. Another bullet pierced his throat. His body was immediately placed in the coffin that had been prepared for him.

No imprecations, no condemnations will come from our mouths against the judges who pronounced the sentence or against the civilians who bear the responsibility for what happened, but to deny that our bodies felt a shudder from the tremendous shock of this unexpected, barbaric, and indescribable act would be to deny the sunlight that shone on this mournful scene that unfolded at the moats of Montjuïc Castle, because nothing can erase from our minds the idea that Ferrer was killed because he stood in the way of clericalism and autocracy, which would rather have Spain drown in blood and shadow than see it bask in radiant liberty.

But along with a country's conscience, there is the universal conscience, and, already alarmed as we saw in the previous chapter, by the reprehensible government repression, it was shaken to the core by news of the sentence. It could not contain its indignation when it became known that the sentence was carried out—and not because Ferrer had been killed, but because the situation his enemies had placed him in made him a symbol, a symbol of the great, new ideals of human liberty.

Chapter 11

Serious Disturbances in Front of Spanish Embassies and Consulates •
Paris Under Martial Law • The Mayor of Rome • A Wave of
Indignation Erupts all Over Europe and the Americas • Spain

The sound of the eight shots that left Ferrer's body inert in the moats of Montjuïc was a shock wave to every conscience in every nation. The demonstrations of protest that we mentioned previously resumed tumultuously. Hundreds of thousands of demonstrators went to Spanish embassies to bear witness to their indignation at this iniquitous execution.

In documenting the magnitude of this universal and angry display, we cannot be as thorough as we might have liked. We would need many volumes. On the table here, we have an enormous pile of French, Italian, Belgian, German, English, Austrian, Portuguese, and North and South American newspapers that have reported the magnitude of this protest in their respective nations.

In this wave of indignation, Paris came under martial law.

The Solidarity Committee for the defense of the victims of Spanish repression and the newspapers *L'Humanité*, *La Guerre Sociale*, *Le Libertaire*, *La Voix du Peuple*, and *Temps Nouveaux* published extraordinary sheets inviting Parisians to demonstrate in front of the Spanish Embassy.

The streets of the great city were packed with demonstrators, and the Prefect of Police issued the strictest orders to keep from upsetting the Spanish ambassador. A company of the 28th Infantry Division, another from the 76th, a Republican Guard squadron, two platoons of cuirassiers, and numerous officers and guards on foot.

All these precautions were useless. The demonstrators, men and women, advanced toward the Boulevard de Clichy shouting, "Murderers! Murderers! Vive Ferrer!" and a few groups were singing the Internationale.

Streetcar and carriage traffic was interrupted, and when officers and republican guards tried to stop the crowd from advancing, there was a tremendous conflagration in which one officer was killed and the Prefect of Police, M. Lepine, was injured.

The protesters were enraged, and small groups ran along adjacent streets destroying trees, streetlamps, kiosks, and two streetcars (pieces of which were used to make barricades).

Security forces made several arrests and many charges were filed. Shouts of "Murderers! Vive Ferrer!" were ceaseless.

The reactionary newspapers and a few that called themselves liberal and democratic reduced these events to the insignificant proportions of a riot instigated by troublemakers, but the truth became known when it was repeated the next day during a massive demonstration that began in the Latin Quarter.

The demonstrators insulted the Spanish Government, calling on France to sever all ties with Spain as long as the clergy remained in control of it. They advanced along Boulevard Saint-Germain, and when the police tried to stop them, they destroyed kiosks and streetlamps, initiating a violent fight. There were injuries on both sides.

A small group of university students from the Sorbonne advanced to the Spanish Embassy, which was guarded by the military, and at the same time, another group positioned itself in front of the Spanish chapel on Avenue de Friedland, shouting vitriol against the Vatican, the reaction, and Spanish reactionaries.

If the truth of what happened was being concealed by those whose political leanings clearly meant they should have let the public know, how can we trust the official entities? What moral force do they think their words have? Every individual has the right to approve or disapprove of an action or an event, but in condemning that event, they do not have the right to omit the truth, as they have done.

Better evidence of the state of outrage in Paris is provided by the powerful and admirable demonstration that took place two days after these previous events, in which Parisians also protested against the repression exercised by the French Republican Government.

Surrounded by police forces, over one hundred thousand demonstrators marched through the streets of the *Ville Lumière* in the direction of the embassy. As they approached the building, two battalions of republican guards surrounded it along with four infantry battalions (the 24th, 28th, 102nd, and 104th), and a squadron of cuirassiers. A colonial infantry company, a squadron of municipal guards, and a brigade of security officers took a position along Avenue de Villiers.

Steadfast, the protesters marched in front of the embassy holding small white signs that said: "Vive Ferrer! For the glory of Ferrer! Long live Free Spain!" Groups singing the *Carmagnole* and the *Internationale* made the action feel solemn and grandiose.

The demonstration dispersed at the Place de la Concorde, and due to the Parisian people's resolve, there was no major rioting. They would not allow their legitimate feelings of indignation to be repressed.

During the events in Lyon, stones were thrown at the balconies of the Spanish Consulate.

The police charged the crowd, which scattered throughout the town's streets, continuing their protest there. It then returned to congregate in front of the consulate and tried to destroy the coat of arms.

Several people were wounded.

In Toulon, demonstrators marched through the streets shouting, "Vive Ferrer!" and "Down with the zucchetto!"[1] They overwhelmed the gendarmes and penetrated into the cathedral, knocking down effigies and candelabra. They also attacked several churches.

At town hall buildings, the flags were flown at half staff, and at the offices of *Le Petit Var*, it was replaced by a black tie.

In Amiens, Lille, Reims, Béziers, Saint-Étienne, Clermont-Ferrand, and Bordeaux, demonstrators expressed their indignation at Spanish consulates. Police confirmed several arrests.

---

1. A Roman Catholic cleric's skullcap, invoked as a symbol of Catholic power.

There was also some protest at Rouen, Montpelier, Maury, Besançon, Cherbourg, Valence, Nice, and Narbonne, where workers centers flew their flags at half staff in some points. Over the protest of the local sub-prefect, the provincial council at Bouches-de-Rhône agreed to the following resolution:

> This Council is deeply disturbed by the execution of Ferrer and outraged that in the twentieth century, in civilized Europe, a government can still sentence and apply the capital punishment to a man who has committed but a crime of opinion, since Ferrer did not threaten the life or property of another. We protest vigorously against the evil committed by the Spanish Government; we would like to express our pain and our hope for the future to Ferrer's family and to Spanish democracy; and we adjourn this session in mourning.

The union at Les Docks de Marseille decided to declare a boycott of all Spanish goods.

The National Association of Freethinkers agreed to erect a monument to Ferrer's memory. The mayor of Paris, the president of the provincial council, and several deputies endorsed this proposal.

Sixty-four attorneys of the Supreme Court expressed their protest. The Council of the Grand Orient de France did the same during a formal session.

M. Flaissières wished to have his protest recorded in the Senate.

A teacher at the École Polytechnique in Paris, M. Laisant, returned his diploma from the Academy of Sciences of Madrid.

When the deputy and mayor of Cherbourg, M. Mahieu, learned of Ferrer's execution, he sent the Spanish Embassy his Commander Insignias of the Order of Isabella the Catholic, which the Spanish king had honored him with.

In Italy, we see political agitation across every region.

During the space of a few hours on the 12th, the city of Rome stayed silent. There was no streetcar or carriage traffic, which paralyzed work. This occurred before the sentence against Ferrer was carried out.

Close to 10,000 people gathered across from the botanical gardens. A railway bridge was utilized as a podium, and various orators spoke.

Afterwards, a very large group went to the Piazza di Spagna and wanted to approach the Spanish Embassy, near the Vatican, but the Palazzo, as an islet, was inaccessible and was surrounded by numerous forces. There were some clashes: several officers were wounded and some demonstrators were arrested.

When Ferrer's execution became known, the emotion was tremendous, and people shouted insults at Spain. More demonstrations crossed on the streets, with black flags appearing at some points.

The mayor issued a leaflet with a mournful tone. It said:

CITIZENS:
Rome joins the civilized world in grieving for Francisco Ferrer.

The death of this thinker, this devotee of schooling, is an offense against the sanctity of human life, the freedom of conscience, and the progress of civilization in the fight against reaction.

Dedicated to the freedom of conscience, to the progress of civilization, Rome raises its voice against the barbarity of this act. May this expression of feeling be an affirmation of your character.

The victim, whose blood will fecundate the idea for which he lived and died, will acquire a halo from the citizens' peaceful, dignified, and solemn demonstrations.[2]

Rome, Capitoline Hill, October 13, 1909. Municipal mayor: *E. Nathan.*

In Genoa, Bologna, Turin, Parma, Milan, Perugia, Verona, Naples, Cortona, Florence, Ravenna, and Venice, there were work stoppages and the crowds went to Spanish consulates shouting, "Death to Jesuits!"

---

2. A direct appropriation of Tertullian's phrase "the blood of the martyrs is the seed of the Church," often invoked in anarchist martyrology in this period.

Workers engaged in boycotts at some ports, the first being in Livorno, where they refused to unload two ships from Spain.

Rallies were held everywhere.

Ravenna was the first city to name one of its piazzas after Francisco Ferrer.

Many political and community associations went to the town hall with 70 banners cheering for Ferrer and yelling "Down with the Spanish Government."

Deputy Barcilai presented an appeal before the Chamber, asking if Italy had offered the gestures required by human reason. This appeal led to the Spanish Government rushing to print a file of documents related to Ferrer's sentence, which did not convince anyone.

The Genoa Bar Association passed a resolution protesting vigorously.

Holland, Switzerland, and Austria-Hungary contributed to this worldwide demonstration of protest with extremely large rallies.

Socialists in Holland organized public events in Amsterdam and The Hague, expressing their disgust before the consulates.

In the Swiss towns of Zurich and Geneva, demonstrations at Spanish consulates were violent. The police intervened, and some officers were injured.

The Bern City Council unanimously approved a motion of mourning.

Professors at the University of Geneva also signed a protest.

In the Austrian towns of Vienna, Trieste, Fiume, and Prague, many trades went on strike and held several rallies. In Trieste and Prague, there were serious riots. The Fiume city council canceled their session as a sign of mourning.

A proposal to discuss the Ferrer case was put before the Budapest House of Representatives. The government refused. In the Hungarian capital, as well as in Pressburg and Temesvar, the demonstrations had a violent character.

We would have dispensed with many of these details and others that follow if we didn't know what has been written to distort the nature of this universal protest. Reactionaries from every country have tried to voice their hateful fury in books and other types of publications, trampling the truth with false information that history must not record. This is why we are patiently gathering information in these paragraphs on the real demonstrations, the true enthusiasm, and the reliable data, which, taken together, form the grandest monument to human solidarity in these new times—a monument where the people have witnessed the insidiousness, the falsehood, and the meanness of the clerical authorities turn to ashes.

In Belgium, there was also a lot of anger. Two thousand students tried to tear off the coat of arms at the Spanish embassy in Brussels, but the police were able to stop them.

A rally was organized. At the end of it the students marched to the Nunciature.

The police stood against them, but at that moment, another group of students arrived, and they were able to invade the boulevards. They attacked a religious house.

In Liège, two religious houses were attacked by demonstrators. The same thing occurred in Seraing. The police intervened, charging several times. The crowd marched along the streets shouting, "Down with the murderers! Vive Ferrer!"

The International Socialist Bureau in Brussels called for a boycott of Spanish goods. They also agreed to encourage all workers of the world to adopt the same measure.

Héctor Denis, a professor and deputy in Liège, made a proposal to close the Spanish diplomatic mission in Brussels.

The rue d'Espagne was given the name of Francisco Ferrer.

In Berlin, Germany, the Democratic Union held a protest rally, and Doctor Breitscheid spoke against the Spanish Government. Demonstrators wanted to go to the Spanish Embassy, but they were opposed by gendarmes, who made several arrests.

Other such demonstrations took place in Halle and Frankfurt am Main.

When the session began in the Reichstag, a socialist deputy unfurled a banner with thick letters: "Viva Ferrer!"

No less worthy of mention was the displeasure of the English people brought about by the death of Ferrer.

In London's Trafalgar Square, it was confirmed that there was an outstanding rally against the inquisitorial terrorism. Speakers from diverse countries hurled furious insults at the most powerful figures in Spain.[3]

Numerous groups carrying banners with terrible threats headed to the Spanish embassy. The police cut the demonstration off several times, but the demonstrators made it to the building. They threw rocks and shouted, "To hell with the murderers!"[4]

Once they reached their objective, the demonstrators dispersed at Parliament Square. Similar demonstrations occurred in Liverpool, Cardiff, and other points.

They demanded that the ambassador of Spain hand over his passport.

The International Committee of the Social Democratic Party condemned the injustice of the execution.

Many deputies made appeals to the government.

Despite censorship by the authorities, it was known that the demonstrations in Portugal were powerful as they were attended by a large number of individuals.

In Lisbon, Porto, and Coimbra, when they read telegrams reporting that Ferrer had been executed, groups were formed so they could express their indignation at demonstrations before the Spanish diplomatic missions and consulates. The Portuguese authorities severely repressed the demonstrations, arresting many individuals.

Various republican and workers centers flew their flags at half staff.

The incredibly just anger that was expressed in Europe reverberated intensely throughout the Americas. In all the capital cities, towns, and villages, we saw a unanimous outpouring of emotion, as if wanting to re-conquer their symbol, liberty, which was viciously trampled on by fanatics who should have already ceased to exist.

The demonstrations of protest were replicated in all of

---

3. Through the 1890s and early 1900s London had become a center for political exiles, including many hundreds of anarchists across Europe, who were attracted to Britain's relative tolerance for "foreign" radicalism (which was far less evident for Irish radicalism in this period). See Constance Bantman, *The French Anarchists in London 1880-1914: Exile and Transnationalism in the First Globalization* (Liverpool: Liverpool University Press, 2013).

4. Translated into Spanish as "Mueran los asesinos!"

Argentina, paralyzing work in almost every town. The work stoppage lasted three days in Buenos Aires, where massive rallies were held. At the last of these rallies, held at Plaza de la Constitución, the number of demonstrators was enormous. Reports agreed that the number of people reached 25,000. People were in trees, hanging over each other, eager to hear the speeches from the podium. The spot chosen for the speakers was a small flat surface in the grotto that was constructed there, a couple of meters high. Above, below, to the left and to the right, everywhere, a sea of people formed an imposing picture. A banner was unfurled higher up in the grotto which said, "Montjuïc, with the crimes you committed, you spread the truth!"

Other signs and small banners stood out in every direction. Their inscriptions alluded to the event and encouraged a boycott of Spanish goods.

All the workers associations expressed their protest, as did the Universal Republican Alliance, the Argentine Socialist Party, and the Spanish Republican Federation.

Analogous demonstrations were held by workers associations, socialists, republicans, and anarchist groups in Rosario de Santa Fe, La Plata, Mar del Plata, Mercedes, Bell Ville, Chacabuco, Bahía Blanca, Junín, Cañada de Gómez, Marcos Juárez, Córdoba, Zárate, Laboulaye, San Fernando, San Martín, and other towns.

In Montevideo, the demonstrations had the same character, although there was a violent event in the Uruguayan capital. The strike was generalized. This was according to the Workers Federation and the International Center. Twenty thousand people, many from bordering towns, joined in a demonstration at the Maciel Wharf. There were speakers at three different podiums condemning the Spanish reaction.

When the speeches ended, some groups of people thought to go to the Spanish Embassy, but they were attacked by police and a cavalry squadron before they made it there. Eight demonstrators were injured by gunfire and many were arrested.

Forty-eight Uruguayan deputies condemned Ferrer's execution.

In Santiago, Chile; Asuncion, Paraguay; Rio de Janeiro and São Paulo, Brazil, there were equally large rallies and public demonstrations. The same was true in the United States, in New York, Vermont, and Los Angeles and San Francisco, California.

In this twentieth century crossroads, every thinking and working person on the island of Cuba also joined in this heroic push to raise a glorious banner to the martyrs of Montjuïc.

The bourgeois press was able to isolate itself in silence, thinking that would favor the fanaticism that is the scourge of some parts of the Greater Antilles to this day, but the efforts of those who always advance progress made the protest proud and dignified.

In their columns, ¡*Tierra!*, ¡*Rebelión!*, and *La Voz del Dependiente* launched serious threats against the reactionary Spanish clergy, calling on the Cuban people to demonstrate in solidarity with their victims.

Extremely large public events were held in Havana and replicated in Cruces, Cárdenas, Matanzas, Sagua la Grande, Santiago de las Vegas, and other Cuban towns, where every social sector was represented.

***

In the middle of this great worldwide anti-reactionary movement that we have just reflected on, Spain could no longer remain silent and tolerate the permanent insults to its governing community. It had been quiet too long. It was sick and tired of having to keep its arms crossed.

Even before Ferrer's execution, the lungs of some free individuals had grown tired from so many efforts to change the situation and restore justice but in order to get to this point, universal action condemning this execution was necessary.

So at the same time as this global movement, we saw republican political parties in Spain joining with young rebels, socialists, and workers from different regions, initiating campaigns, making resolutions, writing calls to action, everything for the purpose of toppling Maura and all the organs of reaction. This being the mood there, the demonstrations in favor of Ferrer also took on notable importance.

Several councilors recorded their protest at city halls in Madrid, Santander, Seville, Valencia, Tarragona, Zaragoza, Eibar, and Alzira, and some councils canceled their sessions in mourning. In Gijón, A Coruña, Bilbao, Ferrol, Santander, Zaragoza, and Elche, workers associations organized well attended rallies. Republican parties joined with socialists in some cities to plan large demonstrations against the government of Maura.

The thick atmosphere darkening Spanish skies after twelve terrible weeks was beginning to clear.

And stepping in the way of this rebirth, which heralded the defeat of political reaction and religious fanaticism, were dark forces such as Sr. Luca de Tena from Madrid's *ABC*, who took issue with the great demonstrations against Ferrer's execution in Europe and the Americas.

That repugnant and abominable trilogy prevalent in Spain—immorality, false devotion, and the satisfaction of base instincts—regurgitated its angry rage in the pages of the abovementioned newspaper, at the behest of its audacious director.

Out of all the protests against the heroic efforts of honorable people from every country, none appearing in the pages of *ABC* were more insulting and none lied as shamelessly as the one signed by about two dozen individuals from the town of Aznalcóllar, (province of Seville), which congratulated Sr. Luca de Tena "for his patriotic campaign against the infamous protest of foreign nations in support of a coward."

We believe that those who have inflicted such significant harm to our sense of humanity, taking their hate beyond the grave to the founder of the Modern School—they should be ashamed of their sad acts, since only blind rage can cause a person to be cruel to the dead, and even worse, to lie like the above signers did, regrettably.

Some neighbors of this same town of Aznalcóllar wrote a well-deserved and worthy correction to this offense, this outrageous insult, espoused, we repeat, by a dark force aiding the Spanish Government's barbarity, Luca de Tena. Admirers of the truth, these neighbors widely circulated a leaflet addressed to *El Pueblo*, in which, after highlighting the courage and serenity with which Ferrer confronted the terrible moment of his death (in Chapter

10), which completely destroyed the crude assertion of cowardice proffered by the signers of the aforementioned defamation campaign, they define the true nature of the international protest in this way:

This international protest has never been against the true Spain created by those who, with their work, with their blood, their intelligence, contribute to the growth of an educated Spain, a Spain that should march in unison with the other European nations. No! This protest is against those in Spain who want to destroy everything: they want to destroy culture, trade, industry, and dignity, taking us backwards to the shameful times when thinking was a good enough reason to be burned over a low flame. So, good Spaniards, those who love the soil on which we were born, instead of taking offense at the protests of foreigners, we should be glad that solidarity is expressed across the border to prevent us from speeding into an inquisitorial abyss.[5]

And why do they congratulate the director of *ABC*, that is, Luca de Tena? Well, they congratulate him, as we said earlier, for the falsehoods they describe as a "patriotic campaign." Let's prove it again:

> To counteract the healthy influence of the foreign protests against the reaction led by Maura and La Cierva, Luca de Tena, director of *ABC* and extremely sagacious devotee of Maura, telegraphed the large newspapers abroad telling them that Ferrer was sentenced legally and rightly for leading the movement in Barcelona, in which "children were killed and nuns were violated by the revolutionaries."
>
> But the information contained in these telegrams, which is so pleasing to the enemies of freedom and the people, was false. It was false because in the first place, the alleged leadership of Ferrer has not convinced anyone due to the lack of evidence, and the process is being appealed since Ferrer's role is denied even by the very people who were part of the executive board of the general strike committee.

---

5. A further reference to "Black Spain," contrasted here with what Bonafulla considers the "true" Spain: European, "modern," freethinking.

The information in the telegrams was false because the children that were killed and the nuns that were violated do not appear anywhere. *El País*, a republican newspaper in Madrid, has called on *ABC* to clarify and cite who verified these facts, and this newspaper, this director who should have been more well informed if he was going to hurl accusations, has had to send an editor to Barcelona to find out and look for evidence in what might more clearly be called "had to send an editor so he could come out looking good." We expect some sort of crooked deal.[6]

The signers of the *ABC* protest may call us meddlers, but they do not realize that they have offended everyone of liberal sentiment.

Staying silent would be a sign of complicity with those who are falsifying the truth, whether because of ignorance or bad faith (we are inclined to think the latter), and we are not prepared to do that in any way—one can give a sincere opinion on any matter, but without offending, without injuring a people who are for the most part aware of what happened, a people who have read about and understand our social struggles and who know the causes of the consequences of the events in Barcelona and the death of Ferrer.

Now, a plea or a challenge: Among the signers of the *ABC* protest, among the twenty signers in this town, there are men of learning, men of knowledge. And the humblest and most insignificant person who now resides in our town, José Sánchez Rosa, who considers himself offended, challenges the twenty signers or any one of them (or anyone else who will accept the challenge) to a public, rational debate on the following points[7]: What caused the events in Barcelona? Was Ferrer the leader of the movement? Was he a coward? Who was the international

---

6. [Author's note] As a result of this, an extended dispute arose between *El País* and *ABC*. Sr. Luca de Tena blew his own sad, ridiculous horn in the pages of this latter newspaper.

7. A shoemaker and anarchist publisher who opened a workers' school in Aznalcóllar (Seville) in 1905. Sánchez Rosa remained a key figure in the Andalusian movement until his execution by Francoist troops at the start of the Civil War in 1936.

protest against—was it against Spain or against the rulers that dishonor it?

You are invited to a reasoned discussion in which insults are forbidden, which would be appropriate for civilized people. And you would be doing us a great service if either you were to disabuse yourselves of your beliefs if you have been misled or if you were to correct our error if we have been wrong about the points to be discussed.[8]

The signers of this page conclude by dedicating some words in honor of Francisco Ferrer Guardia, praising the struggle and offering their condolences to the victims of it.

The names of those who proclaim the truth and defend justice should be made known regardless of their political and social ideas!

This sublime work was done in Aznalcóllar on November 7th:

Manuel Libero Márquez, José Sánchez Rosa, Vidal Caballero, Rufino Pascual, José Ojeda Suaz, Avelino González, Antonio Domínguez, Francisco Pascual, José Librero Borrallo, José Rodríguez, Manuel Álvarez, Gregorio González, Francisco Moreno González, José Calero, Miguel Enamorado, José Moreno, Juan Sanz, Juan Vega Ojeda, Patricio Sánchez Sierra, Román García Ojeda, B. Sierra, Francisco Guirao, Manuel Bernal, Tomas Calero Gómez, Manuel Losada, Patricio Sánchez Palomo, Eduardo Librero, Carlos Palomo, Francisco Enamorado, Isidoro Casilla, Román Ramírez Vázquez, Eduardo Olea Moreno, Serafin Mateos, Vicente García Álvarez, Juan A. Delgado López, Francisco Segado, Fernando Mateo, Manuel Ortiz, Eulogio Vargas, Eustaquio Moreno, Ventura Ojeda, Pablo Sanz, José Sánchez, Rodrigo Morabel, Crispín Sánchez.

---

8. [Author's note] It goes without saying that those invited to this reasoned discussion did not heed the call.

Chapter 12

Withdrawal of Sr. Maura's Government • Replaced by Moret • Costa
Destroying Maura • Crime of the Advanced Political Parties

The government had anticipated the universal protest movement but what it had not imagined was its magnitude and importance.

Despite all the sophistry used by the reactionary press to prevent Spain's honor from being called into question, it was hard to avoid.

The way this affair looked, its resonance, the impression it made abroad, and at the same time, the severe accusations made publicly by many Spaniards of sound mind and proven integrity—well, this flood of furious condemnation endangered Spanish institutions.

It was impossible to deny the dissatisfaction of the other Spanish political parties with Sr. Maura, and so he could not count on them to re-establish normalcy if he stayed in power. As many people observed, it was then, in these circumstances, that some reflection in the highest circles resulted in a complete political plan to calm the peoples' mood and protect the threatened regime.

Could there be a disadvantage to this plan? From the point of view of the reaction, there was none—their hate and their desire for vengeance had already been satisfied. Did it matter if there were more victims if the horrible spectacle of this misfortune had already shaken the entire world? Those who sought to restore the Inquisition had already anticipated how far their crime could go, and that is exactly how far they went. This truth was expressed by some through tears.

There also couldn't be any disadvantages for the liberal and democratic parties, given their known love for the dynasty.

The only obstacle to the plan depended on the opposition of the republican and socialist parties, with their deep roots among the people, the most harmed by the state of things both before and after the events.

Without digressing, this political plan, conceived in the highest circles, was accomplished with widespread applause, but it left a few people like Joaquín Costa disappointed, people who, having political faith, believed they had sincerely enlightened the people, demonstrating that if those individuals who had spilled so much blood and committed so many iniquities and infamies were able to have Maura's punishment reduced to forcing him to step down, then this would happen[1]:

1. After a few years spent looking in the mirror, he would take back the presidency, knowing from experience that nothing bad would happen to him, and he would return to his old haunts so nonchalant with his politics of bloodletting, because he would be in his element and can't help it, because his petulance, his conceit, and his narcissism are stronger than he is, and he is condemned to being unrepentant.[2] In summary, he is incapable of learning and correcting himself.

2. And every six months, as is customary, one of the four or six presidential leaders who the so-called liberal faction conveniently has at the ready would come in their place, I'm not saying to govern, but to reap the benefits of governing the country.

3. With this tremendous new example of impunity, the last living vestiges of faith would be extinguished in the breasts of Spaniards, that is, if there is still any faith left there.

The same Costa came to show Maura's treason even before setting out this ominously true analysis, adding that "the referenced crimes are more serious, more malicious, and more consequential than the ones committed in July by the subversives in Barcelona.

---

1. Joaquín Costa was a high-profile critic of the Restoration system, who called for an end to endemic political corruption and educational reform to end Spain's "backwardness."

2. An astute prediction: Maura remained a key figure in Spanish politics, attracting a substantial following behind his program of reformist conservativism (known as *maurismo*). He returned as Prime Minister on several occasions during the crisis years of 1918–1923.

However, Sr. Maura and others condemn these subversives for passing laws through violence, but they are in fact in the moats of Montjuïc. So, Maura is already sentenced. He has sentenced himself. They are missing a few people in the moats of Montjuïc."

Costa and public opinion had already decreed Maura's execution, but the Spanish parliament reduced the sentence, simply forcing him to step down. A crisis was declared, and Moret replaced him.

We are not inclined to investigate how this crisis unfolded. It would be better if our readers judged for themselves. That way we can avoid having to lower ourselves to the depths of political immorality.

In summary, in this crude battle between the forces of obscurantism and the lovers of progress, not all Spaniards agreed that Maura should leave defeated. Instead, considering some very different needs, they retreated.

The main thing is that, sadly, because of this political plan, the sacrifice of those who marched in front to nobly and generously fight the cause of the suffering gripping every home went unrewarded—the reaction was not defeated, and its minions were not eliminated.

As enemies of all politics, we might show bias by trying to establish who was responsible for what, but since we are almost at the end, we will, in accordance with the goal of this book and despite our opinions (documented in other chapters), echo a few interesting statements of Deputy Tomás Caballé Goyeneche to determine the conduct of the advanced political parties during the events of July:

I declare that—in one of those calm moments of lucidity that everyone has, even those who in general are called impressionable, impulsive people, who act without reflecting or ascertaining the scope and consequence of their actions—I needed to be my own confessor; I needed to examine my conscience. And my conscience told me that I hadn't done my duty, that I hadn't fulfilled the obligations that are unavoidably imposed on any austere conscience by my position as deputy in parliament and my political significance as member of the governing board of *Solidaridad Catalana*.[3]

As shareholder of *El Poble Català*, member of the left of *Solidaridad Catalana*, maybe out of moral cowardice, or something else (it doesn't matter now), it is true that by my silence, I assented to the campaign of *El Poble Català*, which was evidently a mainspring of the revolutionary protest in Barcelona. Well, *El Progreso* was not the only impetus for the protest, as Sr. Cierva claimed from the blue bench when he intervened during the debate initiated by Sr. Moret several days ago in Congress, a debate which I was not in any way able to take part in. All my attempts to obtain authorization to participate were unproductive, despite the fact that I had the indisputable right to do so according to the rules, since Sr. Moret most kindly humbled himself to honor me, referring to me clearly, bluntly, expressly during his first speech.

It is clear that to proceed now loyally and with honor, I must state that the campaign of *Poble Català* in Barcelona was solely a protest against the sending of reservists to Melilla and against the war in the Rif; they believed the public's opinion was with them.

But to obey the imperatives of my conscience, I must also acknowledge and declare that the revolutionary protest in Barcelona and the terrible consequences of it emerged from that campaign—namely the troubles that occurred during the revolt, the court cases that ended in death sentences and prison sentences. What emerged from that campaign was an extraordinary number of citizens from the humble, the disinherited classes in Spanish society who were expatriated and exiled, and finally the great damage to our social order.

***

The representatives in the Cortes of the left, *Solidaridad Catalana* and the Radical Republican Party of Barcelona, had,

---

3. A coalition of bourgeois Catalan political parties, which dissolved following the Tragic Week.

in my judgment, a firm duty to endorse the revolutionary protest in Barcelona, in order to channel and guide it, to obtain the benefits created by revolutions, when those benefits are holy and honorable. Our duty was to stand behind and devote ourselves to the leaders and the planners, who we must assume acted in a spirit of sacrifice and selflessness.

Later, the moment the government began its extraordinary repression, it became our duty to demonstrate collectively against these measures, which we considered a declaration of war against Catalonia, that epitome of liberal and democratic values, and we would answer this declaration with all-out war, using every means and resource at our disposal to ensure that our ideas and aspirations would triumph.

It was also our duty to appeal to the government to free Ferrer from death's clutches if we thought he was innocent, or to ask the government to sentence him but improve his terribly painful situation if we thought he was guilty.

Anything other than standing with our hands crossed, impassive, coldly and stoically contemplating how some people, how the government, fought with itself, stuck between what it considered fulfilling its duty and its humanitarian sentiments.

***

Would Alfonso XIII be ruling in Spain today if republican leaders, particularly the radical republicans of Valencia and Madrid, had seconded the revolutionary protest in Barcelona, as they were obliged by their programs and their commitments to do (according to their speeches and their actions in Parliament and at demonstrations)?

Would they have behaved better in the service of and for the benefit of Alfonso XIII if the monarchy had recruited people to serve and defend it and remunerated them handsomely?

Something else the advanced political parties are responsible for is that they did not heed the sincere call of the poet Gabriel Alomar, who made an effort to find a way to shut the inquisitors up during the weeks of deathly silence. We therefore have decided not to include the movement of the liberal and republican press from Madrid and a few other provinces, in which, in aid of this movement against Maura, Pérez Galdós, Sol y Ortega, Azcárate, Melquíades Álvarez, Soriano, and other deputies lent their support. We also did not want to echo the rowdy parliamentary sessions that ended with a declaration of crisis because all of these accidents were advantageous to the political plan we have discussed.

Consider, all of you, the weeks of silence only interrupted by the gunfire of the firing squads who extinguished precious lives in the moats of Montjuïc; consider the sad sacrifice of Spanish youths led to the foot of the rugged mountains of Gurugu; and finally, consider that great emotions are not always assimilated and the necessary remedies are not always conceived in silence.[4] Opportunistic stalling hinders the fight against injustice, but nevertheless, this did not stop the government from holding captive our nation's thinking and violating human dignity both during and after the events. Does this mean that the path of prison or escaping abroad is preferable? Besides the fact that the answer to this question lies in the impulses of our natural conscience, we should also note that a people falls into disgrace sooner out of weakness than out of conceit.

The assumption that we were working or writing from a biased perspective, unfairly, with a desire to favor our ideas, however noble they might be, might have devalued our analyses and our attacks against the absurd policies that were prevalent after the events. It would be foolish to assume that. You may have already noticed our exceptional interest in making sure we do not appear exclusive with respect to everything concerning the defense of truth and dignity, which has been so scorned; we have included newspapers and individuals whose ideas are different than ours, whose participation we consider extremely honorable.

We believe our work is truly fair.

---

4. Gurugu is a mountain in Morocco close to the Spanish territory of Melilla.

Chapter 13

The Reaction Survives Maura • Imprisonment • Military
Tribunals Continue • Path to Prison • Amnesty is Granted

After Ferrer's execution and Maura's shameful withdrawal from government, and once the suspension of constitutional guarantees was lifted, it was thought, since nothing else seemed possible, that there would be a complete restoration of normalcy, that the people would be released from the painful moral weight falling on their shoulders, which forced them, hour after hour, day after day, for weeks and weeks, to continue watching the last gasps of numerous families buried by the military tribunals, families made to quiver with hate and indignation by the clerical authorities.

Although the recently ousted government was universally declared to be the cause of the rebellion and the human decency of the revolutionaries was praised, the jails were still packed with prisoners, and the military tribunals continued, coolly handing down sentences of life imprisonment and death, making life even harder and more terrible for the victims, who were transferred from their jail cells to even harsher prisons just when they thought their ordeal would be over.

Having previously chronicled the military tribunals that took place the day after the revolt, it would not be useful to interrupt our reporting, so we will give an account of the others that followed.

In summarizing them, our readers can rest assured that reining in a state of repression is not the same as ending it. We therefore presume that the fall of the government, rather than being an act of justice and humanity, was advantageous to the interests of the ruling institutions, now shaken. We have mentioned something about that elsewhere in this book.

And this presumption will gain the force of reality if, after reading the reports on the military tribunals and their sentences, we stop to reflect on the prolonged school closures (which continued despite the resources given to Sr. Moret's government for their reopening) as well as the prisoners kept in Madrid, Barcelona, Mataró, Vic, Sitges, Sabadell, Logroño, and other points, well-known individuals who should never have been there in the first place.

One of these prisoners, the libertarian Mariano Castellote, who, like his comrades Cardenal, Herreros, and Alluard, was imprisoned for the crime of professing advanced ideas, said this:

> The crowds still sound vibrant and joyous after the liberals' rise to power, but when the jails are still filled with supposed subversives and arsonists, many of whom have not even made a statement, what can be the effect of this "popular" joy over the triumph of liberty and even revolution? What do so many innocent exiles think about this cheering and uproar? What do they think of all the people wrongly imprisoned, all the children without bread, and all the families driven to poverty and desperation over a nuisance complaint by the Committee?
>
> Isn't it ironic that after those same people came to power who shouted and demanded that the suspension of constitutional guarantees should be lifted, they became the very people who could return those guarantees, and meanwhile prisoners are still suffocating in their cells, the exiles are far from their homes and their children, Barcelona and Girona are without constitutional guarantees, and the reaction is represented by and is in the hands of the police and directed by the Committee of sad remembrance?
>
> And isn't it appalling and horrible that thousands of unfortunates are in such conditions even for one extra moment, when it would be so easy to grant them the freedom they have every right to have? Have they thought about this, those that can and should make this current state of affairs end?
>
> We do not doubt that there exists a desire for justice, but

we want to believe that it will be fulfilled with the same intention as the gypsy from the story.

Certainly we do not think, like many others, that Maura's
exit from power means liberty has triumphed, and we do not
think that in spite of it, in spite of the enthusiastic demonstrations, the deafening shouts and the applause for the liberals, we
do not see liberty anywhere and we do not believe the time will
come when innocence will be given the applause it deserves.

If liberty has triumphed, it is necessary to demonstrate it
with deeds, not with shouts or banners or demonstrations. And
if not, there is no reason to be excited, since numerous innocent citizens are dying of poverty and desperation, as they are
being accused by the reaction.

Let the Spanish people refocus their enthusiasm into soliciting a broad amnesty, the most effective way to wash away so
many tears.

In case more grounds were necessary to support the case for
amnesty, the statements in this next document are included here:

It should be easy for readers to remember what happened on
the morning of July 22nd at the Mediodía Railway Station on
the occasion of the embarkation of troops for Melilla. That
popular outburst of anger against the war is common knowledge. As a result of it, several individuals were arrested at the
station, but that was not the case with us. Our arrests occurred
two days after these events, the last one being before the constitution was suspended. Who is accusing us, and what concrete act are we accused of having done? We do not know. Up
until now, we have only been interrogated one single time:
Caraballo, D'lom, García Prieto, and Cruz del Olmo were interrogated by their examining magistrate, while the others
were interrogated by his chief secretary. Solera and Barón declared that they had been at the station. They said they had not
taken part in what happened there and were nothing more than
one of the innumerable spectators who watched the embarkation of the troops. The others denied they were there and gave

the names of witnesses, who until very recently had not been called to make a statement (up to now only a small number of them have done so). All of us have been interrogated on our ideas, but we believe that since only actions fall under the purview of the Codes, these questions must have to do with some legal formality that we are not aware of—if this is about judging our actions, our ideas should not matter much. Up to now this is everything we know about our situation, but we should add that during the captain general's visit, a chief of joint staff added the observation that one of the undersigned who was there at the time was accused of being the leader of the subversives. We could not have been more surprised by this. But despite this, we kept silent hoping this affair would end quickly, in a way that was favorable to us, since the absurdity of this accusation would make our innocence even more obvious.

We will make a few clarifications that could shed light on this affair.

We must make this known:

First: Our arrests began after the publication of a short news item in *El Imparcial* that said that what had occurred was part of an anarchist plot that the police were unaware of.

Second: In the days leading up to our arrest, we were continuously in our residences, and so if we had committed a crime, and the police had witnessed it, they did not do their duty if they did not arrest us in the act. And if they were not able to do it then because of the exceptional circumstances at the time, they could have done it the next day, as long as they knew where we lived.

Third: While we were under arrest, other individuals were being sought, and as soon as they found this out, they could have tried to hide. They were then jailed, but since the constitution was suspended by then, it was possible to keep them in prison without having to process them. Thus, they were saved from our same fate, which would have happened to them if they had been arrested at the same time as us.

Fourth: We will leave the accusation of the supposed

leadership role for the consideration of those reading these lines, since it can only be useful to those who may have wanted it to appear that they have lent a relevant service so in keeping with the news item we referred to.

The police, who so clumsily go about their business arresting murderers, could not bear it that a newspaper would say that they were not aware of the *terrible* plot that was hatched (in the mind of a journalist), and since none of the arrestees had any reason to hide, the service was carried out with great ease. What happened was a worthwhile lesson—we now know that whether we were guilty or innocent, we had to be fiercely hunted in any way possible.

The other defendants arrested at the station are still in prison. Only four have been released, and we do not know whether that was provisional or definitive. Of these, one or two have lost their brothers in the war. A sad freedom—it has been at a high cost!

Let us take advantage of this occasion to commemorate those that have died during the Maurist repression and send our best wishes to the others who have been jailed, exiled, and are being tracked. We are grateful to everyone in and out of Spain who has been concerned and still is concerned about the situation of the thousands of victims of this most cruel, unchecked reaction.

Madrid Prison, November 14, 1909. Fernando Ramos, Alfonso Barón, Miguel D'Lom, Cruz del Olmo, Ricardo García Prieto, David Solera, César Caraballo.

Many others suffered this same way in different Spanish jails.

In summary, the reaction survived Maura, preventing Moret from instituting a liberal government.

The military tribunals that followed handed down rulings that we will summarize as follows:

In the days preceding Ferrer's execution, the military tribunal sentenced the following people to the death penalty:

José Álvarez Señalada, José Giné, Natividad Rufo, José Regás, José Bel Plá, and Francisco Ramírez.

To life imprisonment:
Antonio Sanz, Valentín Cornet, Inocencio Emperador, Carlos Pasalamar, Eugenia Ruiz, Ramón Giró Pijoan, José Traver, Pedro Acosta, J. Ginés Perca.

To twenty years in prison: Concha Ortíz; to less than six months in prison: José Moreno and three others from the district of Gràcia.

Later, the following people were sentenced to death: Ramón Ballonga Bernet, Victoriano Sagués Artigas, Joaquín Tomás Centellas, Juan Tomás, Esteban Roig y Roig, and Pablo Homs Romeu.

To life imprisonment:
Vicente Guillén, security officer, for not showing up to work, Patricio Prades, José Traver, Pedro Acosta, Francisco Monreal Sacristán, Antonio Terrades, Manuel Rivas Pla, José Canals, León Farras Pallarés, Isidro García Bou, Rafael Fernández Serra, Silvestre Poch Balada, Salvador Lloret Ardriles, Domingo Ferrer March, Olegario Abeu, Federico González Marcet, Leandro Conesa, Jaime Pou, Delfín Martí, Sebastián Dalmau, Pedro Guardiola.

To several years in prison:
Trinidad Altés, Luis Zurdo Olivares, Enrique Manresa Martín, Santiago Blanch, Francisco Cabrera, Vicente Botarell, Petra Just, Encarnación Avellaneda, Manuel García Igual, Martín Fernández, Francisco Ortega, Agustín García Moret, Eugenio Casado Bargallo, Ángel Fernández Santiago, Antonio Juncosa, Rosa Curto, Domingo Rius, Mariano Portolés, Arturo Gallifa, Manuel Chiva Bou, Manuel Chiva Negre, Salvador Ardid, Domingo Monfort and his son Antonio, Miguel Mermení, Juan Riera, Ramón Escuder Viñas, Joaquín Palmada, Mercedes Monje, Henriete Braza, Pío Monfort, Juan Rafí, Mariano Montaña, José Ribalta, Luis Plans, Jaime Limón, Manuel Rovira, José Franch, and J. Rubiols.

In reviewing these and many other military tribunals that took place after November 25th (the last day used for this report), we found people were prosecuted based on hearsay: "so and so said, 'so and so spoke to his friend and he said,'" "so and so reads such and such newspapers and such and such books," "I heard him say," "It seemed to me."

Many of these military tribunals barely lasted twenty minutes. How much pain and humiliation!

It would be endless work, listing all of the injustices that were sowing distrust among those who until recently had cheered for the change of government. Sure, no one else was executed in the moats of Montjuïc, but who can count the victims who died in silence in dignified homes, where sadly days and weeks passed as they waited in vain for a sibling or a child's father to return? By chance, regarding the people mentioned previously in this chapter, doesn't holding them in jail for long periods of time indicate a cruelty that is not different from the cruelty that was prevalent under the previous government of the arrogant Maura? Can something more painful and humiliating be conceived of than what the eight prisoners transferred to the prison at Santoña went through when they arrived at the station in Lleida and their feet were chained tightly and their arms were tied with rope? When they were kept hungry, thirsty, and cold, and during every break along the way, they were thrown in a foul cell from the Palencia prison? And the weight of their chains destroyed their wrists and made it impossible to sleep? Do you want a more painful situation than the one we see on the other side of the border, where they wait anxiously for completely honorable fathers and beloved children, honorable criminals who could escape their pursuers' fury, to return to their cold homes to bring them the warmth that was missing?

All this cruelty and these atrocities created such an atmosphere of indignation that the government—which some say had come to liberalize Spain—tried to contain the anger by opening the gates of the prisons for some, declaring by the way, that they couldn't do that for everyone because such a pardon would have to be approved by the parliament, and it was closed.

Was this reservation of theirs sincere? What could possibly be the objection to reintegrating the revolutionaries into their homes on the very same day that the people were cheering Sr. Moret's rise to power? Who else but he himself and his ministers had condemned Sr. Maura's abuses before the nation, considering that to be the cause of the misfortunes that dispirited the Spanish people? But what is the point of all these inquiries when we have already said that the ministerial changes came from above, not from below, not to calm the people, but for the protection of the institutions. It was not an act of justice to condemn Maura, but a political plan to absolve him.

El País of Madrid fittingly reminded us:

For the slightest reason (a king's wedding, a prince's birthday, a princess's wedding, the queen's days, the centennial anniversary of Columbus, etc.) general pardons have been given out, true amnesties as Sr. Maura has said, which covered the entire penal population, opened the jails to those who were under arrest, and suspended the proceedings against certain criminals.

This has been done often, and this has always been done, as Sr. Moret well knows. During the Restoration, pardons of this type were given to celebrate: the end of the Civil War, the wedding of Alfonso XII, the birth of his daughters, the Barcelona Exposition, the centennial anniversary of the discovery of the Americas, the birth of Alfonso XIII, his entry into adulthood, and the marriage of the unfortunate princess Mercedes. Aside from these general pardons, which differed from amnesties in name only, less extensive (but not partial) pardons were granted in commemoration of birthdays and the King's Day.

In a country where, behind the parliament's back, young men are sent to wage war against the Riffians, add the disturbing state of indecision, the terrible delays fostered by qualms and reservations that do not take the people's profound distress into consideration—if only we understood the harm that was caused by urging the people to appeasement and moderation in circumstances where our conscience demanded sublime intransigence, that precursor to healthy and desirable transformations.

All of the human heart's most noble sentiments and all of the spectacular work of the international movements, which came to rehabilitate the spirit of liberty that had been trampled on by the modern devotees of the Inquisition, were abused and abandoned the very day that the people placed their trust in Moret and stopped trusting themselves.

No one doubts that the prisoners will be freed, but when? How? Ah, another humiliation! They will be freed once the political plan that we have discussed has been fully executed. For it to come to its conclusion, we are still awaiting the dissolution of the parliament and new elections.

Luis Zurdo Olivares, who was sentenced to six years in prison, was not unaware of this. He said to me, from behind the bars of his prison cell:

"Bonafulla, we haven't been prisoners since yesterday."[1]

"What?"

"Now we're electoral fodder."

"So in the end you understood the trick. Moret has made a mockery of you republicans."

"We all allowed ourselves to be fooled . . . ."

We will finish. What matters is for the prisoners to be released so they can return to their homes and kiss and embrace their loved ones. And since that happy moment will come shortly after this book comes out, we will finish our work.

Everything we have narrated, fought against, and praised in these pages will have been engraved in the memories of our readers.

The synthesis of the events of July goes hand in hand with a sacrifice of blood for a most noble aspiration that became a protest against governmental tyranny and against the unpopular, grotesque, and deadly religious institutions that impoverish the land that shelters them.

Was this sacrifice productive? The oppressed psychological makeup of contemporary people—one day they are heroes, the next they are resigned—means not as much as we would have hoped, but the path is now open, and the sick egoisms of tradition will never be able to stop the overwhelming flood of new ideas.

---

1. [Author's note] He is alluding to January 23rd, the king's name day, when it was thought there would be an amnesty decree, after massive demonstrations were held in Barcelona, Valencia, Coruña, Tarrasa, Mataró, and Sabadell, as well as the petitions from other towns handed in to the government to publish them.

AK PRESS is small, in terms of staff and resources, but we also manage to be one of the world's most productive anarchist publishing houses. We publish close to twenty books every year, and distribute thousands of other titles published by like-minded independent presses and projects from around the globe. We're entirely worker run and democratically managed. We operate without a corporate structure—no boss, no managers, no bullshit.

The **FRIENDS OF AK PRESS** program is a way you can directly contribute to the continued existence of AK Press, and ensure that we're able to keep publishing books like this one! Friends pay $25 a month directly into our publishing account ($30 for Canada, $35 for international), and receive a copy of every book AK Press publishes for the duration of their membership! Friends also receive a discount on anything they order from our website or buy at a table: 50% on AK titles, and 30% on everything else. We have a Friends of AK ebook program as well: $15 a month gets you an electronic copy of every book we publish for the duration of your membership. *You can even sponsor a very discounted membership for someone in prison.*

Email **friendsofak@akpress.org** for more info, or visit the website: **https://www.akpress.org/friends.html**.

There are always great book projects in the works—so sign up now to become a Friend of AK Press, and let the presses roll!